MERITOCRACY AND ITS DISCONTENTS

MERITOCRACY AND ITS DISCONTENTS

Anxiety and the National College
Entrance Exam in China

Zachary M. Howlett

CORNELL UNIVERSITY PRESS   ITHACA AND LONDON

First published 2021 by Cornell University Press

Library of Congress Cataloging-in-Publication Data

Names: Howlett, Zachary M., 1976– author.
Title: Meritocracy and its discontents : anxiety and the national college entrance exam in China / Zachary M. Howlett.
Description: Ithaca [New York] : Cornell University Press, 2021. | Includes bibliographical references and index.
Identifiers: LCCN 2020025194 (print) | LCCN 2020025195 (ebook) | ISBN 9781501754432 (hardcover) | ISBN 9781501754463 (paperback) | ISBN 9781501754456 (ebook) | ISBN 9781501754449 (pdf)
Subjects: LCSH: Gaokao (Educational test)—Social aspects. | Universities and colleges—China—Entrance examinations. | Achievement tests—China.
Classification: LCC LB2353.8.C6 H68 2021 (print) | LCC LB2353.8.C6 (ebook) | DDC 378.51—dc23
LC record available at https://lccn.loc.gov/2020025194
LC ebook record available at https://lccn.loc.gov/2020025195

Contents

Acknowledgments

My experience writing this book demonstrates one of its central premises. We often credit people's accomplishments to their individual merit; however, the foundations of merit are social. My name appears on the cover of this book, but countless people contributed to its formation. First thanks go to all the people in the Chinese high schools where I conducted my fieldwork. My students in these schools were my tireless teachers, and many of the teaching staff and administrators became close friends. Although I cannot name them in public, this book owes its existence to them.

My advisers Steve Sangren, Magnus Fiskesjö, and TJ Hinrichs nurtured me throughout my time at Cornell University. I owe each of them a great intellectual debt. Many other teachers at Cornell also inspired me: Dominic Boyer, Sherman Cochran, Petrus Liu, Robin McNeal, Hiro Miyazaki, Viranjini Munasinghe, Terence Turner, Sofia Villenas, and Andrew Willford, to name a few. I also thank classmates, friends, and staff at Cornell who helped and supported me, including Kevin Carrico, Jack Chia, Donna Duncan, Lim Wah Guan, Pauline Limbu, Laura Menchaca, Margaret Rolfe, James Sharrock, Nguyet Tong, Erick White, and Taomo Zhou.

Funding for my research came from many sources. The US Department of Education financed my graduate training with a four-year Jacob K. Javits Fellowship. My fieldwork was supported by the Mellon Foundation, which stepped in to fund projects selected for the Fulbright-Hays Doctoral Dissertation Research Abroad (DDRA) Fellowship when Congress suspended the program in 2011. The funding was administered by the Institute of International Education (IIE), and I owe special thanks to the IIE program manager in Beijing, Janet Upton, who kindly shared her wisdom about fieldwork as a fellow China anthropologist. In addition to external funding, I received generous support from Cornell University. Two summers of preliminary fieldwork were funded by a Mario Einaudi Center Travel Grant and an East Asia Program Lam Family Award for South China Research. The Cornell East Asia Program also supported the writing phase of my research with a Hu Shih Fellowship in Chinese Studies.

In China, a variety of institutions and individuals provided crucial support. In the Department of Anthropology of Xiamen University, I was hosted by Zeng Shaocong, now at the Chinese Academy for Social Sciences. Professor Zeng welcomed me into his community of friends and students and helped me secure the tricky permissions necessary for a foreigner to conduct fieldwork in a rural school. In the Department of Social Work, Yi Lin served as a vital sounding board for ideas and made many helpful introductions. At the Institute of Education of Xiamen University, Liu Haifeng and Zheng Ruoling shared their profound knowledge of the College Entrance Examination and inspired me with their distinctive style of scholarship, which investigates the contemporary exam in tandem with China's imperial era civil exams.

I received invaluable mentorship as a postdoctoral fellow at the Harvard Academy of International and Area Studies. Elizabeth Perry generously agreed to read my whole manuscript and chair a book workshop on it. Susan Blum, Andrew Kipnis, Karrie Koesel, and Ajantha Subramanian took part, giving me countless incisive critiques. I am deeply grateful to them for their insights, which run through every chapter. Cristina Florea and Malgorzata Kurjanska brightened my days with their friendship. Many other colleagues and friends helped make my time in Cambridge convivial, productive, and intellectually inspiring, including Brinton Ahlin, Rabiat Akande, Sophia Balakian, Yael Berda, Chantal Berman, Lina Britto, Melani Cammet, Steve Caton, Rishad Choudury, Arunabh Ghosh, Julian Gewirtz, Chris Gratien, Jason Kelly, Egor Lazarev, Adam Leeds, Noora Lori, Casey Lurtz, Eduardo Montero, David Szakonyi, Arne Westad, and Amy Zhang, among others. The academy administrators Bruce Jackan and Kathleen Hoover gave tremendous logistical support, which was always infused with their spirit-lifting humor and kindness.

I have received suggestions on various parts of this book in many different forums. I am deeply grateful to Michael Szonyi and Tarun Khanna for inviting me to attend workshops on meritocracy in China and India organized by the Fairbank Center for Chinese Studies and the Lakshmi Mittal South Asia Institute of Harvard University. They and the other attendees—including James Lee, Cameron Campbell, and Liang Chen—gave me invaluable critiques. I thank Kaori Urayama for giving me the opportunity to present my work at the Asia Fellows Seminar of the Harvard Kennedy School. In panel presentations, I benefited from the insightful suggestions of Fida Adely, Kathryn M. Anderson-Levitt, Elena Aydarova, Sara Friedman, Gerry Groot, DJ Hatfield, Jill Koyama, Huwy-min Lucia Liu, Ellen Oxfeld, Robert Weller, Wu Jingting, and Roberta Zavoretti, among others. Sections of chapters 3 and 4 expand on ideas first developed in a chapter that I wrote for an edited volume: "China's Examination Fever and the Fabrication of Fairness: 'My Generation Was Raised on Poisoned Milk,'" in *Emptiness and Fullness: Ethnographies of Lack and Desire in Contemporary China*, edited by Susanne Bregnbæk and Mikkel Bunkenborg (New York: Berghahn Books, 2017).

At Yale-NUS College and the National University of Singapore, I have been blessed with many extraordinarily kind and supportive senior colleagues, including Joanne Roberts, Jeannette Ickovics, Jane Jacobs, Anju Mary Paul, Nomi Lazar, Naoko Shimazu, Terry Narden, John Driffill, and Christina Tarnopolksy. Many other colleagues and friends contribute to making teaching in Singapore an immensely collegial and fulfilling experience: Emily Chua, Jessica Hanser, Annu Jalais, Rohan Mukherjee, Ben Schupmann, Risa Toha, Christine Walker, Chitra Venkataramani, Huong Tam, Jolene Tan, Ashlyn Thia, Daniel Yeo, and Robin Zheng, among many others. Steve Oliver created the map charts in this book. My Anthropology colleagues at Yale-NUS—Cecilia Van Hollen, Gabriele Koch, Stuart Strange, and Neena Mahadev—have given me a steady source of camaraderie and intellectual fellowship. I owe special thanks to Cecilia Van Hollen for her constant support and sage advice as well as for being such an inspiring model of kindhearted equanimity. I am likewise extremely grateful to Marcia Inhorn who, while visiting from Yale, graciously and unstintingly supported me and other junior faculty in countless ways. Erik Harms also provided invaluable mentorship and encouragement while on leave from Yale. My undergraduate students at Yale-NUS inspire me constantly with their curiosity, passion, and diligence. An undergraduate student assistant, Liu Chengpei, read my manuscript in its entirety and provided helpful feedback. Publication of this book was made possible, in part, by a Yale-NUS College subvention grant.

At Cornell University Press, I am profoundly grateful to my editor, Jim Lance, for his enthusiasm and support, which saw me through the final stages of this project. He is a paragon of kindness and professionalism. I thank him from the bottom of my heart for believing in me and this book. I also wish to thank Clare Jones for her skilled editorial assistance. Two anonymous readers for Cornell gave generously of their time to provide many important and insightful suggestions. My production editor, Karen Laun, and copyeditor, Monica Achen, improved the final product substantially.

The love and support of my friends and family has made all my life journeys possible. At every stage of my research, the stalwart friendship of Wang Yuanchong has given me a wellspring of strength. My friends Kyle Rand and Josh Morsell traveled halfway around the world to visit me in the field. Lee Calkins spent his vacation time reading my manuscript. Merry Li supplied crucial help at every turn. My parents have been pillars of care since the beginning. Throughout my life, my mother and stepfather, Judith and Brooks Mencher, have nurtured my curiosity. When I was a child, they dedicated themselves tirelessly to creating opportunities for me. Brooks was my first writing teacher and continues to guide me. He read every word of this manuscript at least three times. Although my father, Joe Howlett, did not live to see the completion of my graduate studies, I know that he would be very proud. My sister, Malinda Wagner, is a constant ally, and I thank her husband, Roger, and my niece and nephew, Emily and Eli, for being so understanding of my absences through the years. My redoubtable cousin Margaret Ronald showed me that getting a PhD was possible. My parents-in-law, Ong Mei Tuan and Lau Liak Koi, have embraced me into their family, giving me a warm and welcoming home in Southeast Asia. I am likewise grateful to my brother- and sister-in-law, Kai Yang and Yie Hui, for accepting me so warmly into their family. Finally, I owe a special debt of gratitude to my partner and collaborator Lau Ting Hui, who is my biggest support. She inspires me constantly with her insight and strength.

Note on Translation and Orthography

From time to time in what follows, I provide translations of important Chinese terms and phrases. In some cases, it is to disambiguate terminology for other researchers. In other cases, I use these translated phrases to distill important aspects of the examination experience. Metaphors are more than mere figures of speech; they reveal how people conceptualize their worlds (Lakoff and Johnson 1981). In particular, it is significant that warfare metaphors abound regarding the College Entrance Examination.

When referring to the original Mandarin, I follow the Pinyin system of transliteration, the standard in China. Readers can usually approximate the sound of Mandarin by following English rules of pronunciation, but the following four consonants require special guidance: "zh" is pronounced like the "j" in "judge"; "c" is pronounced like the "ts" in "cats"; "q" sounds like the "ch" in "launch yourself"; and "x" sounds like the "sh" in "push yourself."

Mandarin is a tonal language, which means that pronouncing the same syllable with a different tone literally produces a different word. To disambiguate homonyms for students and researchers, I use the standard Pinyin tone notations for the four basic tones: high, rising, low, and falling. Thus, for example, the syllable *ma* means something different depending on whether it is pronounced with a high tone, *mā* (mother); a rising tone, *má* (hemp); a low tone, *mǎ* (horse); or a falling tone, *mà* (to scold).

To protect confidentiality, I employ pseudonyms for most people and places.

Selected Twentieth-Century Timeline

1905   Imperial civil exams are abolished
1911   China's last imperial dynasty, the Qing, is overthrown
1912   Republican Period commences
1919   May Fourth Movement starts
1949   People's Republic of China is founded by Mao Zedong (1893–1976)
1952   First College Entrance Examination (Gaokao) is held
1966–76   Gaokao is suspended during the Cultural Revolution
1977   Gaokao is reinstated
1978   Post-Mao era of economic reform begins
1989   Tiananmen protests take place
1999   Higher-education expansion begins
2013   Xi Jinping assumes power

Prologue: The Final Battle

Every year some ten million high-school seniors take the National College Entrance Examination in China, and for two days in early June, the exam, known as the Gaokao, transfixes the nation.[1] Police appear outside school gates to ensure order. Temples fill with family members and teachers praying for success. Normally penny-pinching taxi drivers deliver examination warriors (*gāokǎo zhànshì*) to their battlegrounds (*zhànchǎng*) for free, and schools, transformed into examination halls, become sacred spaces. Apart from exam supervisors, only test takers may enter. Biometrics may be used to verify identities, and signal-blocking equipment and even aerial drones may be deployed to foil cheats. Sidewalks throng with nervous parents and gawking onlookers. TV crews and newspaper reporters interview spectators. The state media hold forth on exam conditions. Some cities even reroute aircraft to reduce noise.

As the warriors line up, their clear plastic pencil cases in hand, they are grim and determined; many tremble with anticipation and anxiety. For them, there is no clear distinction between education and the Gaokao. Their twelve years of schooling have all led up to this final battle (*zuìhòu yī zhàn*).

Following the big day, examinees wait anxiously for their scores. Newspapers conduct lengthy postmortems, debating the test's difficulty and fairness. When the names of top scorers leak out in July, these exam heroes (*kǎoshì yīngxióng*) are feted like star athletes, sometimes in public ceremonies. They receive the same exalted title—examination champion (*zhuàngyuán*)—bestowed on first-place examinees in late imperial China (960–1911 CE), when the country used an elaborate system of civil examinations to select its ruling mandarins.

As in imperial times, the examination is a fateful rite of passage. Even those who do not compete follow the exam with rapt attention, and China's highest leaders intervene directly in its management. The Gaokao is what anthropologists call a total social fact—an activity that "involve[s] . . . a large number of institutions," reverberating through the economic, political, legal, and religious spheres of society (Mauss [1925] 2000, 78–79). As a newspaper reporter told me, "The Gaokao concerns every family and is directly related to the stability and harmony of the country and to the image of the government." And as a rural high-school principal said, "Without the Gaokao, there would be social revolution in China."

The Gaokao's significance might be compared to national elections in a liberal democratic country. But China is an authoritarian one-party state. What accounts for the great importance that people attach to the Gaokao? And what can China—the historical birthplace of competitive examinations—reveal about similar systems in other places? China preceded Europe in the transition from aristocracy to merit-based leadership by many centuries, and most countries now follow some form of meritocracy. People almost everywhere believe that hard work and intelligence, rather than hereditary privilege, should bring honor and success. In most places, this meritocratic aspiration includes educational credentials based partly or wholly on exams.

Still, since the 1980s, the world has experienced a period of rapid social, technological, and political change. Although life has improved for countless millions, social inequality has also increased. The gap between rich and poor is widening in China and around the world, resulting in what some critics call a hereditary meritocracy. Is meritocracy, then, more myth than reality? Meritocracy produces unquestioning believers but also growing numbers of discontents—those for whom the reality of this social system never quite lives up to its promise. The title of this book is a play on Sigmund Freud's ([1919] 2005) *Civilization and Its Discontents*, which argues that modern societies breed guilt and anxiety as people strive to live up to impossibly stringent cultural ideals. Some anxiety is inevitable, but the ideal of academic-driven social mobility becomes ever more difficult to realize as inequality increases.

The Gaokao raises broader comparative questions as well. People in China liken the Gaokao not only to examinations elsewhere but also to other types of fateful (*gǎibiàn mìngyùn de*) events such as war, athletic competitions, and high-stakes gambling. Cross-culturally, many occasions that are both consequential and chancy may be seen as fateful. Such events include modern institutions like elections and trials as well as traditional forms of total social exchange like Kula (Papua New Guinea) and potlatch (North American Pacific Northwest). What do these occasions have in common, and what accounts for people's fascination with them? How do individuals use these events to gain recognition and imbue their lives with meaning? And what does this process reveal about what people are and how societies are organized?

This book, based on two years of immersion in Chinese high schools, is my attempt to unravel these puzzles. My answers are partial or preliminary in many cases, but if nothing else I wish to convey a nuanced understanding of the Gaokao as a complex social phenomenon that both resembles and differs from similar institutions in other places. Appreciating these differences and similarities is a step toward building stronger bridges of understanding in our globally interconnected and rapidly transforming world. As we enter the third decade of what many predict will be the Chinese century, this task assumes even greater importance.[2]

MERITOCRACY AND ITS DISCONTENTS

1

A FATEFUL RITE OF PASSAGE

The Gaokao and the Myth of Meritocracy

Study changes fate.

—common Chinese saying

It was Sunday morning in the third week of April 2013 in Ningzhou—a backwater prefectural capital in China's southeastern Fujian Province. Only forty-seven days remained before the Gaokao. I was accompanying Ms. Ma, a head teacher at Ningzhou Number One High School, on home visits to students' families. So close to the exam, Ms. Ma focused on students whose practice-test scores were fluctuating wildly. She aimed to calm their nerves and boost their morale.

The stakes of the Gaokao are high, and test takers must cope with tremendous pressure. Many see the exam as their only opportunity to achieve social mobility or, as they say, to change fate (*gǎibiàn mìng*) or transform destiny (*gǎibiàn mìngyùn*). The Gaokao occurs annually, and retaking it is difficult and expensive. In China, where students are Gaokao athletes, head teachers are a combination of coach, counselor, and surrogate parent. Ms. Ma knew who was falling in school rankings because of a personal problem or family crisis, and who did poorly on low-stakes exams but, as teachers say, unleashed their latent potential (*bàofā qiánlì*) in high-stakes ones. She used this information to provide her flock with moral and scholastic guidance. The home visit—a venerable institution at most Chinese high schools—constitutes an important occasion for such ministrations.

As the Gaokao loomed closer, one student in particular was close to Ms. Ma's heart—a boy named Zeyu. The majority of Ms. Ma's students came from the city, but Zeyu hailed from a peripheral rural county of Ningzhou Prefecture. In front of his classmates, Zeyu referred to his parents as pig farmers. This was a euphemism. Several years earlier, Zeyu's parents had migrated from the countryside to an urban shantytown in Xiamen, and they made a living by collecting garbage from all-night street restaurants to sell as pig slop. As with the children of many migrant parents, Zeyu and his younger brother were left behind (*liúshǒu*) in the care of their rural grandparents (Murphy 2014).

In light of his humble background, Zeyu's scholastic accomplishments were impressive. He had spent much of his childhood with his paternal grandmother, who did not speak Mandarin but only her native Minnan dialect. His mother and grandparents could not read. Zeyu's father had been forced to quit school in the third grade because his parents could no longer afford book fees and tuition. Nevertheless, Zeyu was one of only a handful of students from his home county to test into the best high school in the prefectural capital, Ningzhou Number One.

Zeyu's father called the boy "good stuff" because he possessed great diligence (*nǔlì*), self-discipline (*zìlǜ*), and persistence (*jiānchí*). Clearly, however, the middle-aged man's unfulfilled ambitions also played an important role in Zeyu's success. Thirty years after dropping out of school, Zeyu's father still proudly recounted getting perfect scores on his third-grade mathematics tests, and he

FIGURE 1. Studying diligently for the "final battle." Photograph by the author.

spoke with gnawing regret about forgoing the big examination. This disappointment fueled his desire to help his children "conquer the Gaokao" (*zhēngfú gāokǎo*).

Zeyu exemplified great diligence and grit, but as the examination approached, his composure, or psychological quality (*xīnlǐ sùzhì*), wavered. He was nervous and distracted. He missed classes and his performance faltered. Ms. Ma hoped to diagnose the problem and boost the boy's morale. Her visit was different from most in that Zeyu's parents were absent, working in the big city. Nevertheless, the boy had his own home of sorts. To provide him with an optimal study environment in the all-important year before the examination, and to avoid noisy school dormitories with eight children to a room, Zeyu's parents rented him an apartment near the school. He shared it with one other high-school student. This luxury was a tremendous expense for the family.

Zeyu showed Ms. Ma and me in. We sat at a folding table in the otherwise empty living room. His face looked haggard, and he fidgeted with a receipt while we talked. He had just returned from a pharmacy with a package of stomach-fortifying Chinese medicine. Ms. Ma expressed concern about Zeyu's having skipped an afternoon of classes. Breaking into tears, the boy complained of stomach pain and insomnia. He was plagued by guilt over his parents' sacrifices. Ms. Ma encouraged him, saying, "I know it's hard, but you can't slack off now. Once you slack off too much, it will be difficult to get back into shape [*huīfù zhuàngtài*]."

After we left, Ms. Ma and I talked about Zeyu's situation. Herself of rural origin, Ms. Ma understood the enormous burden that the boy felt. People from rural places see the examination as their only hope of escaping the farm (*tiàochū nóngmén*), by which they mean obtaining white-collar employment and household registration (*hùkǒu*) in prominent cities. Good jobs, which are reserved for graduates of high-ranking colleges, promise a coveted middle-class existence in urban areas. For most rural residents, university degrees are the only way to obtain official urban residency, which promises prestige, security, and superior marriage prospects. Dropouts and graduates of inferior colleges often either return to the countryside or are relegated to a precarious existence in the floating population (*liúdòng rénkǒu*) of migrant workers, who are second-class citizens. As Ms. Ma observed, "The risks and rewards for someone like Zeyu are different from [those of] most children from the city."

Students and their families are not the only people affected by the exam. Examination scores determine the reputation of teachers, schools, and educational officials. Promotions and salary bonuses are based on exam scores. Keenly aware of the stakes, not only parents and students but also teachers and administrators turn to religion and magic for comfort and guidance. Certain high schools, like Ms. Ma's, even organize temple visits for teachers. These pilgrimages are conducted quietly to avoid flouting China's policy of atheism in schools.

With other head teachers, Ms. Ma made offerings to the gods during school-sponsored temple visits. She prayed that Zeyu would regain composure and have good luck on test day. But Zeyu was not alone in her thoughts. Even some of Ms. Ma's more privileged urban students—including her top student, the daughter of a local police detective—were wilting under the pressure of the impending ordeal. By contrast, the latent potential of some underperforming students showed promise of surging (*bàofā*) before the final battle. Such dark horses (*hēimǎ*) achieve sudden renown by delivering a "clutch" or game-saving performance on the fateful day.

Thus exam results can be highly capricious. Indeed, head teachers observe that Gaokao results routinely fluctuate twenty points or more from students' expected scores. Such variations have far-reaching consequences, easily meaning the difference between attending a prestigious Project 985 college (China's top forty) and an ordinary first-tier university (*yīběn yuànxiào*), of which there are about two hundred.

The fickleness of test scores has many sources. On the one hand, performance is affected by mood or nerves. On the other, factors outside the individual's control influence performance, including test questions, weather, health, and even seat location. For these reasons, the exam is a chancy undertaking. As one student said, "Your hand moves a little, five points are gone, and your whole fate is different."

As it turned out, Zeyu performed poorly, scoring thirty points lower than his teacher had anticipated. Instead of 620 out of a possible score of 750 points, he got 590. Zeyu himself attributed his poor showing to an "uneven attitude" and to a lack of composure or "psychological quality." His family doubted his ability to endure the stress of retaking the examination, and they did not have the money to fund such an endeavor. They decided to "come to terms with fate" (*rènmìng*).

Zeyu's thirty-point drop translated into a fall of over ten thousand places in the provincial rankings. Upon graduation from a respectable but unremarkable college, he began working as a traveling salesman in a minor city with no guarantee of an urban household registration. By contrast, his classmates who scored in the low-to-mid 600s—his initial target score—went to Project 985 colleges. Many obtained stable long-term jobs in centrally located cities like Beijing, Shenzhen, and Xiamen.

Zeyu's father had few illusions about the social inequalities that plague the education system in China. Over tea in his cramped Xiamen home, he discussed his struggle to get Zeyu's younger brother into a good public school. He talked about the great disparities between rural and urban schools. He complained about the protectionist system of regional admission quotas, as a result of which people from ordinary provinces like Fujian are far less likely to test into a top university than are students from Beijing or Shanghai. Nevertheless, he retained faith in the big exam, insisting on the test's power to "change fate." Despite Zeyu's performance, the man felt sure that his family's destiny had improved. In his view, the Gaokao offered ordinary people like him a chance to fight back against a corrupt and unequal world. As he explained, "The Gaokao is China's only relatively fair competition" (*wéiyī xiāngduì gōngpíng de jìngzhēng*).

The Myth of Meritocracy

Many people share this assessment of the Gaokao. It is a constant refrain heard all over China. People see the results of ordinary social competitions as determined ahead of time backstage through social connections, or *guanxi*. Thus they say such competitions are empty (*xū*), fake (*xūjiǎ*), or counterfeit (*zuòjiǎ*). By contrast, people see Gaokao scores as decided during the examination frontstage— that is, publicly—according to universal, rules-based measures of merit. Accordingly, they say that the Gaokao is relatively true (*shí*), real (*xiànshí*), and genuine (*zhēnshí*).[1]

By one path or another, China's white-collar elite and many of its government officials are drawn from graduates of its top colleges. It is common belief that the competition for status and power is heavily corrupted at the higher levels. Yet in this world ruled by guanxi, the test gives ordinary people hope of mobility and even of social and political power. Since its reinstatement in 1977 after a ten-year hiatus during the Cultural Revolution (1966–76), the exam has played an important role in reinforcing people's impression that anyone can change fate. The Gaokao reassures people that competition can rest on a fair foundation, and many in China regard it as the cornerstone of meritocracy. By meritocracy I mean a society in which the ruling elite are selected on the basis of merit through open competition.

Unfortunately, meritocracy is largely a myth. In the post-Mao era of reform and opening (1978–present), the country has developed rapidly, lifting hundreds of millions out of poverty. But social inequality has also skyrocketed, leading to wide chasms in educational opportunity and in test scores between different regions and socioeconomic groups (Hannum 1999; Yasheng Huang 2008; Khor et al. 2016; Y. Liu 2013; Obendiek 2016; X. Wang et al. 2013; Yeung 2013). Under such conditions, one's social background and other accidents of birth matter more than the ideology of meritocracy would have us believe. When I say that meritocracy is a myth, therefore, I am mainly referring to this problem of social equity. I do not mean to denigrate successful examinees as somehow lacking merit (though precisely what kinds of merit an education system should encourage is subject to debate). Quite the opposite, I argue that top scorers display great distinction. But the opportunities to accumulate this merit are unevenly distributed.

There is another, closely related sense in which meritocracy is a myth. As a system of beliefs and practices, meritocracy feeds off narratives of success—stories of dark horses who transform destiny. These stories themselves form potent myths. Without them, people's faith in meritocracy would fade and die. Of course, a skeptic might object that these narratives refer to an objective reality. The Gaokao system really does produce extraordinary examination athletes who transform their destinies through virtuosic displays of merit. Without doubt, such people exist. Zeyu himself came close to embodying this ideal. But Zeyu's story also highlights the problem. Narratives of dark horses are myths because their promise outstrips their reality. In the real world, near misses like Zeyu's are far more common. For a few years in the 1980s, it appeared as though the Gaokao could be a substantial path to mobility for people of rural origin (Liang et al. 2012). But in recent decades, this pathway has narrowed (X. Wang et al. 2013; Yeung 2013; D. Yang 2006). The exceptions just prove the rule.

But what accounts for the remarkable resiliency of Gaokao success stories, these myths of meritocracy? The answer is complex, but a key point to recognize is that examination scores, although they are often presented as the accomplishment of individuals, are in fact socially produced. Individuals do not achieve high scores in a vacuum. Rather, they benefit from a variety of social resources, which educational sociologists, following Pierre Bourdieu, refer to as various forms of capital (Bourdieu and Passeron 1977; Bourdieu 1977, 1986, 1990). Families rely on social connections to get children into good schools (social capital). Similarly, children with educated parents get a leg up on schoolwork because of their family's academic knowledge, which is regarded as providing a superior home environment (cultural capital). And parents who are wealthy—that is, have large amounts of economic capital—are able to transform this wealth into other forms of capital. For example, they can compensate for deficits in social capital by bribing school officials or make up for deficits in cultural capital by paying for after-school lessons. The goal is to acquire what sociologists refer to as symbolic capital, of which educational credentials form the paradigm (Bourdieu and Passeron 1977; Bourdieu 1977, 1986, 1990, 1991).

The net result of these arrangements is that people who achieve remarkable educational success usually have something special in their backgrounds that makes it possible. People tend to see the stories of dark horses and examination champions as reflecting the heroic capacities of isolated individuals. But usually these extraordinary test athletes could not have achieved their accomplishments alone. The farmer's daughter who tests into Tsinghua University (tied with Peking University for first place in the Chinese college rankings) is also the niece of a high-school principal. The son of a migrant worker who gains admission to Peking University (also known as Beijing University) was fostered out from a young age to a well-educated aunt, who willingly accepted this duty because her less educated sibling financed her through college. In Zeyu's case, his father's extraordinary motivation certainly played a role in his own qualified success.

But the Gaokao and exams like it essentially render moot the contribution of parents, relatives, teachers, and schools. By discounting these contributions, test scores exaggerate the degree to which people pull themselves up by their own bootstraps and allow parents and children to think of these scores as individual accomplishments.

The Gaokao not only selects individuals according to merit, it also produces a belief in individual merit. In an important sense, I would argue, the exam also thereby produces individuals. This creation of individuals is an important cultural function of the exam. People have always possessed individual bodies, desires, personalities, and so on, even when they have belonged to highly egalitarian, community-based societies. But people inevitably belong to a social context; they exist only in dialog and interaction with others. It is important to disaggregate such common human experiences of possessing a body, personality, and so on from culturally specific beliefs in individualism. The latter revolve to a large degree around conceptions of individual merit, which seem to be particularly prevalent in complex, market-based societies like China.

Chinese society is especially fascinating because it combines a large degree of individualism with great emphasis on family ties and social relationships. In recent years, anthropologists of China have argued that the country is losing the latter focus, becoming increasingly individualistic as a result of its economic reforms (M.H. Hansen 2015; Y. Yan 2003). This is certainly true. With market reforms, broader and broader swaths of the population have been drawn into the atomizing cultural ethos of dog-eat-dog economic competition and the narcissistic pursuit of personal happiness. To some degree, however, this body of scholarship underemphasizes the history of individuals and individualism in China. China has long possessed a highly developed form of impersonal bureaucracy (M.M. Yang 1994). Centuries before such exams were adopted in the West, the imperial civil exams in China (as well as similar systems in Korea and Vietnam) furthered and valorized the myth of individual merit through open, anonymous, competitive examinations (Elman 2013; Woodside 2006).

Now as before, this myth has profound social and psychological effects. Much like the imperial exam system before it, the Gaokao transforms the social labor of parents, teachers, and schools into a measure of individual merit—a test score or examination ranking—that for the successful candidate embodies cultural over-tones of charisma, a quality akin to divine favor (Weber 1946). Bourdieu would say that the examination encourages people to misrecognize social labor (in the forms of social, cultural, and economic capital) as individual merit (Bourdieu and Passeron 1977; Bourdieu 1986, 1990). Thus the myth of individual merit forms what social thinkers call an ideology. In popular usage, of course, this concept generally refers to a set of beliefs or ideas that a government, party, or organization advances. But anthropologists and social theorists give this con-cept a more specialized definition. Most simply, ideology is a cultural system of beliefs and practices that reinforces an unequal status quo (Marx [1846] 1970). Marxian thinkers sometimes refer to ideology as "false consciousness." Seeing merit through the distorting lens of ideology, people tend to credit themselves too much for their successes and blame themselves too much for their failures. Zeyu lamented his lack of psychological quality, but social inequality surely also played a role in his inability to achieve his dreams.

In short, the two sides of the myth of meritocracy point to a contradiction. Despite the false promise of a socially equalizing effect (the first myth of meritoc-racy), the Gaokao recruits the majority in China into a belief in individual merit (the second myth of meritocracy). Why do examinees and their families continue to believe in the relative fairness of the Gaokao—and, by extension, the fairness of the lot that falls to them in life—despite China's great chasms in educational opportunity and achievement? This is the central question of this book.

In answering this question, the theory of misrecognition—of individual merit as ideology—only goes so far. As useful as it is, this theory tends to offer an axiom rather than an account. The process of how social labor is transformed into individual merit is largely a black box. An influential explanation is that the labor of parents, relatives, and teachers (and accompanying forms of capital) is embodied in students (Bourdieu 1977, 1984, 1986). But this approach tends to flatten the various kinds of merit that examinees possess. It does little to explain, for example, how the merits of diligence or persistence are embodied differently from, say, those of composure or luck. Nor does it shed much light on the dif-ferent roles that these qualities play in the experience of the exam. Just as this conventional account flattens merit, it also flattens labor. The work of parents, relatives, and teachers is much more complex than the language of capital trans-formations would suggest. Rather than a simple injection of capital, this labor involves a large component of what Teresa Kuan (2015) calls the artful disposi-tion of things, that is, the creation of conditions that are conducive to success.

Another shortcoming of the theory of misrecognition is how it tends to focus on the determination of individual destinies and personalities by objective social structures, giving short shrift to personal agency and moral effort. Much social theory revolves around specifying the relationship between structure and agency. But the theory of misrecognition tends to tip the scales too far in the direction of structure. In Bourdieu's sociology, one's class position and social environment more or less predetermine one's educational outcome. This is a useful model for identifying patterns of inequality, but it tends to flatten human experience to the mechanical fulfillment of social destinies. To do full justice to the exam, I leave room in my account for random events, forceful personalities, and extraordinary moral efforts.

If the Gaokao is like a machine for transforming social labor into individual merit, my goal in this book is to peer into this black box to examine its workings. In particular, I wish to emphasize the role of test takers themselves. The misrecognition of social labor as individual merit does not happen automatically but rather requires an enormous moral investment by those who are at the center of this drama. Gaokao examinees work diligently for twelve years (which, at their age, represents most of their lives) to acquire the cultural capacities and virtues that it takes to compete in the exam. It is largely this labor, alongside that of parents, schools, and others, that drives the machine of misrecognition.

This point brings me to another important aspect of the exam that conventional accounts underemphasize, namely, the question of motive. Without doubt, the Gaokao system helps justify and reproduce a highly unequal society, but what drives examinees to work so hard? Are they merely duped into believing in an ideology? In my view, this formulation does not do them enough credit. Rather, examinees and those who support them (teachers, parents, and administrators) strive to realize the myth of meritocracy despite all its contradictions, of which they are often painfully aware. To some degree, the examination is forced on examinees; many feel that they have little choice but to compete. Further, most examinees have an inflated conception of their chances. But they also understand that education in China is unfair. Nevertheless, the majority fervently desire to achieve the recognition that the examination confers and thus willingly submit to its discipline. To gain this recognition, they work tirelessly to train themselves in the capacities and virtues that success requires, and most revere the Gaokao despite any lingering ambivalence toward China's education system in general.

This book shines light on these moral and ethical dimensions of the Gaokao and similar exams. Conventional accounts tend to stress the immorality of standardized exams, which are much maligned for reducing human beings to a test score and for diminishing education to a competition (Kohn 2000). I share this critique. But to have lasting success in reforming examination systems, it's necessary to understand their cultural significance, particularly how examinees themselves use these occasions to imbue their lives with existential meaning. In taking this approach, I build on work in the anthropology and sociology of education that focuses on the implicit lessons of schooling—the often unconscious values, habits, and character ideals that children acquire by going to school (Foley 1990; Bourdieu and Passeron 1977; Demerath 2009; Stafford 1995; Willis 1981). These lessons often assume greater importance in children's lives than the explicit contents of their textbooks. Whereas the latter is something that they may forget, the former sticks with them for a lifetime.

Another contribution of anthropology to the study of education is how it enables analyzing education systems from a broadly comparative perspective. The Gaokao can be fruitfully compared not only to other exams but also to broader types of events cross-culturally. Adopting such a comparative perspective, my main argument in what follows is that the Gaokao is a fateful rite of passage. This is a common kind of social occasion in which people strive to achieve social recognition by personifying high cultural virtues. In the Gaokao, these virtues include diligence, persistence, composure, filial devotion, and divine favor or luck.

Fateful Rites of Passage

As sociologist Erving Goffman (1967) observes, most events are either undetermined or consequential, but not both. By undetermined, Goffman means unpredictable. Undetermined events are structured in such a way that their outcome is uncertain. By consequential, he means significant. Consequential events create or destroy value (whether conceived as money, fame, status, prestige, or whatever), leaving people enhanced or diminished in some way.

Think of driving a car. This activity is highly consequential—one can lose one's life at any moment. But as long as people more or less follow the rules, driving is ordinarily not all that chancy. By contrast, other events are unpredictable but not consequential. Take for instance a chat with friends. The unscripted quality of such an occasion means that people can easily say or do things that they later regret. Ordinarily, however, these mistakes are of little consequence.

Fateful events are special because they combine consequentiality and chanciness. Examples of such events include examinations, elections, athletic competitions, duels, war, and trials. Seduction can be fateful, as can a marriage proposal. Certain high-stakes performances, such as the opening night of a play, also fall into this category. And various economic activities—including fishing, hunting, harvesting, stock market bets, and certain business transactions—combine unpredictability and consequentiality in this way. In addition to such planned activities, unorganized happenings and calamities can also have fateful significance. Accidents and natural disasters place people suddenly in unpredictable situations in which every action may have life-or-death consequences. Finally, life decisions can be fateful. Economic migrants, for example, make a fateful gamble when they decide to leave behind everything that is familiar to try their fortune in a foreign place. The Gaokao forms just such a fateful intersection of indefinite outcome and profound consequence—a fateful trial of merit with Chinese characteristics.

All fateful events are rites of passage, or rituals. Many non-anthropologists use rite of passage to refer to a specific type of rite of passage: initiation rites, which mark the transition between childhood and adulthood. Without doubt, the Gaokao performs this role. But in the anthropological nomenclature, rite of passage has a broader meaning. It describes any event that solemnizes people's shift from one status to another. In addition to initiation rituals, the most famous examples include weddings and funerals (or mortuary rituals as anthropologists term the latter). But even normal, everyday events can be analyzed as rites of passage.

Take the example of bumping into someone in the hall—a mundane but potentially troublesome incident. In an instant, the status of both parties is thrown into ambiguity. A moment earlier, they were social equals with equal rights to move unmolested in public space. But this sudden mishap raises the possibility that this status is being challenged. If the situation is not to become a conflict or, at minimum, an embarrassment, one or both parties must conciliate the other by formulaically apologizing for the accident. This apology is a small ritual—a little rite of passage.

All rites of passage share a basic three-part structure—separation, transition, and reintegration (Van Gennep [1909] 1960; Turner 1977). During these rituals, people first separate from their old status, upon which they enter a transitional or liminal state. After a period, which can be long or short, they then reintegrate into the normal flow of social life. In the example of bumping into someone in the hall, the goal is to erase the transitional ambiguity that follows the accident, thereby returning both parties to their normal social status.

But many rites of passage aim to transform or change status. In a wedding, for example, people transform their status from unmarried to married (thereby linking two families together). In most funerals, people are mainly concerned with the orderly transition of souls into the afterlife, as well as with giving mourners a socially sanctified occasion to grieve.

As these examples highlight, societies are not static places. Even in simple, small-scale communities, the status of individuals is in constant flux. Life is a risky business. The status quo is never permanent but constantly faces various threats. One such threat consists in people's personal ambitions to accumulate status and fame, which frequently upset the status hierarchy. But many other threats come from relatively involuntary causes, such as the inevitable aging of children, who must be reintegrated into society as adults. Finally, accidental or random occurrences constantly appear in human life, presenting people with various dangers that must be overcome or opportunities that can be grasped. Consider a natural disaster or an unexpected attack. Because they throw the normal flow of events into disarray—into a liminal state—such events present people with a rite of passage—a particularly risky and consequential one, in fact.

All fateful events are rites of passage but not all rites of passage are fateful events. Take, for example, a wedding. If a wedding has an unexpected outcome, this is generally a bad thing, meaning that either the bride or the groom has gotten cold feet. Thus, a wedding, though consequential, is not ordinarily all that chancy. Upon closer investigation, however, a surprising number of rituals contain an uncertain or fateful aspect, especially when considered from the perspective of the participants. Think of initiations. It's common to view these occasions as foregone conclusions, like weddings. But in many cases, they involve a great component of uncertainty or chance and thus constitute fateful trials of merit that require the demonstration of cultural virtues like bravery, composure, and knowledge.[2] Many people think of initiations as a type of event that only occurs in relatively simple, small-scale societies, or perhaps in a club or gang. But rites of initiation also play an important role in complex, market-based societies like China. In such societies, school can be viewed as a prolonged series of interlinked initiation rites in which initiates, much like their counterparts in many traditional small-scale societies, are promoted through a series of transitional age grades. When children enter the system, they are separated from their pre-school childhood. After twelve years, they emerge on the other side as legal and (to a somewhat more varied degree) social adults.

In China as elsewhere, examinations are central to this process. Promotion through school is contingent on passing exams, which, as they increase in difficulty, gradually become more intensive training for the big test, the Gaokao. Between junior high school (grades 7–9) and senior high school (grades 10–12), examinees take a particularly fateful transitional examination, the high-school entrance exam, which determines what kind of high school they will attend. Those who succeed (about 50 percent) undergo three years of additional drilling in academic high school, after which they face the final battle.[3]

The Gaokao, then, is the culminating rite of passage within a long series of such rites. And similar to participants in rites of initiation elsewhere, those facing the Gaokao consider it a fateful trial of merit that enables them to display their superior moral character.

Performance Character and Ethical Character

Merit involves both performance character and ethical character.[4] The former refers to virtues required to succeed in fateful events, the latter to moral aspects verified by that success. In practice, much slippage takes place between these two aspects of merit. For example, people in China consider diligence both necessary for successful performance on the Gaokao and a character ideal. Nevertheless, the distinction between performance character and ethical character remains a useful heuristic.

As Zeyu's test experience illustrates, Gaokao performance character includes at least four aspects—diligence, persistence, composure or psychological quality, and divine favor or luck. In modified form, similar virtues are important not only in the Gaokao but also in other fateful events in China and elsewhere. Cross-culturally, these qualities manifest themselves differently, and different types of fateful events demand them in different proportions. But fateful events everywhere possess basic structural similarities, partly because most people everywhere possess similar basic equipment (most fundamentally, a body). Thus performance character demonstrates much cross-cultural similarity.

Fateful events usually demand special techniques of the body and habits of the mind, which often can only be acquired through long years of training. In China, diligence reflects the assiduousness needed to acquire such primary capacities. By the same token, success in moments of fateful action often necessitates perseverance in the face of setbacks, disadvantage, or defeat. People in China usually call this characteristic persistence. Growing bodies of research refer to it as grit (Duckworth et al. 2007) or resilience (Luthar, Cicchetti, and Becker 2000). Moreover, participants in fateful events everywhere must conquer their nerves. In the heat of the fateful moment, people confront their bodies—hearts racing, skin sweating, hands shaking—almost as alien powers that must be mastered. Composure refers to this self-control.

Finally, factors beyond individual human control inevitably impact performance. Fateful events are undetermined—they are chancy and precarious, and random happenings can intrude with fateful consequences. In many types of fateful events, such as high-stakes gambling, randomness is even cultivated and foregrounded. But chanceful outcomes cannot be accounted for through appeals to ordinary forms of performance character alone. Thus people everywhere have some conception of luck, fate, or divine favor.

As I suggest above, merit includes not only performance character but also ethical aspects of personhood, which exhibit great cultural variability. In China, the virtues of performance character—that is, diligence, persistence, composure, and luck—are often understood to index filial devotion (*xiàoshùn*) to parents as well as the nobility of the scholar or cultured person (*jūnzǐ*). In recent years, test designers have attempted to reform the Gaokao to emphasize various aspects of all-around quality (*zōnghé sùzhì*), including creativity and innovation. But the ethical values that the exam promulgates are circumscribed by its individualistic focus. In China and elsewhere, fateful events that involve community and teamwork may emphasize strikingly different conceptions of ethical character, such as coordination, empathy, self-sacrifice, and so on.

The Paradox of Character and the Question of Structure and Agency

Goffman (1967) notes how our commonly accepted or folk notions of character present a paradox. On one hand, people tend to see character as something that endures through time and thus is characteristic of people. On the other, they think of it as something that periodically requires demonstration or proof. Goffman suggests that this paradox corresponds to two important social needs that all societies must fulfill. One is to provide people with morale and motivation, that is, to give them the impression (true or mistaken) that something can be won or lost in life's moments; that the game of life, in other words, is worth playing. The other is to maintain social continuity and order by ensuring that people reliably personify important social values.

Fateful rites of passage are important to fulfilling both social needs. Not only do they provide occasions for people to demonstrate their character, they also require people to undergo the special training and preparation that builds the character in the first place. This character-building function is particularly pronounced in fateful rites of initiation, like the Gaokao, which select and educate leaders. Such events also have an important legitimizing function. Preparation for them socializes those who will not be selected into accepting those who will.

I suggest that fateful rites of passage can have these effects because, from the perspective of individuals, they help to resolve a common existential dilemma— the question of structure and agency. This question is usually conceived as one for the social theorists, as I note above. Indeed, much theoretical work in anthropology and allied disciplines centers on this question, which asks to what degree people determine their own destiny and to what degree their destinies are determined by their social circumstances. My goal here does not lie in adding to these accounts. I do not attempt to present a better mousetrap for grasping the relationship between social organization and personal agency. Rather, I wish to highlight how the question of structure and agency is not only one for the social theorists but also one of ordinary people themselves.

In their everyday lives, people are constantly presented with this dilemma, which could be summarized as an existential question: Did I create my destiny or did my destiny create me? Of course, it is always both, and thus the question cannot be answered definitively in one way or the other. From the existential point of view, the goal is rather to hold these two poles of existence—the subjective and the objective—in a productive tension (Jackson 2005; Winnicott 1991). If one moves too far toward the subjective pole, attributing to oneself too much destiny-making power, then the danger of psychosis looms. One stands on the precipice of slipping into one's own private fantasy world. If one moves (or is forced to move) too far toward the objective pole, focusing on circumstances beyond one's control, then one faces a set of equally scary but complementary hazards—those of alienation and neurosis. One risks becoming a living automaton who is determined by others and thus dead to the world (Lacan 2006).

We can now see that the paradox of character that Goffman identifies is symptomatic of this fundamental existential concern. The need for continuity of character represents the objective pole of existence (the demands of society) and the need for demonstration of character the subjective pole (the striving of individuals). This paradox is given potent expression in the Chinese word for destiny (mìngyùn), which is formed from the combination of fate (mìng), which people conceive as divinely determined, and motion or luck (yùn), which they see as containing a controllable aspect.[5] This compound indexes the question of structure and agency by combining reference to both sides of existence: objective determination, continuity, and stasis on one hand, and individual striving, change, and mobility on the other. When people seek to change fate or transform destiny with the Gaokao, they are posing for themselves this question of structure and agency. They do so not in theory, but in fact, through their ritual practice.

To some degree, all rituals—fateful or not—enable people to address the paradox of structure and agency. Even small, mundane rituals can create a liminal, transitional space in which people can experience existential plentitude and self-transformation by collaboratively creating a reality (Puett 2015; Seligman et al. 2008). Creative play also has this quality (Winnicott 1991). But fateful rites of passage present people with particularly significant opportunities for achieving existential meaning. This is why fateful events cross-culturally form the object of so much daydreaming and fantasy, ranging from children's games and popular culture to the great traditions of high literature.

The existential significance of fateful rites of passage is particularly pronounced in those that form what anthropologist Marcel Mauss ([1925] 2000) calls total social facts. These are social events that concern almost every member of society and mobilize vast economic resources, becoming an object of general political, social, and religious concern. Mauss and his followers mainly analyze total social facts in relatively simple, small-scale societies. The classic touchpoints of anthropological thinking on the topic include the potlatch of the Pacific Northwest and the Kula exchange in Milne Bay Province of Papua New Guinea. Both these events display the typical characteristics of fateful trials of merit.[6] But large-scale social rituals in complex, market-oriented societies can also be analyzed as total social facts. In a democratic society, elections constitute an institution of analogous social significance (at least, that is, when people actually vote). In China, the Gaokao forms just such a total social fact.

Mauss proposes that total social facts are moments of generalized social reciprocity. What he means is that people use these events to compete for social recognition by marshaling immense economic, social, and cultural resources. As people say in China of the Gaokao, one goes all out (*pīnmìng*) or, literally, "puts fate on the line." But the curious and defining quality of recognition is that one cannot provide it for oneself; rather, it must be granted by others. Fateful rites of passage—particularly those of the total variety—are occasions in which people earn this recognition through their display of high cultural virtues. These are moments of reciprocity because people receive recognition in exchange for merit, which they acquire or demonstrate in various direct or indirect ways through their mobilization of resources.

The Politics of Recognition

By proposing that the question of structure and agency forms a humanly common experience, I do not mean to flatten the cultural diversity that exists in the world. This existential question can be asked in myriad ways, yielding a limitless variety of answers. But it is nevertheless important to identify cultural commonalities in addition to investigating cultural differences. First, understanding commonalities gives us a better appreciation of diversity. Commonalities are like the ground against which the figure of diversity emerges. Second, without an understanding of commonalities, we face the danger of overestimating differences. Commonalities can provide a foundation for achieving cross-cultural understandings about right and wrong. For example, cultural diversity itself forms one of those human commonalities, suggesting that diversity is something that we should all value.

The desire for recognition forms another such human commonality. Indeed, this desire can be inferred from certain basic qualities of personhood. As I suggest above, people are never individuals in the strong sense; that is, they are never selfsame sovereign subjects who exist before discourse and language. Rather, people always exist in dialog and relation with others, and this is why people cannot achieve existential meaning by just staying at home and recognizing themselves (down that path lies psychosis). Like Gaokao examinees, they must go out in the world and risk fate. Thus the phrase "desire for recognition" is actually redundant. Desire is precisely this constitutive lack of human beings—the paradox that we cannot recognize ourselves but must be recognized by others (Butler 1997).

My concern about the Gaokao and similar events is that opportunities for social recognition fall unequally onto different social groups. This process works differently in different societies, which are ruled by different ideologies. But in the Gaokao, as in such events in other meritocratic societies, the organizing ideology is that of individual merit. As I note above, some people are better positioned to achieve individual merit than others. But because of the way that this fateful rite of passage encourages people to take individual responsibility for their displays of character, it tends to reinforce this unequal status quo.

The Gaokao also reinforces this status quo in another way, namely by encouraging people to attribute to fate things that are within human control. Fateful events contain two types of uncertainty, which I term "agonistic" and "aleatory." The first type—agonistic uncertainty—is the product of interpersonal competition. This is the uncertainty that surrounds the result of two evenly matched boxers in the ring, or two well-prepared test takers. One will prevail, but which? This can't be known until they duke it out. The second kind of uncertainty—aleatory uncertainty—refers to events outside of human control, such as one's health or the weather on test day (until recently, most test-taking venues were not air-conditioned). Of course, this distinction between agonistic and aleatory uncertainty is mainly heuristic; it should be regarded as forming a spectrum rather than a clear division. But the key point here is how people conflate these two types of uncertainty, attributing to fate and other magico-religious categories things that are humanly produced. In particular, people tend to blame the effects of social inequality on fate, when social inequality actually results from the social competition for resources. Of course, accidents of birth are not within one's individual control. No one chooses whether to be born a man or a woman, the child of a farmer or of an official. But the differing opportunities of these groups result from their differing social positions, which are not the product of fate but of culture and history. In recognizing fate, people obscure the social origins of inequality. Thus the idiom of recognizing fate forms an important aspect of the Gaokao's ideological role.

By highlighting the ideological roles of fateful rites of passage, however, I do not mean to impute to all people in all places and times a universal desire for freedom. The concept of ideology, which derives from the work of Marx, has been rightly critiqued for universalizing what is (culturally and historically speaking) a parochial human concern—the desire for liberation from various social bonds, including religion, the family, social class, and so on. Critics contend that this kind of liberatory politics is the narrow cultural product of modern Western subjects (Mahmood 2012; Strathern 1988). I agree, with the caveat that Western societies do not have a monopoly on this politics; rather, it seems to emerge in one form or another within any sufficiently complex, market-oriented society, including late imperial China.

Although modern liberatory politics is not common among human societies, the politics of recognition is. Ironically, even people in relatively open, meritocratic societies must discipline themselves into becoming paragons of cultural virtue to achieve agency and recognition. Consider the example of a virtuoso pianist, who must practice for years to gain recognition in fateful moments of performance (Mahmood 2012, 29). Similarly, Gaokao athletes prepare for over a decade—their whole childhoods—for examination glory. The recognition that they achieve through the pious demonstration of virtues in meritocratic competition facilitates their performance of piety in the private sphere of the family, where they strive for recognition as daughters and sons, wives and husbands (Howlett 2020).

The Cultural Logics of Meritocracy: Credentialism, Hegemony, and Filial Piety

Insofar as every society socializes people into conceiving of their elites as exemplars of superior merit, all cultures might be conceived as meritocracies. But I primarily use this term in a more restrictive sense. In this book, meritocracy refers to cultures in which educational credentials play an important role in certifying the status of elites. These are usually, if not always, complex market-based societies.

Cultures of meritocracy display much variation across time and place, but their ideological foundations possess similarities. People in all meritocratic cultures believe that success reciprocates individual merit as judged by universal, rational authorities, the evidence of whose favor must be sought in the fruits of diligent earthly labor. Such authorities include rule-based institutions like the examination, the courts, and the market. But believers in meritocracy understand these institutions to ultimately be regulated by even greater transcendental authorities—the nation, the invisible hand, nature, or divine beings.

In such societies, credentials perform an important gatekeeping function by reinforcing the ideology of individual merit. In so doing, they ensure that social elites can maintain a relative monopoly on social and economic power, while also reinforcing the myth of open competition. But elites do not form a homogenous class. Rather, they consist of groups whose interests may overlap or conflict. A large-scale society like China has local elites, regional elites, and national elites. Other social divisions are also important, including ethnic ones (China has fifty-five officially recognized minorities, most of whom underperform the Han majority in education). And to some degree, even the genders may be considered separate status groups. Like most places, China is a patriarchy. In China's centuries-long history of examinations, women only recently received the right to compete. Although they outperform men in school, women in China, as elsewhere, continue to be locked out of the highest levels of social and political power.

No single status group ever dominates the competition for monopoly over credentials. Rather, elites negotiate with one another for a piece of the pie. This includes negotiation over the content of examinations, especially gatekeeping examinations like the Gaokao. On the surface, this negotiation concerns people's character ideals. On a deeper level, however, it is a social struggle. Different groups strive to secure canonical status in the educational curriculum for contents that will be friendly to their interests. I refer to this negotiation as hegemonic because relatively dominant groups (regional and national elites) must obtain the often grudging consent of weaker groups (such as local rural elites). The concept of hegemony, as theorized by Marxist social thinker Antonio Gramsci (1971), refers to this kind of elite alliance. Local elites may lack certain forms of social and economic power, but dominant elites need their acquiescence to ensure social stability. Even in an authoritarian society like China, the contents of examinations must be negotiated. In fact, negotiation may be especially important in a society like China, where the exam carries so much weight in buttressing the myth of meritocracy.

The stated purpose of the exam is the fair selection of people of merit according to objective, universal criteria. But because the contents of the exam are always the result of a hegemonic negotiation between different elite interests, its supposedly objective judgment inevitably reflects particularistic interests. Thus standardized exams, like other calculating rationalities (bureaucratic ranking mechanisms), can never do full justice to the singularity of human existence

(Derrida 1989). The personal history of each individual is too varied to be represented fairly by a test score.

As a result of these cultural logics, meritocracy gives rise to a double anxiety. On the one hand, the pollution of various particularistic influences always haunts the impossible ideal of universalistic selection. The feverish asceticism of the examination ritual—twelve years of regimented practice, all for the final battle—derives from the futile desire to erase all traces of this contamination. On the other hand, every individual feels personally responsible for his or her merit—for achieving recognition in the eyes of others, the market, the state, and (in many cases) ultimately divine beings or God. This terrifying sense of personal responsibility means that each member of a meritocratic society ultimately faces his or her destiny alone.

For these reasons, meritocratic cultures assign great spiritual value to assiduous labor. In the European context, Max Weber ([1905] 1992) points out that the German word for profession or occupation—*Beruf*—literally means God-given calling. I suggest that an analogous Chinese term might be found in *shìyè*, which people usually translate as undertaking, cause, occupation, or mission. Like *Beruf*, this term evokes the notion of forging one's own fortune through diligent devotion to an occupation. In imperial China, aspirants to examination glory described preparing for the examination as their occupation (*yè*) (Chaffee 1995, 4).

But now, as in imperial times, the most sacred of all occupations in China consists in rearing the next generation—traditionally, sons, but increasingly also daughters. Meritocratic societies everywhere present the paradox that people pursue individual success to fulfill social obligations. But this irony is particularly pronounced in China, which combines highly developed cultures of meritocracy and filial piety (*xiào*). The latter term refers to the cultural duty of honoring parents and ancestors, which scholars widely regard as a legacy of China's Confucian heritage. But filial piety is also instituted within Chinese families (Sangren 2013). Whatever calling people pursue, they commonly assert that their real mission in life lies in fostering filial children, who will take care of them in old age and extend their lineage. In this way, children provide parents with meaning, security, and a spark of immortality. For children, however (and every parent is simultaneously a child), this situation presents an existential double bind (Bregnbæk 2016). Children's sense of agency and autonomy is closely entwined with their pious fulfillment of the filial ideal.

To be properly filial, children must be successful. For this reason, people typically direct whatever resources they can accumulate in other endeavors toward educating their children. This educational desire is remarkably general in China

(Kipnis 2011). As Zeyu's father, the garbage collector, said, "My genuine calling [*zhēnzhèng de shìyè*] is educating my sons. All my life's sacrifices are for them." For many people such as Zeyu's father, success in the calling of educating children serves as a touchstone for success in life more generally—success that ultimately constitutes proof of divine favor or karmic merit. Therefore, the examination forms the central endeavor around which people organize a broad array of economic and social activity ranging from migration to marriage and from home-buying to entrepreneurship.

Each of these activities themselves possesses moments of fateful action that test cultural virtues. But the examination remains the central activity around which families organize their search for mobility and around which social elites justify their status. Vast segments of the population pursue what historian Benjamin Elman (2013) terms the examination life—a life devoted to preparing for, taking, and readying one's offspring for examinations.

Meritocracy in the Mirror of History: Disciplinary Revolutions East and West

In both Europe and China, the rise of meritocracy went hand in hand with the decline of aristocratic authority. In Europe during the Reformation and Enlightenment (approximately the sixteenth through eighteenth centuries), the aristocracy weakened as monarchs made alliances with a new social group, the rising middle classes or bourgeoisie. In China, society underwent a similar social transformation several centuries earlier during the Tang-Song transition (approximately the eighth to twelfth centuries CE) (Bol 2008; Hartwell 1982). During this period, the old aristocratic families declined and a new meritocratic status group—the literati gentry (*shì*)—developed a symbiotic relationship with the imperial house. In both societies, these changes coincided with commercial, technological, and economic revolutions. Under these changing social conditions, people of humble social origin could accumulate vast sums of wealth. As social mobility increased, the ascribed status of birth and blood gradually lost much of its luster. Instead, the new elites increasingly justified their positions through the achieved status of meritocratically earned titles and credentials (Linton 1936), and new meritocratic rites of passage were required to manage the process.

These economic and social transformations accompanied increasing bureaucratization, which heralded another kind of revolution—a disciplinary revolution (Gorski 2003). In both societies, the sovereign's power to inflict prohibitions and punishments receded in importance as significant swaths of the population increasingly dedicated their lives to the ascetic discipline of meritocratic self-cultivation. These developments had a strong religious inflection. In Europe, the Protestant clergy was bureaucratized two centuries before the state, and many early bureaucrats were clergymen's sons. In China, the rise of the mature civil examinations during the Song dynasty (960–1279 CE) accompanied a Confucian religious revival, known as Neo-Confucianism or Way Learning (*Dàoxué*) (Bol 2008). According to this creed, every (male) member of society bore personal responsibility for the moral development of the empire through personal cultivation (Bol 2008).

In Tang times (618–907 CE), the privilege of competing in the exams had been restricted to the aristocratic elite, who were known personally to their examiners. By contrast, the late imperial exam was open, competitive, and anonymous. Almost all men could participate, and their identities were carefully anonymized (Elman 2013; Miyazaki 1981). Armies of scribes copied and recopied examination papers so that no examiner could recognize his students' handwriting. This process erased the social origins of examinees, enabling them to compete through individual merit alone. Although conflicting views of merit persisted, it was largely thought of as the product of diligent study rather than innate talent. This way of thinking built closely on the egalitarian impulse in Confucian thought—the notion that, as the sage said, "education does not distinguish between classes" (*yǒujiào-wúlèi*) (Ho 1962; Munro 2001). Correspondingly, the curriculum of the examination gradually shifted from one that emphasized the composition of poetry, which required immense levels of cultural capital, to one that stressed the regurgitation of classics and the production of highly formalized eight-part or "eight-legged" essays. Although achievement in the exams no longer required lyrical brilliance, successful examinees were nevertheless highly charismatic figures. The Chinese pantheon of popular deities is a celestial bureaucracy composed largely of deified former officials. Achieving examination success, especially at the higher levels, was one step short of becoming a god (C. K. Yang 1967).

The civil examination comprised a complex system of exams supported by a nationwide network of government schools. Climbing the ladder of examination success entailed traveling up the geographical hierarchy of towns and cities from rural places to urban ones. Examinees were sojourners, constantly on pilgrimages to test centers. The entry-level licentiate or Distinguished Talent (*xiùcai*) examinations were held in the seats of local counties or prefectures. The next level, the Elevated Man (*jǔrén*) exams, were held triennially in provincial capitals. And the highest achievement—the Advanced Scholar (*jìnshì*) degree—was conferred by the emperor himself in Beijing.

Only the Elevated Man and Advanced Scholar degrees qualified candidates for official office. Few people succeeded at these higher levels of competition, but by the Qing dynasty (1644–1911 CE), a licentiate degree had become an important marker of elite status, with approximately 1 in 540 people holding this degree (Elman 2013, 106). Remarkably, this figure is of the same order of magnitude as elite university degree holders in China today. This correlation is especially noteworthy considering that women—half the population—were not allowed to compete in the imperial exams. Fewer than 1 percent of China's children achieve admission to a Project 985 university, the current hallmark of elite success.[7] Now as then, strict quotas limit the number of elite degree holders to a small but influential portion of the population.

Like today's college graduates, licentiates were not immediately eligible for government service. But their lives changed radically upon donning the special cap that marked their status. They received immunity from corporal punishment and were exempted from performing mandatory labor (corvée) in service of the state. In effect, these Distinguished Talents graduated from a world governed by punishment to a world governed by discipline—that is, from being feudal subjects to being modern ones (Foucault 1995).

The civil examinations were a startlingly modern form of disciplinary technology. Upon entering special examination halls, examinees were searched for unauthorized mnemonic devices, which included undershirts that were painstakingly hand-printed with canonical texts. One surviving such cheat shirt displays printing so small that it is barely legible without magnification (figure 2). Examination halls consisted of row upon row of cubicles, resembling lines of crops.[8] Inside these cubicles, examinees worked, slept, ate, and attended to their bodily functions for the duration of the examination, which could last several days (figure 3). The similarity of these buildings to contemporary penitentiaries and schools is striking, anticipating the appearance of such institutions in Europe by hundreds of years (figure 4). Some scholars even argue that the civil exams had an important but underappreciated influence on Europe, where competitive written exams are not documented before the eighteenth century. The mandarinate of China, supported by its system of merit-based examinations, was admired by European Enlightenment thinkers and European colonizers (Jacobsen 2015; Teng 1943). In the case of the US civil-service exams, which were instituted in the late nineteenth century, there is evidence of direct Chinese influence (Teng 1943, 306–8).

Ironically, however, just as other countries had started to modernize their systems of education and governance by introducing open, anonymous, competitive exams, China abolished its exams also in the name of modernization. Facing the threat of Western colonial incursions and having recently lost a war

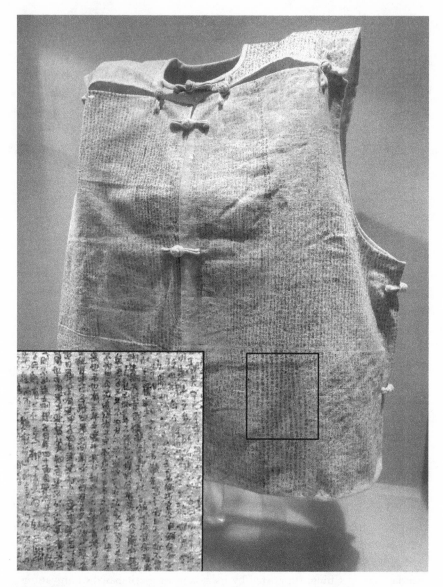

FIGURE 2. Imperial-era cheat shirt. Photograph taken by the author at the Shanghai Imperial Civil Examination Museum.

with Japan, Chinese state reformers worried that the exam system was the source of China's weakness. They fretted that the bureaucratic rationality of the exam isolated people into competing monads, thereby diminishing the social solidarity that modernization and national self-strengthening required (Woodside 2006). But by abandoning the exams, the state dismantled an institution that had helped

FIGURE 3. Mock-up of imperial-era examination-hall cubicles. Photograph taken by the author at the Shanghai Imperial Civil Examination Museum.

FIGURE 4. The imperial examination compound in Beijing, circa 1899.

Source: Sarah Pike Conger, *Letters from China: With Particular Reference to the Empress Dowager and the Women of China* (Chicago: A.C. McClurg, 1909), 56–57.

to ensure social stability for centuries. In 1911, two millennia of imperial rule abruptly ended with China's republican revolution. As China looked to the West for answers to its pressing social questions, the precocious modernity of the civil-exam system was lost, along with six hundred years of experience with governing a large bureaucracy (Woodside 2006).

Historians now question the assumption that the Chinese state needed to abandon the civil exams to modernize (Elman 2013; Woodside 2006). The civil examinations served as a cultural gyroscope—a stability-providing mechanism—that united even its failures around a common aspiration and pursuit (Elman 2013). This institution also bound the gentry-elites together with the government in a politics of mutual recognition—a "nexus between state and scholar" (Perry 2020, 7). By conferring the elites with examination credentials, the state recognized the elites' merit. The elites thus naturally recognized the authority of the state.

The abolishment of the civil examination in 1905 dissolved this relationship, presaging social chaos. During the Republican Era (1912–49), the country entered a period of weak central control, warlordism, and civil war. Newly founded Western-style institutions of higher education administered separate entrance exams. During this period, the absence of national examinations contributed to the alienation of Chinese elites from state power (Yeh 1990). Following the Communist Revolution of 1949, one of the new government's first priorities was to implement a unified national examination system. In 1952 the Communist government held its first Gaokao, bringing elites firmly back into the orbit of a newly consolidating state.

The renationalization of examinations under Communist rule—albeit now under the influence of Soviet and Western models—accompanied the reestablishment of centralized state authority after decades of disunity. In the following years, the state has constantly tinkered with the examination to adapt it to changing circumstances, and except for the hiatus during the Cultural Revolution (1966–76), the Gaokao has formed a perennial national ritual to this day.

The Lost Educational Legacy of the Cultural Revolution

The Cultural Revolution was a period in which people earnestly questioned the ideology of individual merit. Students decried examinations as a right-wing, capitalist institution. They tore up their examination papers and demanded that they be allowed to take tests in teams. Following the height of activism from 1966 to 1968, universities were closed completely. For a few short years from their reopening in 1972 to the end of the Cultural Revolution in 1976, admission to college was based on a recommendation system that gave preference to the children of manual workers and farmers.

Critics complain that these ideological changes turned back the clock on China's development by throttling the training of technocratic talent (H. Liu 2007). Without doubt, the Cultural Revolution caused immense suffering, unleashing domestic strife and setting neighbors against one another in "struggle sessions," a form of public humiliation in which victims were forced to admit crimes while being verbally and physically assaulted before a crowd. But historians now recognize some underappreciated achievements of that tumultuous time. In particular, the Cultural Revolution was also an educational revolution—a period of rapid improvement in equity of access to school (Andreas 2004; Thøgersen 1990).

Before 1966, Chinese schools mainly focused on preparing a small minority for success in competitive examinations. But during the Cultural Revolution, reformers dismantled this hierarchical system, known as "the little pagoda" (Andreas 2004). In the countryside, villages mobilized to build vast numbers of new schools. Enrollment soared, with teachers emphasizing practical skills and basic literacy. But without fateful examinations to motivate them, students needed other reasons to study, so teachers appealed to patriotic ideals of serving the village and country.

When the Gaokao was reintroduced in 1977, state planners reassembled the ladder of success. As the pendulum swung back in the direction of elite education, many local schools were shuttered. The state established a new category of highly selective keypoint schools (*zhòngdiǎn xuéxiào*) to train the next generation of leaders (Thøgersen 1990). But ordinary people fell behind. When children who were born in the 1980s came of age in the early 2000s, China's literacy rates suffered a marked drop (Yasheng Huang 2008). A national policy declared nine years of education compulsory in 1986, but China did not make significant progress toward this goal until the 1990s, when the effect of state-imposed controls on population growth—the one-child policy—began to be felt (Andreas 2004, 33). Introduced in 1979, this policy reduced the number of children, especially in urban areas, making it easier to implement education for all.

Literacy rates have recovered, but compliance with compulsory education is much lower than rosy government statistics suggest (Andreas 2004; Khor et al. 2016; Wu 2016). The state claims that nearly all students finish ninth grade. But these numbers are vastly exaggerated, particularly in rural areas, where many leave school to work (Chung and Mason 2012; H. Yi et al. 2012). In the countryside, governments continue to shutter schools in the name of consolidating resources.

During the first two decades of the twenty-first century, the state has attempted to increase the availability and quality of vocational education (Woronov 2015). But schools remain focused on preparing children for exams. Critics argue that this emphasis on the Gaokao does not serve the educational needs of people in rural places and other marginalized groups (Andreas 2004; D. Yang 2006). But many in China continue to pursue the elusive dream of Gaokao success for themselves and their children. As in imperial times, examinations form a sacred rite of passage for millions of Chinese. Now as before, vast segments of the population pursue the examination life, and the National College Entrance Examination remains a remarkably effective cultural gyroscope.

Managing the Cultural Gyroscope in Post-Mao China

With the resurgence of examination-based meritocracy in post-Mao China, the composition of the elite has changed substantially. In the Maoist era (1949–76), the elite largely consisted of party cadres from the Communist Revolution, which itself formed a fateful rite of passage. In the post-Mao era of economic reform (1976–present), an entrepreneurial elite of wealthy business people has emerged. Simultaneously, the party has become increasingly technocratic, filling its ranks with Communist engineers, lawyers, and economists (Andreas 2009). Party membership has become strongly correlated with success in meritocratic competitions.

Prior to the 1990s, college graduates were virtually guaranteed employment for life—which they termed an "iron rice bowl"—in a government work unit. People in China often compared graduates of that time to imperial-era licentiates, who were guaranteed an annual stipend paid in rice. In the 1990s, however, officials accelerated the dismantling of the state-planned work-assignment system (fēnpèi zhìdù) and expanded higher-education enrollment, producing rapid degree inflation. Now only a degree from an elite college provides comparable prestige and security. Although the definition of an elite degree has shifted many times from the Qing era to the present, the importance of possessing one has not. Now as before, acquiring such a degree secures one's status within a state-certified national hierarchy of credentials.

Western scholars may reject the likeness between the civil exams and the Gaokao, but few people in China regard this comparison as strange. With much justification, they see their country as the birthplace of examinations. For them, the Gaokao is the continuation of this legacy. In Xiamen, a whole research organization—the Institute of Education—is largely devoted to mining China's imperial exams for insights into contemporary education problems. And education officials, echoing the sentiment of the rural principal whom I mentioned in the prologue, compare the Gaokao to the civil exams in their socially stabilizing effects. As a provincial education official said to me, "The purpose of the Gaokao, like the civil exams of old, is to give the common people hope."

Skeptics might say that the Gaokao differs from the imperial-era exams because the Gaokao does not qualify people for official office. According to this view, the true parallel with imperial China, if any exists, is the contemporary civil-service exams, which were instituted in 1991 on the model of South Korea (Woodside 2006). But the imperial civil exams formed not just one exam but an integrated system of exams, only the higher levels of which qualified candidates for official service. Similarly, examinations in contemporary China should not be analyzed in isolation but rather as a social system, of which the Gaokao builds the base. Like the licentiate exam of old, the Gaokao is a threshold examination (*ménkǎn kǎoshì*). Passing the exam qualifies candidates for a lifetime of competition in more advanced trials of merit, including the modern civil-service examinations (provincial and national), the State Judicial Examination or bar exam, the teacher's qualification and recruitment exams, and the notoriously difficult Certified Public Accountant Exam. In particular, many in China today spend years taking and retaking the various civil-service exams in the hope of acquiring a job in the system (*tǐzhì nèi*). The system refers to any kind of stable employment within the state or state-backed institutions. During the present period of economic uncertainty, working in the system has become particularly desirable. Still, people widely regard these other examinations as heavily corrupted, whereas they persist in their view of the Gaokao as relatively fair.

Of course, epochal gaps separate the imperial and contemporary examinations. Over the last 150 years, China has experienced multiple social revolutions, civil wars, and international conflicts. In the twentieth century, massive state-sponsored social engineering projects catalyzed China's ongoing transformation from an agrarian society into an urban one. In the thirty years between the beginning of China's reform era and the start of the recent economic slowdown, gross domestic product per capita increased over thirty-fold and China became the world's factory. Although Confucianism is making a comeback, the Confucian classics play only a muted role in the Gaokao. Instead, today's students train themselves in math, science, and English, among other subjects. Examinees no longer need to make pilgrimages to examination halls in the provincial and national capitals; rather, these exams travel to them through modern technology. Using the same modern technology, administrators and education officials collect vast amounts of statistical data in their efforts to scientifically manage student and teacher resources. And whereas women were completely excluded from examination competition in imperial times, they now make up more than half of China's university graduates.

Such differences, although huge, could easily be exaggerated. Now as before, the examination system connects local elites to central-state power. Now as before, it helps to unite a linguistically and ethnically diverse country around the study of a common written and spoken language. Now as before, people grant the exam great authority but feel shocked when they catch a glimpse of its messy backstage reality. And now as before, it pulls even examination failures into its cultural gyroscope.

Evidence for the Gaokao's social and political significance can be found in how the highest echelons of state power routinely intervene directly in its management. In 1989, the student-led Tiananmen protests—partly a response to runaway inflation—threatened to topple the regime. The state responded by massacring protesters. But afterward it pursued a seemingly contradictory strategy. Instead of clamping down on college enrollment, state leaders continued to increase the number of college students, which rose from 670,000 in 1988 to 980,000 in 1993.[9] To be sure, the state reintroduced ideological control throughout the education system, reversing the liberalization that characterized the 1980s. As Chinese leaders watched the former Soviet Union collapse and Eastern Bloc regimes fall one after another in a series of velvet revolutions, the importance of such control could not have escaped them. But raising enrollment during a period of student unrest seems to be a peculiarly Chinese response—one that recognizes the significance of the nexus between state and scholars.

Around the same time, the state radically increased investment in higher education. Starting in 1995, President Jiang Zemin's administration poured billions of dollars into China's top universities to form Project 211, an abbreviation of twenty-first century and one hundred, the approximate number of participating universities. The more exclusive Project 985—named for the year (1998) and month (May) of its inception—funneled even greater sums of money into China's forty most elite research universities. These investments aimed to jumpstart China's innovation economy and to strengthen the ties between state and scholar (Perry 2020). At the same time, the format and content of the Gaokao began shifting to emphasize examinee quality. To further stimulate innovation, the authority to design examination papers was delegated to individual provinces, each of which became a laboratory for experimentation in education reform. China's leaders hoped that these measures would preserve social stability while increasing China's competitiveness in a global market.

In the late 1990s, the regime experienced another threat to its survival when the Asian financial crisis shook public confidence in party-led national development. The Politburo, the highest decision-making body of the Chinese Communist Party, responded by ordering another expansion of higher-education recruitment, overriding the gradualist plans of the Ministry of Education in an extraordinary exercise of autocratic power. This time the expansion assumed epic proportions. Over the next decade, the number of students matriculating to college increased over five times, from 1 million in 1998 to 6.3 million by 2009. By taking this measure, state leaders hoped to improve the economy by increasing consumption (Q. Wang 2014, 151). In this Confucian society, higher education was one of the few sectors in which demand far outstripped supply. And as a result of population controls, more families than previously had only one child, sometimes dubbed "little emperors," in which they were eager to invest (Fong 2006). But expansion also drew greater numbers than ever before into the orbit of the entrance exam's cultural gyroscope, giving ordinary people hope of a better life under Communist rule. As a result of the expansion, the majority of examinees (around 80 percent) now get into some kind of college.

Yet many of these college admission letters are only consolation prizes. In most provinces, fewer than 15 percent of students attend a first-tier college and fewer than 2 percent go to a Project 985 university.[10] But if graduates of first-tier institutions are hard-pressed to find jobs, this is a fortiori true of alumni of the thousands of lower-quality colleges.[11] Under expanded enrollments, therefore, college admission in China forms an example of what Bourdieu calls delayed selection (Bourdieu and Passeron 1977). Instead of being filtered out at the college level, so-called failures are now eliminated in the employment market, where those without an elite degree struggle to find a good job. Thus people still describe the Gaokao as "a great army crossing a narrow plank bridge" (*qiānjūn-wànmǎ guò dúmùqiáo*). On one side of the bridge are the masses clamoring for an opportunity to change fate. On the other side are the elite colleges, with their promise of a bright future and a good job (figure 5).

Today, China faces another brewing economic storm, which threatens to aggravate this employment crisis. The state staved off the worst of the 2008 global financial crisis by injecting credit into China's economy, but this action produced colossal levels of bad debt and exacerbated already high levels of corruption. At the same time, China's economic expansion is finally slowing after decades of double-digit growth, largely fueled by cheap labor. As wages rise, many industries are automating or moving abroad, and leaders worry that China may not be able to jump over the middle-income trap that bedevils developing countries (Shambaugh 2016). As one response to these challenges, officials are

FIGURE 5. "A great army crossing a narrow plank bridge." The sign on the desk at the end of the bridge reads "Prestigious Schools Admissions." Cartoon by Ensheng Han (2006).

pursuing another round of examination reforms under Xi Jinping, the current party leader. Like earlier reforms, these measures aim to accelerate China's transition to a consumption-based innovation economy. But they are also congruous with the anti-corruption campaign that has largely defined Xi's presidency (D. Cohen and Beauchamp-Mustafaga 2014). By reclaiming central-state control over the test, which is widely perceived to have fallen prey to corrupt local politics and special interests, these reforms aim to bolster people's faith in this pillar of China's meritocracy.

Such state intervention in the exam system reveals the degree to which central-state leadership considers the legitimacy of the examination to have implications for the legitimacy of party rule. Party leaders take the exam so seriously because of its central role in maintaining belief in meritocracy. China watchers often suggest that Chinese political legitimacy rests on a tacit bargain: people acquiesce to party-state rule in exchange for wealth. In this view, people in China support the party because economic development has improved their lives. But this focus on development gives short shrift to merit. People do not so much expect their lives to improve under party rule as they expect to have *opportunities* to improve their lives. In other words, people expect the state to guarantee the conditions for the meritorious to advance. At minimum, it must ensure the perception that such conditions exist.

Although the current economic slowdown may eventually change this perception, people commonly say that the party is doing a relatively good job of providing economic growth and social stability—basic prerequisites for mobility. They consider this achievement to be especially admirable in light of China's national circumstances (*guóqíng*) of overpopulation and underdevelopment (*rénkǒu duō, dǐzi báo*). Although widespread ambivalence exists with regard to party rule, people view alternatives such as electoral democracy as fraught with risk.

Note on the Gaokao System and Corresponding Terminology

People see all twelve years of schooling as one long road toward the Gaokao. But only the last three years, senior high school, focus directly on preparing students for the exam. Nationally, around half of students test into senior high school, a passing rate that is set at the central-state level (Woronov 2015, 5). Those who do not make it are branded failures, either attending vocational school or dropping out (M. H. Hansen and Woronov 2013; Ling 2015; Woronov 2015).

In what follows, I employ the Chinese usage, referring to the first year of senior high as senior one, the second year as senior two, and the third and final year as senior three (*gāoyī, gāoèr, gāosān*). Administratively, high schools are divided into subunits by grade, each of which is termed a year-section (*niánduàn*). For the sake of brevity, however, I customarily refer to these administrative subunits as years, for example, the senior-one year, the senior-two year, and so on. Each year is headed by a section leader (*duànzhǎng*) who oversees head teachers (*bānzhǔrèn*). Each head teacher manages a class (*bānjí*), which typically contains forty to fifty students. Head teachers coordinate the efforts of subject teachers (*kēmù lǎoshī*) and, in addition to these administrative duties, instruct their classes in an academic subject. Most teachers—including head teachers and section leaders—follow their students through the three years of high school.[12] After a cohort of senior-three students finishes the Gaokao, the whole year-section cycles back to instruct a new senior-one class—a welcome break from the stress and pressure of senior three.

During the first two decades of the twenty-first century, the Gaokao followed a 3+x model in most provinces, including Fujian, the site of my fieldwork. The

3 meant that all students were tested in that number of compulsory subjects—Chinese, math, and a foreign language (almost without exception English). The x referred to one of two comprehensive exams—the humanities comprehensive or the sciences comprehensive. At the end of senior one, students chose a humanities track or a sciences track, the selection of which determined the comprehensive exam that they would take. The humanities exam consisted of history, geography, and politics (a mixture of ethics and Marxism); the sciences exam consisted of chemistry, physics, and biology.

Under the newest round of Gaokao reforms, which the state plans to roll out in most provinces by 2022, a 3+1+2 model is becoming the standard. Chinese, math, and English continue to be compulsory, but instead of being divided into humanities and sciences tracks, students select their noncompulsory subjects individually as electives. The +1 means that students must choose between history and physics, and the +2 means they can select any two subjects from the remaining four—biology, chemistry, geography, or politics. The exam is still held every year in June, but the authorities are planning to implement a system in which students can take the English section twice yearly starting in senior two and keep their best results.[13]

This new structure aims to give students greater autonomy and flexibility. It is also meant to help address the common complaint that a single exam performance can determine life outcomes (*yī kǎo dìng zhōngshēng*). But many teachers and parents say that the reformed system is just "the same medicine in a new soup." As before, the exam constitutes a unified national ritual. As before, it is the conducting stick (*zhǐhuībàng*) of the whole education system. And as before, its main purpose is to select winners and losers.

Fieldwork and Methods

My research is primarily ethnographic; I learned about the Gaokao by interacting directly with students, teachers, administrators, and officials. I conducted fieldwork for two continuous years from 2011 to 2013 in the Minnan region of southeastern China's Fujian Province, across the strait from Taiwan. To gain an understanding of rural-urban variation in the exam experience, I carried out research at three different sites: the coastal metropolis Xiamen (pop. ~4,000,000), the backwater prefectural capital Ningzhou (pop. ~700,000), and a rural county seat in Ningzhou Prefecture, Mountain Town (pop. ~80,000). In each of these places, I immersed myself in the community as a volunteer teacher at under-resourced schools. I taught general English conversation courses to students and English teachers, at times teaching fifteen to twenty hours per week. I occasionally also served as a substitute teacher in students' regular English classes, which gave me firsthand understanding of the challenges that instructors face in teaching to the test.

Although I usually tried to speak English during my lessons, I kept to Mandarin outside of class.[14] I interacted with students, observed courses, and accompanied worshippers to pray for examination success. I also interviewed teachers, parents, administrators, and officials. In Xiamen, I conducted focus groups of college students, which offered insight into the experiences of Gaokao veterans from elsewhere in China. In all three places, I shadowed head teachers. These priests and priestesses of the Gaokao initiated me into many secrets, including the backstage manipulation of exam scores and the practice of school-sponsored temple pilgrimages.[15]

My access to schools and communities differed. In Xiamen, a major national economic center in China, foreigners are common. It was relatively unremarkable for a foreigner to visit Xiamen high schools, the most prestigious of which even employ foreign English teachers. But I primarily worked at a low-ranking school, Dragon Gate High School, located in a recently urbanized district of the city. As my contacts expanded, I visited other schools. In addition, I benefited greatly from dialog with researchers and students at Xiamen University's Institute of Education, and I joined conversation groups hosted by researchers in the Xiamen Municipal Institute of Educational Science.

In contrast with the relative anonymity that a foreigner enjoys in Xiamen, I was the only foreigner in Mountain Town, seat of Mountain County, where my presence required official government permission. Mountain County is a peripherally located, sparsely populated county of Ningzhou Prefecture, with about 350,000 people spread out across 2,000 square kilometers. In the lowlands, the main product is bananas. In the highlands, people grow bamboo and sugarcane, among other crops; however, the mountainous terrain does not lend itself to large-scale agriculture. In the Chinese Civil War, which lasted intermittently from 1927 to 1949, the region was a staging base for Communist guerrilla fighters. During imperial times, it was a refuge for bandits. As in other places in rural Fujian, locals fortified their community by building rammed-earth strongholds called earth buildings (tǔlóu), which still dot the countryside.

I generally spent two weeks per month in Mountain Town teaching at Mountain County Number One High School, the best of three public senior high schools in the county. I lived in student dormitories and took most of my meals with students.

When I traveled between Mountain Town and Xiamen, I typically stopped for a few days in Ningzhou, the prefectural capital, which formed the midpoint of my commute. Although Ningzhou consists of a built-up urban area with a population of about 700,000, locals describe the place as a backwater agricultural city (*bìsè de nóngyè chéngshì*). During my stays, I socialized with teachers, visited families, and surveyed schools.

At all three places, my role as teacher gave me a certain status and responsibilities. As the training ground for the big test, senior high schools are prestigious institutions in China. My association with high schools transformed me from a stranger into a known quantity, facilitating my interaction with community members.

After my first year of fieldwork, I scaled back my teaching activities somewhat, maintaining my presence in schools while expanding my footprint in the communities. In particular, I spent more time observing popular-religious activities and socializing with parents. I also visited schools in other parts of Fujian. Eventually, officials in the Provincial Education Ministry took an interest in my research, which gave me the opportunity to have candid conversations with provincial-level bureaucrats.

Fujian Province is relatively representative of people's experience of the Gaokao throughout China. The province neither rushes ahead nor lags behind in introducing reforms, and it performs near the national median on the Gaokao. The southeast coast of China is relatively prosperous, but vast gaps in opportunity loom between Xiamen and the rural areas of inland Ningzhou Prefecture, reflecting the general nationwide trend of rural-urban inequality.

Mindful of G. William Skinner's (1964–65) central-place theory, I selected my three field sites to form a representative cross section of this rural-urban hierarchy. According to this theory, China consists of a networked system of central places that follow regular patterns of geographical variation. This approach enables me to make cautious generalizations about the experience of the Gaokao in other parts of China. A county seat in Fujian will have more in common with a similar-sized town in Jiangxi than with a big city in either place. There are, however, limits to this method. China is vast, consisting of several distinct macroregions (Skinner 1964–65); so when my field sites exhibit potentially large divergences from other regions—for example, in the strong influence that popular religion exerts in southeastern China—I strive to draw attention to these differences.

Following Skinner (1980), I see central places not as isolated units but as command posts of economic activity, broadly conceived. Much of this activity consists in the movement between these centers of various social actors, including drivers, tourists, migrants, parents, pilgrims, teachers, students, officials, officers, salespeople, workers, and many others. Some of my most illuminating encounters occurred in transit, sharing buses and taxis with other travelers. Thus moving up and down the hierarchy itself constituted a method, enabling me to observe firsthand the manifold connections between these places.

Global Convergence and Cultural Variation

Although individual cultures of meritocracy vary greatly, meritocratic examinations have become a hallmark of modern life all over the world. They play a prominent role in everything from college admissions to civil-service recruitment, from intelligence testing to military enlistment (Hanson 1993). High-stakes national college entrance exams like the Gaokao evolved independently in the four Asian Tigers (Hong Kong, Singapore, South Korea, and Taiwan) as well as in Vietnam, all of which share a Confucian cultural legacy (Kipnis 2011; Seth 2002; Zeng 1999). These societies represent relatively extreme examples of meritocracy. But few if any modern societies operate without some kind of merit-based selection in higher education and government service, regardless of the political system. Meritocracy is embraced by authoritarian and liberal democratic societies alike. As in the Gaokao, family background and wealth are often the best predictors of achievement (Bourdieu and Passeron 1977; Lemann 1999; Soares 2007). Nevertheless, people generally persist in seeing success as a reflection of individual merit. And societies that embrace strong forms of this ideology—like China and the United States—tolerate especially high levels of social inequality (McNamee 2009; Whyte 2010).

Inequality has been rising everywhere in recent decades (Milanović 2016). This increase has complex causes. Among other factors, scholars point to the spread of laissez-faire economics, which critics term neoliberalism; technological change; and the rise of a top-heavy, extractive financial system (Harvey 2005; Milanović 2016; Piketty 2013). In many places, the power of the welfare state is eroding and that of multinational corporations and other transnational organizations is increasing (Readings 1996). In developing countries like China, many elites are sending their children to developed countries to be educated (Fong 2011). These trends are producing a transnationally mobile group of corporate technocrats even as ordinary people everywhere remain relatively restricted by national boundaries (Robinson 2012).

By bolstering the myth of meritocracy, competitive exams provide a justification for inequality. But people are pushing back. In both China and the United States, critics decry the emergence of a hereditary meritocracy.[16] In both places, they bemoan an intensifying ethos of technocratic professionalization and cutthroat educational competition. And in both places they worry that this ethos devalues humanistic pursuit, causing people to worship performance over authenticity and utility over wisdom (Blum 2009; 2016; Bregnbæk 2016; Readings 1996; X. Zhao 2015).

Despite these global convergences, policymakers in China and the United States are making momentous decisions based on cross-cultural perceptions that are often defined less by objective analysis than they are by mutual idealization or demonization.

In the United States, people fear falling behind the "big red dragon" (Yong Zhao 2014). The sense that the United States might be losing the international education race has helped galvanize a renewed emphasis on standardized testing in US schools (Ravitch 2010). When Shanghai topped the charts of the Paris-based Organization for Economic Cooperation and Development's 2009 and 2012 Programme for International Student Assessment examinations, US officials called it a Sputnik moment (Finn 2010). Ironically, however, people in China widely perceive US education to be superior. They are astonished to hear that standardized exams have been expanding in the United States. In their minds, the strength of Western education lies in the rejection of exam-based education (*yìngshì jiàoyù*) in favor of nourishing the whole person. In recent decades, reformers in China have been striving to introduce education for quality (*sùzhì jiàoyù*), which they see as largely inspired by Western models. In high schools and colleges, American-style liberal-arts curricula are proliferating. Meanwhile, the demand for study abroad is so great that even public high schools now commonly include special classes for students who plan to go overseas.

People see this Western approach to education as exemplified by US-style multifactor college admissions. They admire how the system considers a variety of inputs, including essays, grades, recommendation letters, and extracurricular activities. But they say that this system would never work in their country. In a society dominated by guanxi, they argue, multifactor admissions would be quickly corrupted. They have a point. In the United States and elsewhere, admissions officers complain about the high levels of fraud they see among Chinese applicants. In response, they are increasingly basing their admission decisions on Gaokao scores.

But this irony raises another question. It is up for debate whether or not multifactor admissions accomplish their stated goal of selecting people of merit while promoting diversity (Guinier 2015; Karabel 2006; Soares 2007; Warikoo 2016). Elite US colleges are admitting increasing numbers of minority students and those from public high schools. But the number of the "doubly disadvantaged"— those who come from poor backgrounds and went to public school—remains exceedingly small (Jack 2016).[17] Moreover, the 2019 college admissions scandal in the United States showed how the US system, too, is vulnerable to corruption. Wealthy parents pay fixers top dollar to secure places for their children in elite

US colleges through unethical means, for example by bribing collegiate athletic coaches to recruit them under false pretenses (Medina, Benner, and Taylor 2019). In light of these revelations, the Chinese critique of guanxi in multifactor admissions seems prescient. There is some evidence that the Gaokao, flawed as it is, may do a better job of encouraging social mobility (Liang et al. 2012).

This book provides a much needed ethnographic perspective on these policy debates. It is intended not only to be read by anthropologists and China scholars but also by educators, policymakers, and general readers. I am confident that readers will leave it with a greater appreciation for the Gaokao as a complex cultural phenomenon. People interested in education will acquire a better understanding of the exam as a fateful rite of passage interlaced with society beyond the school gates. China scholars, including historians of the civil exam, will gain a fresh perspective on the role of examinations in the moral life of the individual and the community. They may also gain new appreciation of how present-day arrangements, in addition to breaking with the past, also continue imperial-era legacies (Chau 2006; Puett 2006; Sangren 2000). And though I cannot dwell on the broader comparative implications of my project here, I hope that anthropologists and members of allied disciplines will see fateful rites of passage as a useful tool for analyses of societies beyond China.

The book is organized into six chapters. This chapter contextualizes the Gaokao culturally and historically and explains why it forms a fateful rite passage. The following chapters each focus on one aspect of the exam as a fateful event. Chapter 2 analyzes the high stakes of the exam, which, together with its undetermined outcome, forms a pillar of its fatefulness. (Recall that fatefulness = far-reaching consequences + uncertain result.) People see the exam as consequential because it enables them to migrate from rural to urban places, expanding their capacity to realize important life projects like marriage, childbirth, and eldercare. The value to people of this migration relates intimately to how they perceive it as a journey forward in time toward modernity and national development. Chapter 3 turns to the other pillar of fatefulness, uncertainty. It investigates people's false confidence in their ability to see through state proclamations of educational fairness. In this post-belief society, little is holy. Still, despite their cynicism, people have an inflated view of their examination chances. Sincere belief in the relative fairness of the Gaokao continues to play an important ideological role. Chapter 4 turns to ideals of character. This chapter shows how diligence and quality form competing ideals in a hegemonic negotiation between rural and urban interests. It examines how the rural character ideal of diligence is gendered and ethnicized, reinforcing the dominance of an urban, male, Han elite. Chapter 5 moves on to the fateful moment of examination itself, investigating the important role of attitude and composure in examination success. It shows how head teachers personify an educational contradiction, both helping children to overcome their deficits in cultural capital and encouraging them to take individual responsibility for their examination results. Chapter 6 investigates the popular-religious and magical dimensions of meritocracy. Whereas chapter 3 focuses on the agonistic aspect of uncertainty (the uncertainty that derives from interpersonal competition), this chapter concentrates on its aleatory aspect (the uncertainty that derives from uncontrollable random events). It explores how people employ magical concepts like fate, luck, and karmic merit to explain the vicissitudes of success and failure. This magico-religious dimension of meritocracy is not an unscientific holdover of superstitious thinking but an integral part of the examination life. A brief epilogue looks at a growing epidemic of lostness and confusion in China and speculates on the future of the Gaokao and similar meritocratic institutions in our rapidly changing world.

MOBILITY, TIME, AND VALUE

The High Stakes of Examination and the
Ideology of Developmentalism

Water flows downward and people move upward.

—Chinese adage

At Mountain County Number One High School, I frequently sat in on the lessons of my Chinese colleagues. During my first year of fieldwork, I attended a geography lesson on urbanization. This particular lesson was for a class of farm children with poor test scores—a "slow" class, or, as teachers sometimes called such groups in secret, a "garbage" class.

I settled into my desk at the back of the room. The teacher, Ms. Hu, directed students to turn to page 29 of their textbooks. She explained that we would be examining "the service functions of cities of different hierarchical levels." Opening my book, I was surprised to discover an introduction to central-place theory. As I note in chapter 1, this theory forms an important conceptual tool in my own research.

Anthropologists and historians use central-place theory to model China's complex system of interconnected, hierarchically nested regions and markets. But this theory also corresponds closely with people's native understanding of place. People perceive major cities like Xiamen as economically and culturally superior to prefectural-level cities like Ningzhou, which they in turn see as superior to county seats like Mountain Town. Officials in Mountain Town report to officials in their prefectural capital, Ningzhou. The highest-ranking officials in Ningzhou are ranked lower than their counterparts in Xiamen. But both report to officials in the provincial capital, Fuzhou. These hierarchies extend even to the pantheon of gods—a celestial bureaucracy that mirrors the earthly one (Feuchtwang 1992; C.K. Yang 1967). The city god of Ningzhou, whose temple draws pilgrims from all over the prefecture, oversees local deities, which, with some exceptions, attract worshippers only from their immediate localities.

This urban hierarchy—simultaneously economic, administrative, and religious—has a long history in China. In my field sites, the hierarchy assumed something like its current form after the commercial revolution of the Tang-Song transition in the ninth to thirteenth centuries CE (Hartwell 1982; Skinner 1980). In this era, Chinese settlers from the north displaced, forcefully pacified, or intermarried with aboriginal populations. The colonizers set up market towns, including my field sites, which date to this period. The Chinese annals describe this process as "opening up the wasteland" (*kāihuāng*), and historians refer to it as the Confucianization of the south (Miyakawa 1960; Wiens 1954). Bringing these newly civilized peripheries into the orbit of the examination system and the imperial bureaucracy was an important part of this process. Many of the gods to whom people now pray are officials from this earlier era of settlement and urbanization, deified for their accomplishments in spreading Chinese civilization.

But the geography lesson that day focused on more recent urbanization. To enliven the abstraction of central-place theory, the teacher directed students to a cartoon illustration in their textbook. This picture depicted a father and daughter in the countryside under the caption, "Low income; social services lacking." Nearby, farmers labored in a field next to another caption—"Quick population growth puts great stress on the land." One of the farmers appeared to be gazing thoughtfully at a city in the distance. Hovering over the city, captions proclaimed, "Many opportunities for employment," "Level of social-welfare guarantees high," "Cultural facilities complete," and "Traffic convenient."

"Urbanization can be divided into two types," the teacher explained, "urbanization of places [*qūyù*] and urbanization of the population [*rénkǒu*]. . . . As the population urbanizes, many things improve, becoming more elevated [*tígāo*]—living conditions, everyday habits, thoughts, even level of edification and all-around . . ."

"Quality [*sùzhì*]!" suggested a student.

"Yes, quality, including physical quality," the teacher replied. "The main reason for migration to the cities is that city people have higher quality and a higher education level."

Quality refers to an individual's all-around deportment and sensibility but may be disaggregated into individual components, including moral (*dàodé*), physical (*shēntǐ*), and psychological (*xīnlǐ*) qualities (Kipnis 2006). People in China say that quality is concentrated in urban areas and increases with urbanization. Raising population quality forms a central goal of national development (Anagnost 2004; Greenhalgh 2010; Murphy 2004; Jacka 2009; H. Yan 2008; L. Yi 2011).

Continuing her lesson, the geography teacher presented some historical assumptions that underpin this worldview. She explained to students that urbanization forms an inevitable global trend that commenced in Europe around the time of the Industrial Revolution in the eighteenth and nineteenth centuries. Developing countries like China must "catch up with the West" (gǎnshàng Xīfāng), seen as the origin of modernity. For people in China, catching up with the West would erase the "national humiliation" (guóchǐ) that Western imperialism inflicted on the Central Kingdom starting with the nineteenth-century Opium Wars (1839–42, 1856–60).

The desire to erase national humiliation is widespread in China (Z. Wang 2012). People see this mission as an effort to return the Central Kingdom to its former glory. Government propaganda refers to this endeavor as the peaceful rise (hépíng juéqǐ) or the great restoration (wěidà fùxīng). This national longing has fueled China's rapid development since the 1980s, which state policymakers have pursued through vast projects of social engineering, including industrialization, infrastructure construction, qualified market liberalization, population control, and, beginning in the late 1990s, the expansion of higher education.

As the teacher explained, these projects have transformed the central-place hierarchy. In the post-Mao era of reform and opening (1978—present), urban areas have swollen, many doubling in size. The percentage of China's urban dwellers increased from 20 percent in 1980 to around 50 percent in 2013 and continues to rise (Goodman 2014). Hundreds of millions have moved to urban areas or become part of a "floating population" of urban sojourners.

During the same period, China has undergone a demographic transition from relatively high to relatively low birth and death rates. Falling birth rates are causing China's population to age rapidly, precipitating a demographic crisis (Feng 2010). In response to this crisis, China has substantially loosened its controls on population growth. As of 2015, the one-child policy has become a two-child policy. In minority areas, parents are encouraged to have more than two children. But these moves are likely to have little effect. Despite decades of draconian controls, including forced abortion and sterilization, the looming demographic crisis probably owes as much to rapid development as to the effects of population control (Hesketh, Lu, and Xing 2005: 1172). Even though families are now allowed and even encouraged to have more children, many complain that the cost of child rearing has become prohibitively high. Social scientists warn of a coming "elder quake" that will curb China's growth, stressing families and social services to the limit (Keimig 2017).

Nevertheless, many in China continue to subscribe to the maxim that China suffers from "overpopulation and a weak foundation" (rénkǒu duō, dǐzi báo) or, in other words, overpopulation and underdevelopment. People say that this dual malady forms the core of China's national conditions (*guóqíng*). These national conditions provide an incontrovertible, ready-made explanation for every necessary evil of development, including corruption, pollution, authoritarian rule, and the Gaokao itself. When people are pressed to account for these necessary evils, they almost inevitably exclaim, "There's nothing to be done [*méi bànfǎ*]. China just has too many people." Like the belief in individual merit, this notion that China is overpopulated and underdeveloped constitutes an *ideology*—a distorted view of reality that justifies the status quo. I term this ideology *developmentalism*.

By referring to developmentalism as an ideology, I do not mean to dismiss the value of development. People everywhere wish to improve their lives, and poverty alleviation is a noble goal. Without doubt, development has vastly improved the lives of many in China, making them more affluent and mobile (Kipnis 2016). But state-imposed development often reinforces inequalities and creates new problems even as it reduces certain kinds of poverty (Ferguson 1990; Hobart 2002). By analyzing developmentalism as an ideology, I add my voice to those who envision more equitable and just forms of development (e.g., Ferguson 2015; Kubiszewski et al. 2013).

Of course, developmentalism is not unique to China. Readers who are familiar with this ideology from other cultural contexts will notice many similarities with how it manifests in China. At the same time, the Chinese version of developmentalism possesses much that is distinctive.

In China as elsewhere, developmentalism maintains a firm grip on people's minds because it co-opts their most intimate desires. The desire for national development (*guójiā fāzhǎn*) is undergirded by an even more fundamental desire—the desire for individual development (*zìwǒ fāzhǎn*). In a kind of neo-Confucian logic, the collective efforts of individuals toward self-development are an important source of national development but also the main way in which people accumulate quality or individual merit. In this way, the ideology of developmentalism becomes entwined with that of individual merit. People are critical of the Chinese Communist Party, which they perceive as corrupt. But their personal aspirations nevertheless hitch their life projects to the cart of national development under party-state rule, thus reinforcing the party's authority.

Since at least the 2000s, central leaders have been moving beyond a singular focus on economic growth toward a wider array of objectives, including corruption control, social welfare, and environmental protection (Perry 2014). To some degree, stability maintenance (*wéiwěn*) has superseded developmentalism as a legitimating ideology of the party-state. Although the Chinese state has long been focused on social harmony, stability maintenance became an explicit watchword of the regime after 2008.[1] This term refers to a raft of policies combining coercive techniques of social control, such as censorship and suppression of dissent, with softer approaches, such as conflict resolution and pacification of marginalized groups through welfare guarantees (Benney 2016; Lam 2019; Y. Wang and Minzner 2015). But economic growth is an important part of stability maintenance, and developmental logics and rationales continue to animate official discourse and popular experience.

For the majority in China, individual development is synonymous with urbanization. People associate personal transformation (positive or negative) with movement up and down China's geographical hierarchy of central places. Most desire to move up the hierarchy from relatively peripheral places, which they see as lacking opportunity and value, to relatively central places, which they say possess these qualities (Xin Liu 1997; Nyíri 2010; Skinner 1976). An oft-repeated adage—the epigraph of this chapter—attests to the force of natural law that people attribute to this aspiration: "Water flows downward and people move upward" (*shuǐ wǎng dīchù liú, rén wǎng gāochù zǒu*).

As this maxim suggests, people see the urban hierarchy as a hierarchy of talent (*cáinéng, réncái*). By extending their reach—their center of activity—up the hierarchy of places (from villages to towns and from towns to cities) people increase their status, reputation, and earning potential. For this reason, people see geographical mobility (movement through space) as synonymous with social mobility (increase of status). Following Julie Chu (2010), therefore, I analyze mobility as a variant of what anthropologist Nancy Munn (1986) terms the spatiotemporal extension of self. But unlike Chu, who focuses on the material and semiotic dimensions of mobility, I highlight its existential ramifications. By achieving mobility, people earn recognition. They do so by enhancing their self-efficacy—their potential to get things done in the world—in both spatial and temporal ways.

It is perhaps self-evident how people's mobility expands their self-efficacy through space. But mobility also extends self-efficacy through time. By moving up the hierarchy, people improve their ability to enact future life projects, including marriage, education of children, and care of elders. In short, achieving mobility is changing one's fate.

In a memorable turn of phrase, a friend of mine—the principal of a local junior high school, Mr. Jian—summarized these arrangements as follows: "Fortune is a type of movement" (*yuánfèn shì yī zhǒng yùndòng*), he said. In Chinese cultural conceptions, fortune (*yuánfèn*) is similar to such terms as fate (*mìng*) or destiny (*mìngyùn*) but emphasizes serendipitous connections between persons, places, and things.[2] By referring to fortune as a form of movement, Mr. Jian made explicit the cultural logic that links the pursuit of mobility with the propitious unfolding of fate. By pursuing mobility, parents and children aspire to create what Mr. Jian called a "better platform for fortune" (*gěi yuánfèn yīge gènghǎo de píngtái*). Creating a better platform for fortune means extending one's sphere of self-efficacy to more centrally located destinations, which is the main way in which people create value for themselves and their families. In sum, these cultural conceptions equate mobility with the expansion of self-efficacy, and thus with the creation of value. This link exists in other cultural contexts, but it is particularly strong in China because of the great geographical salience and cultural significance of the urban hierarchy there (Skinner 1964–65).

In the modern era, this link between mobility and value is both spatial and temporal in a further sense. People have increasingly adopted a linear view of time, largely borrowed from the West. According to this view, history develops toward a telos or goal—usually communism, socialist modernity, or simply modernity. As a result, people associate movement up the hierarchy with becoming more modern. Moving to the cities is moving forward through history, and mobility and its various trappings constitute an important way in which people express their modernity (Chu 2010). At the same time, the cities are expanding to meet the migrants. This dual process of urbanization—the urbanization of people and places—entails the simultaneous development of individuals and the nation as a whole.

These close associations between mobility, value, and time form the warp and weft of developmentalism's ideology. China's massive new cities, eating up China's farmland at a breathtaking pace, testify to the enormous resources that the state has poured into this vision of development. Through decades of breakneck urbanization, the ideology of developmentalism has become objectified—that is, physically instantiated—in the hierarchy of places (Bourdieu 1990). Advanced cities draw migrants from their so-called backward hinterlands—a Manichean divide that the household registration system enshrines. Following a circular logic, people see the consequences of developmentalism—an increasing rural-urban divide—as incontrovertible evidence of the correctness of this ideology.

But people's experience of mobility complicates this developmentalist narrative of linear movement through space and time. Extending the self upward on the hierarchy does not necessarily mean abandoning places lower on it. Most families maintain a dispersed existence (M.L. Cohen 1970). They stay connected to their places of origin while attempting to open up new platforms for fortune in more centrally located, modern places.

The Gaokao is China's main state-sanctioned or orthodox strategy for creating these new platforms for fortune. For this reason, the Gaokao is particularly consequential. As an orthodox mobility strategy, the exam gives people an opportunity not only to move to the city but also to acquire the status and stability that they associate with urban life—a secure white-collar job and an urban household registration. But families must pave the way for their pursuit of orthodox mobility through unorthodox mobility strategies, including undocu-mented sojourning in cities. By the same token, state policymakers employ the Gaokao to direct and control mobility, for instance, by limiting where migrant children can go to school and where they can take the exam.

This chapter examines these relationships between mobility, time, and value. Its main purpose is to explain why the Gaokao matters to people—that is, why the stakes are so high. My argument requires me to unravel some historical and cultural underpinnings of developmentalism. In addition to discussing Western imperialism, I examine China's own history of imperial expansion and internal colonialism. In particular, I argue that developmentalism is not as unprecedented as many think, including the Chinese geography teacher. I see developmentalism as China's newest iteration of earlier civilizing missions to cultivate the populace and incorporate the periphery, which has long been regarded as the realm of uncultured barbarians (Harrell 1995; Rowe 1994). Developmentalism is merely China's most recent variant of meritocratic ideology.

Other historical continuities are important to observe. In the collectivist period (1949–77), people were largely confined to their places of origin. After Mao, however, people have returned to patterns of mobility that more closely resemble those of the late imperial era, when dispersal was common (Skinner 1976). This increase in mobility has had a variety of effects. It has improved people's lives even as it has raised their awareness of social problems, including environmental degradation, rural-urban inequality, and the demographic crisis. As people broaden their horizons (*kāikuò yǎnjiè*) and become world-wise (*zhǎng jiànshi*), they become more critical of the status quo.

The Gaokao constitutes a highly effective system for channeling this dis-satisfaction into the pursuit of orthodox goals. But what the Gaokao offers the majority of people—despite the myth of meritocracy—is the promise of limited mobility rather than any radical transformation of destiny.

Orthodox Mobility, Western-Impact History, and Study-Abroad Fever

Water flows downward and people move upward. Just as gravity draws water down into the lowlands, so do central places exert an inexorable attraction in people, summoning them up the social ladder.

From the vantage of Mountain County, this maxim seems especially apt. Imag-ine that you are standing on a hillside in Mountain County. If you are a farmer toiling in the fields, you pause to picture the central-place hierarchy extending into space. In the distance, ridge after ridge of terraced hills disappears into the smoggy lowlands below. Invisible beyond the mountains lies the prefectural capital of Ningzhou and, beyond that, the coastal metropolis of Xiamen. Farther in the distance, even greater cities beckon—Shanghai and Hong Kong, with their glittering towers and endless shipyards, and the hazy behemoth of Beijing, magnet of political and cultural power. In the minds of parents and students, each move up this ladder represents better resources, better welfare, better schools, better jobs—in other words, greater status and more value.

Many children of rural origin devote themselves to succeeding in the exam because, as they say, they fear becoming farmers (*pà dāng nóngmín*). This fear can have fateful repercussions. When a girl in a rural locale committed suicide after failing the Gaokao, people remarked, "She could not be a farmer, and she did not know how to study, so suicide was her only way out."[3] But disappointment and humiliation certainly also factored into this girl's tragic decision. In rural areas, a college degree offers more than a reprieve from the back-breaking labor of farming; this credential also confers great prestige. As another girl from a poor farming family explained: "In my village, my father always gets beaten up. Last month he lost two teeth in a fight. My aunt told me that if I get into college, people will stop hurting him. That's an important reason we study so hard—the prestige of getting into college." In another village, a man was selected as village head because three of his four children (two of them girls) had attended college. These anecdotes dramatize some of the profound consequences of exam-based mobility for ordinary examinees and their families.

The Score-Value Hierarchy

The Gaokao creates a close link between exam results and mobility. For this reason, test scores both represent and store value (Woronov 2015). Students with high test scores go to high-ranking high schools and colleges, which provide an opportunity to secure employment and a household registration in big cities. Students with bad scores are relegated to so-called bad schools, bad jobs, or a precarious life of urban sojourning. Their only hope of orthodox mobility lies in toiling to establish the conditions for the examination success of the next generation. At the same time, one's position in the geographical hierarchy is closely correlated to one's test score. Low-ranking schools and colleges tend to be located in peripheral places, which are seen as backward; high-ranking schools and colleges tend to be located in central places, which are regarded as modern. For these reasons, the urban hierarchy constitutes what I term a *score-value hierarchy*.

I elaborate on the score-value hierarchy, including the life chances of people at various positions of the hierarchy, in chapter 3. As I note there, the true extent of test-score disparities is a state secret. But people know that educational opportunities are better in centrally located places. And like parents every-where, parents in China strive to give every possible advantage to their children. Although they tend to misrecognize test scores as a manifestation of individual merit rather than social labor, they are well aware that they can improve the chances of their children by providing them with better opportunities and better conditions—in short, a better environment. In practice, this endeavor usually entails migrating up the hierarchy or sending their children there.

The desire to move up the hierarchy seems self-evident to people in China. But this pattern of mobility is not the inevitable product of natural inclinations. Rather, it arises from specific cultural logics, state policies, and historical trends. Meritocracy has a long history in China. Much as people do today, people in imperial times saw the hierarchy of places as a hierarchy of talent. Before as now, they associated central places with civilization and rural places with a pastoral ideal (Berg 2002; Harrell 1995). But the present version of meritocratic ideology, developmentalism, differs in important respects with imperial-era thinking.

In contrast to imperial-era ideologies, developmentalism encourages people to perceive the spatial hierarchy through the lens of time. Moreover, this is a particular kind of time—a linear concept of goal-directed or teleological time. As opposed to cyclical notions of time, like the seasons or the year, teleological time starts in the past and finishes in the future. When people view the spatial hierarchy through a developmentalist notion of teleological time, they see rural places as lagging behind the city in development. By drawing rural residents into urban centers, the state aims to synch up the rural population with the urban present, accelerating China's economic transition to a middle-income nation of urban consumers.

Such a developmentalist logic may seem intuitive to most Westerners. A teleo-logical notion of time is shared by the Abrahamic religions, all of which possess some concept of end times. A related concept of time characterizes the thinking of Karl Marx, whose notion of development toward the telos of communism was influenced by Christian eschatology via the philosophy of Hegel. In con-trast to these views of time, a cyclical concept of time was common in imperial-era China. China's old lunar calendar was divided into cycles of sixty years that people counted by combining the ten Celestial Stems with the twelve Earthly Branches. On a larger scale, people reckoned history with reference to imperial dynasties. They viewed history through the lens of dynastic cycles of union, when the country was united, and disunion, when it was divided.

But one should not overstate the divide between imperial-era views and contemporary ones (Puett 2014). On one hand, people in China today—particularly in rural areas—continue to reckon major life events (birth, marriage, death) according to the old calendar. Many, moreover, continue to see history as a succession of dynasties, of which the Communist Party is merely the most recent. Even the party's own project of great restoration suggests such a cyclical view of time, pursuing the return of the country to its former glory. On the other hand, it would be untrue to claim that imperial China had no notion of teleological progress. Confucian doctrine states that the goal of enlightened leadership is to develop the world toward a period of great unity when everyone and everything will be at peace. This great unity is modeled after an idealized view of ancient China, but, like communism, it provides a utopian vision of the future. Nevertheless, the notion that rural places are backward and urban places are modern, which dominates China today, is a major departure from older cultural logics. This developmentalist logic represents a hybrid formation of older notions of meritocracy that continue from the imperial era, and linear notions of historical change, which arrived in China via Marxism and other forms of Western developmentalist thinking.

This teleological, developmentalist logic justifies urbanization, including plans to unify backward Ningzhou Prefecture with modern Xiamen into one megacity— one of many such projects across the country. By pursuing such policies, the mission of socialist modernization (*shèhuìzhǔyì xiàndàihuà*) promises—in principle at least—the eventual creation of a monadic contemporaneity in which no person will be backward and no time out of joint with the future. According to this urbanization blueprint, only a small number of residents will need to remain in rural areas, where they will run mechanized farms, extract natural resources, and enact an idyllic pastoral past for urban tourists.

Developmentalism and the Rural-Urban Divide

In China and elsewhere, development was originally conceived as an antidote to the negative effects of global capitalism and Western imperialism (Kipnis 2016). Indeed, development in China has raised hundreds of millions out of poverty. But since the 1990s in China, development under the authoritarian party-state has increasingly enriched a corrupt few by causing vast amounts of wealth to flow up the central-place hierarchy from peripheral places to central ones (Yasheng Huang 2008, 2015).

During my fieldwork, I commuted regularly between Xiamen and Mountain Town. This journey covered only 120 miles, yet it traversed starkly different social worlds. The bucolic and underdeveloped Mountain Town struck a stark contrast with the chaotic streets of Ningzhou and the towering high rises of Xiamen.

As a government official explained to me, Mountain County, like many places in China, was striving to "move all the people from the mountains into the towns." As in other rural areas, the government encourages people to move by providing resettlement compensation, cheap mortgages, and other incentives. Some populations are forcibly relocated. Under Xi Jinping, this urbanization policy has become a major component in a strategy to eradicate poverty by 2020.

From the central state's perspective, urbanization is not only about alleviating poverty but also about making sure that the engines of the economy keep churning. In the wake of the 2008 global financial crisis, Beijing injected a tremendous amount of liquidity into the Chinese economy, dulling the impact of the crisis. This infusion of easy credit fueled a construction boom within China's borders and abroad. As a result, several new apartment complexes sprang up around Mountain Town from 2011 to 2013. In Mountain County as elsewhere, however, many of these new buildings remained empty or unfinished, turning whole neighborhoods into ghost towns (Ulfstjerne 2017). This pattern of development enabled government-connected developers to embezzle vast sums of money.

By 2015, the political winds had shifted in Mountain County. The county magistrate was arrested as part of Xi's anti-corruption drive. Locals said the "big bosses" who had received government money to construct new buildings had run off, leaving behind bad debts and serious overcapacity. As Mr. Wu, a guard at the high school said, "If all these houses were full, the population of Mountain Town would have to double."

Rather than settling in Mountain Town, people from the hinterlands travel to the cities to work. As a local school administrator said, "What are they supposed to do if they stay here? There's no way to make money. And those who can afford a new house would rather buy one in the prefectural capital, where the schools are better."

Located on the outskirts of town, the high school, Mountain County Number One, faces a stagnant irrigation channel and is surrounded by one of the empty housing-boom developments. It is the largest of three functioning county senior high schools left after many rural schools were closed in the 1990s and 2000s. The best school in the county, it attracts many students from rural areas. Approximately half its students are boarders from outside of town, the majority of them the children of farmers.

Teaching at the school, I became intimately acquainted with the ironies that these young people experience in their attempt to get out of the countryside. One such irony expressed itself in the geography lesson that I describe above. The lesson argued for the correctness of pursuing socialist modernization under the party-state's stewardship. But students perceive the party as corrupt, and for that reason ideological catchphrases such as "socialist modernization" strike many as hypocritical and empty. Nevertheless, they regurgitate these slogans to pass examinations, and their goal in doing so is one that they pursue with great sincerity. For them, the Gaokao provides the best hope of a good life in the city, or, in the language of the lesson, of urbanizing themselves. Whether or not students believe in developmentalist ideology is almost immaterial; they enact it in their own life projects, albeit for their own interests. Success on the test is synonymous with self-transformation through migration.

These arrangements present another irony. Urbanization policies have exacerbated certain types of rural-urban inequality. Paradoxically, therefore, these policies frustrate many people's chances of realizing their dream of a comfortable urban existence. As elsewhere in China, the government has closed many rural schools. The stated goal of this policy—known as school consolidation (*chèdiǎn bìngxiào*)—is to improve quality of instruction by concentrating resources in central schools (Chan and Harrell 2010). But local educators admit that the policy disadvantages rural children. Few ordinary families can afford to buy or rent a house in town, forcing children to board at school or drop out. The schools that remain open are heavily focused on securing admission to college for a high-scoring few rather than raising the level of education for the many.

Brain drain is exacerbating this unequal trend. The best and most ambitious teachers in Mountain County have fled the countryside. Many now work at newly opened private schools in Ningzhou, where the education bureau has supported the partial privatization of education. Still others have moved to Xiamen, taking advantage of municipal programs to accelerate the city's urbanization by introducing talent (*yǐnjìn réncái*) from rural places. By the same token, students of means and ability (money and high test scores) exploit various loopholes in the system to move to the cities, where education is better (that is, test scores are higher).

Further, higher-education expansion has given vast new segments of the population access to college but has also resulted in widespread underemployment and unemployment—a scourge that disproportionately affects people of rural origin, who generally can only gain admission to low-ranking colleges. In the face of such widening educational and economic gaps, many students of rural origin drop out of school to seek wage labor in urban areas without completing compulsory education (Chung and Mason 2012; Wu 2016; H. Yi et al. 2012).

But in spite of such increasing disparities, the majority in China continue—albeit with increasing ambivalence—to believe in urbanization, meritocracy, and development. Why? A partial answer lies in how developmentalist ideology is objectified in the central-place hierarchy. People find objective proof of the validity of development in their experience of centrally located places as relatively advanced and modern, on the one hand, and peripherally located ones as relatively backward and traditional, on the other. Processes that people associate with modernization—for example, the construction of high rises, the regulation of traffic, the implementation of educational policy—percolate into peripheral places from central ones. Thus, increasingly remote areas appear to exhibit progressively earlier stages of development.

The National Conditions of Overpopulation and Underdevelopment

The ideology of developmentalism is exemplified by the view—nearly ubiquitous in China—that the country suffers from overpopulation and underdevelopment or overpopulation and a weak foundation. This concept requires some explanation. People mainly understand weak foundation to mean underdevelopment, including an overabundance of low-quality citizens. Moreover, people associate low quality and underdevelopment with the predominance of particularistic connections or guanxi, which many consider to be a cultural relic of China's traditional, or in the leadership's official Marxist terminology, feudalistic (*fēngjiàn*) past. People say that the cultural prevalence of guanxi holds back China's development by encouraging nepotism and corruption. This combination of underdevelopment, low quality, and guanxi forms China's "national conditions." This term refers to supposedly irrefutable commonsense truths about Chinese society, which can only be transcended through continuous development. As evidence of the national conditions of overpopulation and underdevelopment, people point to such problems as overcrowded train stations, bad traffic, pollution, rampant corruption, and fierce social competition, which is epitomized by the Gaokao itself. People interpret these problems as evidence for the necessity of continued development, and thus for the inevitability of the current development model—a drive toward modernity shepherded by an authoritarian party-state.

In addition, people's belief in overpopulation and underdevelopment has long drawn strength from another source—the traumatic sacrifices that many families have made to comply with state polices to control population growth. People in China refer to these policies as "birth planning" (*jìhuà shēngyù*). From the early 1980s until 2015, most couples were limited (in theory at least) to having only one child. Most people in the West—where this restriction was known as the one-child policy—assumed it to be a response to the Malthusian specter (real or imagined) of overpopulation. But state planners never saw this policy merely as a way to reduce population growth. They also conceived it as a method of reverse-engineering demographic transition (Greenhalgh 2010). This term refers to the demographic changes that countries undergo as they develop. As per capita wealth increases, birth and death rates typically fall. Economists argue that this transition results in higher parental investments in a smaller number of children (Becker 1993). Chinese policymakers saw population control as a way of accelerating this transition from quantity to quality.

By limiting births, they intended to focus parental and state investment on a limited number of high-quality children. At heart, then, birth planning was a eugenicist aspiration; indeed, an explicit goal of the policy was "superior birth" (*yōushēng*). The "study of superior birth" (*yōushēngxué*) is the Chinese term for eugenics (Kipnis 2006: 305).

In developed coastal areas and large cities, China appears to have already undergone demographic transition. China now faces a demographic crisis that threatens to derail its economic growth. Much of this growth (as much as 15 percent from 1982 to 2000) is attributable to the "demographic dividend" of plentiful workers (Feng 2010: 246–47). As the population ages, however, the number of young workers is plummeting. To combat this demographic time bomb, central planners have relaxed population controls since 2015. Married couples are now allowed—indeed, actively encouraged—to have two children. But this policy change comes too late to reverse the aging trend. Many urban families now decide not to have any children at all. This reluctance is unexpected in this Confucian society, where one of the greatest sins consists in extinguishing the patriline.

From a policy perspective, the most rational response to the problem of an aging society would be to abandon population controls. But population controls remain in effect, though they are looser than before. Moreover, many in China persist in considering the national population to be overly numerous despite this demographic crisis. This inertia in policy and popular opinion has many sources. For one thing, a vast government infrastructure is dedicated to population control—one that includes many vested interests. More fundamentally, however, the belief in overpopulation plays an important cultural and ideological role by forming a central tenant of Chinese developmentalism. The specter of China's national conditions, coupled with the panacea of development, provides a central rationale for the party-state's existence. For this reason, completely abolishing population controls, if done too quickly, might threaten party legitimacy.

The discourse of national conditions has a very similar cultural effect to that of fate. Both terms function as a theodicy—a theory of how divine powers, or in this case the party-state, can be good and just despite the existence of social ills, suffering, and other evils. People blame any problem on overpopulation and underdevelopment. The Gaokao is counted among such ills. Bemoaning the exam's relentless focus on memorization, people wonder if the test truly selects people of high quality. And they criticize the exaggerated role that this one examination has in determining fate. But, as they say, "There's nothing to be done. There are just too many people in China. Competition is too fierce. The Gaokao is the only answer."

When people invoke fierce competition in the context of overpopulation, they mean that this competition takes place within a very specific cultural environment—one dominated by guanxi. They say that basing college admissions on a single exam provides an effective corrective to this culture, which, in their view, would make US-style multifactor college admissions infeasible in China. In other words, people see the Gaokao as counteracting this particular kind of overpopulation, which they say breeds corruption and nepotism.

Individual Fortunes and National Conditions: Raising Population Quality to Transcend Underdevelopment

This discourse of national conditions builds a meritocratic narrative of national redemption, which casts the Chinese people as heroic conquerors of hardship. The Communist Party stakes its legitimacy on guaranteeing the conditions for this narrative to unfold—the ability for the nation to become wealthy—achieve its great restoration—despite the twin handicaps of overpopulation and underdevelopment. This utopian vision of national development relies on the meritocratic logic of social reciprocity—the notion that hard work is rewarded by individual and national development. According to this logic, only through continuous struggle (*fèndòu*), which is simultaneously national and personal, can China and its citizens overcome their national humiliation by catching up with the West. In this discourse, "the West" broadly refers to Western countries, of which the United States is usually considered (despite its high levels of poverty vis-à-vis other developed countries) a privileged and prototypical representative because of its superpower status.[4]

The Gaokao is an important method by which people recruit themselves into this narrative of meritocratic national redemption. Through diligent striving to succeed in the examination, people link the transformation of their individual fortunes to the transforming fortune of the nation. Ordinary people and policymakers see the Gaokao not only as a byproduct of underdevelopment and overpopulation but also as a potential means by which individuals and nation can transcend these conditions.

Indeed, people explicitly link the transformation of individual fortunes (*gèrén de mìngyùn*) to that of the national fortune (*guójiā de mìngyùn*). This linkage constitutes a core component of developmentalist ideology. According to this ideology, individual development and national development go hand in hand. As one high-school student told me,

> National development and individual development reciprocally rely on each other and reciprocally drive each other. The development of the country stimulates individual development; diligent individual struggle further drives national development.

This linkage of personal with national fortunes means that the spatiotemporal extension of the self (the urbanization of people) relies on the spatiotemporal extension of Chinese society as a whole (the urbanization of places). Continuous national development gives every family hope of better opportunities for self-development in the future. As a forty-something Ningzhou taxi driver said, "My father only graduated from primary school. In the 1990s, I made it through eighth grade. My daughter is about to graduate from college. When China was poor, the general education level was bad. As China develops, the education level is rising." As many recount, moreover, this journey of increasing education is simultaneously a journey from village to city.

As a result of these cultural logics, children shoulder the burden not only of developing themselves but also of developing the nation (Bregnbæk 2016). Subscribing to a form of filial nationalism, some conceive of themselves as having a filial debt to their parents and the state (Fong 2011). Tellingly, people refer to the state in Chinese as the "family-country" (*guójiā*). As one girl told me, "Like my parents, the state has raised me [*yǎng wǒ*], so when I graduate from college I will use my skills to repay it."

Developmentalism in Historical Perspective: Western-Impact Narratives and Psychological Colonization

This identification of quality with central places and central places with modernity is new. But people in China have long mapped moral distinctions onto the center-periphery hierarchy. Since early times, people have associated the center with the moral authority of highly mobile, cosmopolitan elites and the periphery with the parochial customs of immobile, benighted locals (Lewis 2007, 11–16). Similarly, people have seen China—the Central Kingdom—as the center of civilization and the country's frontiers as barbarian. The boundaries of the Chinese state have constantly shifted. But the center has always defined itself as civilized vis-à-vis an uncivilized periphery.

By the Tang-Song transition, the center had developed into massive urban settlements of up to a million people. Many historians consider China to have entered a period of early modernity at least by the Ming era (1368–1644 CE), centuries before Western colonialism (Brokaw 2007; Brook 1998; Chow 2004; Miyakawa 1955). Despite this historical legacy, China's high-school curriculum teaches students that modernity and urbanization originated in the West, along with capitalism. As one history teacher explained to students, the whole Chinese world "was rolled into capitalism" (*bèi juǎnrù zīběnzhǔyì*) as a result of Western imperialism in the nineteenth century. This kind of historical narrative, which draws on Marxism and other modernist currents, undergirds the linear view of time that is so integral to developmentalism.

If "capitalism" means industrial capitalism, then this narrative captures an important truth. The Industrial Revolution that started in Northwest Europe in late 1700s was an epoch-making historical event. Such narratives' obsession with the West, however, obscures long-term historical continuities and cycles that have little to do with Western impact. Before the Industrial Revolution, the developed commercial heartlands of China's Yangtze River delta enjoyed the highest quality of life in the world (Pomeranz 2000). And many of the challenges of governance that the modern Chinese state faces—including rural-urban inequality, a massive population, and a vast multi-ethnic territory—are legacies of the imperial era rather than the result of Western imperialism per se (Kuhn 2002; Woodside 2006; Wong 1997).

But Chinese nationalist history and much scholarly historiography continues to revolve around the impact of Western capitalism on China. Drawing inspiration from Paul Cohen's (1984) historiographical critique, I term such narratives *Western-impact narratives.* Although Western-impact narratives are highly influential in China, they are not the only views of history available. In my field sites, religious beliefs enshrine alternative histories. As I mention above, many deities began as historical officials who were worshiped as gods after their death. For example, the patron deity of Ningzhou is an apotheosized Tang-era official who "opened up the wasteland" by exterminating bandits and pacifying aboriginal populations. Citing such popular-religious lore, people suppose that centrally located places have a more ancient history than do peripherally located ones. As a taxi driver told me, "The history of Ningzhou is older than that of Mountain County because Mountain County was opened up for settlement after Ningzhou."

Such popular histories provide an alternative to Western-impact narratives but foreclose other possible histories, such as those of conquered and displaced peoples. Since imperial times, state policymakers have sought to integrate peripheral peoples into the Central Kingdom by bringing civilization to them. Anthropologist Steven Harrell (1995) calls this mission China's civilizing project— a project that continues, in altered form, today. A central plank of this project consists in promoting literacy (L. Yi 2008). Indeed, civilization and literacy share the same root in Chinese—*wén*, which means pattern, writing, or culture. In imperial times, spreading culture to the uncivilized was termed "transformation through education" (*jiàohuà*) (Rowe 1994). This legacy is still visible in my field sites. In Mountain County, peripheral settlements of Hakka—Chinese settlers who intermarried with aboriginal groups—honor the memory of native sons who passed the civil exams by maintaining monuments to them.

In the contemporary era, China's civilizing project has become fused with developmentalism (Fiskesjö 1999, 2006; Xiaoyuan Liu 2004). In broad outline, this project is a colonial enterprise. China's colonialism appears most conspicuously in its development policies toward the southwest, Inner Mongolia, Tibet, and Xinjiang, where ethnic minorities face particularly acute existential challenges under Communist Party rule (Gladney 2004; Harrell 1995; Lau 2020; Makley 2018). But people of rural origin all over China contend with great structural inequality vis-à-vis the center. In this sense, all rural peoples live under a type of internal colonialism.

Colonial domination takes a psychological toll, producing great ambivalence toward the metropole—the putative center of civilization (Fanon 2008). The attitude of rural people in China is characterized by such ambivalence vis-à-vis China's urban centers. Rural people see themselves both as backward and as morally superior to city folk, who they say are advanced but lack warmth and authenticity. By the same token, one of the most enduring legacies of Western colonialism in China is psychological. Persuaded of the effectiveness of Western science and technology by Western gunboat diplomacy during the nineteenth century, early reformers of China's Self-Strengthening Movement (1861–95 CE) in the late Qing era emphasized that China should retain its superior cultural essence while adopting Western function. In the Republican Era (1911–49), the anti-imperialist May Fourth Movement went further, critiquing all tradition as an impediment to modernization. An irony of these intellectual currents is their obsession with the very thing that they resisted—Western impact. But unlike many other countries, China was never fully colonized. Under Western occupiers in the nineteenth century, it is usually described as semi-colonial. This history of relative independence makes its colonial experience different from that of many other colonies, like India (Ong 1999, 32–36), and remains a point of pride in contemporary China. Taken as a whole, these historical contradictions forge the terms of an ambivalent national sensibility that remains ubiquitous today.

Scholarly and popular views of the Gaokao demonstrate this ambivalence. On the one hand, critics perceive the Gaokao as the heir of the imperial civil exams—a tradition that impedes China's journey to modernity. In particular, they critique how the Gaokao emphasizes formulistic regurgitation of useless memorized patterns—one of the same rationales that Qing-era reformers used to argue for the abolishment of the imperial civil exams (Woodside 2006; Elman 2013). On the other hand, people contend that the Gaokao—China's "only fair competition"—is uniquely suited to facilitating the development of the country under its current national conditions of overpopulation and underdevelopment. Thus people say, for example, that the suspension of the Gaokao during the Cultural Revolution (1966–76) represented an interruption of China's national development—an unfortunate event that significantly waylaid the country on its path to modernity. In short, people see the Gaokao as both a spur and an impediment to modernization.

This ambivalence toward examinations typifies people's attitude toward tradition in China more generally—an ambivalence that is symptomatic of the psychological effects of colonization. These effects are real. But Western-impact narratives help to sustain and reproduce them by glorifying the status of the West as the origin and center of modernity. Moreover, Western-impact narratives perpetuate this ambivalent psychology vis-à-vis not only the West but also China's center. People of rural origin are doubly subjugated, psychologically colonized by both China's center and the West. In a sense, China's urban centers, which lead the way in imitating an idealized image of Western modernity, serve as a surrogate for the West vis-à-vis the rural periphery. People from rural areas feel inferior to people from urban centers because those urban centers, seen as more developed, are closer imitations of this idealized image. Ironically, those who have the opportunity to visit the West find the reality disappointing in comparison to the ideal. The West is rarely as modern as visitors from China had imagined it to be. A common refrain of Chinese visitors to New York or San Francisco, for example, is that these cities seem small and dusty compared to the vertical splendor of Beijing or Shanghai.

Altogether, the ideological needs of the Chinese Communist Party probably represent the greatest obstacle to psychological decolonization. To shore up nationalist zeal for development, official discourse emphasizes the humiliations suffered by Chinese in the colonial era. By focusing on a Western bogeyman, the party-state distracts people from internal colonialism, including rural-urban inequality. As I argue above, however, developmentalism merely represents the latest strain of China's civilizing project—a hybrid formation of Chinese center-periphery distinctions and Western development ideologies. Western-impact histories do not constitute a fundamental revision of China's civilizing project; rather, they merely relocate the center of civilization to the West. According to this logic, achieving the great restoration would mean repatriating that center to its rightful place within the Central Kingdom.

Middle-Class Flight: Transcending the National Hierarchy

Developmentalism, which has long shored up Communist Party rule, paradoxically contains the seeds for critique of that rule. Since the opening up of China in the 1980s, people have increasingly followed developmentalism to its logical conclusion. If the center of civilization lies in the West, then people should sojourn or migrate there. As a result, aspirants to middle- or upper-middle-class status, whose numbers are expanding, are sending their children to be educated abroad in rapidly increasing numbers, forming a study-abroad fever (Fong 2011; Kajanus 2015). From 2007 to 2017, the number of Chinese college and postgraduate students studying abroad more than quadrupled from 140,000 to 610,000, with more than half studying in the United States.[5] But many students travel to influential Western countries besides the United States, such as Australia, Canada, France, Germany, and the United Kingdom. And increasing numbers are going to developed non-Western countries like Japan, Singapore, and South Korea. Through their migrations and sojourns overseas, transnational Chinese students strive for "developed world citizenship"—cultural, social, and sometimes legal belonging to the developed world, broadly conceived (Fong 2011, 12–20). Still, the United States plays an important psychological role in China as a paradigmatic Other, giving it a special status in Chinese imaginings of the developed world. Especially in rural areas, people frequently conflate developed countries with the West and the West with the United States. At the same time, non-Western developed countries occupy a special position in Chinese imaginations as places that have already "caught up with the West."[6]

Not only the very wealthy but even many people of relatively modest middle-class backgrounds are participating in the study-abroad trend (Fong 2011). This phenomenon is particularly pronounced in urban areas, where resources are greater. The privatization of urban housing in the 1990s, and the resulting real estate boom, amounted to a huge wealth transfer to urbanites (Tomba 2014; L. Zhang 2010). If they invested wisely, many parents need only sell a second home to finance a child's study abroad. But wealthy people in rural areas, though fewer in number, likewise favor international education—an underappreciated aspect of the study-abroad trend. The children of wealthy Mountain County entrepreneurs, like the above-mentioned school principal, Mr. Jian, also attend college and sometimes even high school abroad.

If the charisma of the West as the center of civilization is a pull factor that contributes to international migration, a number of closely related push factors also reinforce this trend. In China's reform era, the form of capitalism that has emerged combines state patronage with market competition in a way that resembles the economy of the late imperial era (Brandt, Ma, and Rawski 2014). This reliance on patronage spawns intense anxiety among the wealthy entrepreneurial elite, who worry that the state could withdraw its support at any time (Osburg 2013). In addition, elites worry about China's future. They question if the party can maintain social stability during the present period of declining growth. As a steel company executive and Communist Party member told me, "The feeling of insecurity among the upper-middle classes is like a virus." This individual reported that more than half his friends planned to send their children abroad.

Among rural elites, the tendency to educate children overseas has also become common. Mr. Jian's position on Mountain County's Political Consultative Conference—a political advisory board consisting largely of local entrepreneurs—gave him special insight into this development. He estimated that around 70 percent of its members either had foreign passports or immediate family (partners, children) living abroad. Explaining their motivations for leaving China, Mr. Jian said:

> About half of the parents who send their children abroad to study want them to come home. Another half are like me. They want to "diversify their portfolio." For people like me, having family abroad is a way out (*chūlù*). The Party could come tomorrow and take everything away from us. We don't really own anything. Everything is up to the whims of corrupted officials. People don't feel secure. They say "the political macro-environment isn't good" (*zhèngzhì dàhuánjìng bù hǎo*). This is a euphemism for political corruption and for fear of social chaos.

In addition to worrying about the political environment, many middle-class parents worry about the physical environment, including the toxic effects of China's air pollution, which has grown into an acute crisis in the reform era (Lora-Wainwright 2013). As Mr. Jian suggests, just as the Gaokao provides a way out of the countryside, emigration provides a way out of China. Thus many of these children are so-called parachute kids, who set up a beachhead for the family abroad in case China breaks down.

Educational emigration also gains impetus from another source—aversion to the Gaokao. Parents of children with mediocre scores may encourage them to avoid the test, reasoning that a degree from a foreign college is better than one from a second-tier Chinese university. More generally, people question whether or not Chinese education produces children of real quality. By contrast, they see the West as the center of education for quality. As I suggest in chapter 1, this view may be based more on an idealized image than reality, although it follows logically from the Western-impact view of history. If development leads to quality, and if the West represents both the origin and model of development, then quality naturally concentrates in the West.

Under these conditions, widespread criticism of the Gaokao—as well as calls for educational reform—can be read as a critique of economic development under party-state rule. Many middle-class Chinese say that they are voting with their feet by immigrating to foreign countries. Sending children abroad is a way of transcending Chinese problems, indeed of transcending the national hierarchy altogether. This logic even applies to parents who plan to bring their children home after finishing college. These parents cite the great prestige that people in

China associate with a foreign credentials. In many industries, a foreign college degree can provide applicants with a leg up over locally educated competitors, although this advantage is waning as the number of foreign-educated returnees increases. Even if they still see the West as a locus of quality, growing numbers perceive China as the land of future opportunity.[7]

Concerned about the idealization of the West, the Xi Jinping administration has started to shut down school programs that prepare children for education overseas. At the same time, Xi's government is cracking down on textbooks seen to promote Western values. But such repressive measures are unlikely to change middle-class views of the Chinese education system. China's growing middle classes no longer think that the Gaokao is as consequential as they once did. Now as before, they view mobility as the main way to create value for themselves and their families. But they no longer see the value that exists in China as authentic, searching instead for true quality abroad.

As Mr. Jian was fond of pointing out, however, critics of the Gaokao mainly hail from the relatively privileged classes. As significant as the study-abroad trend is, the numbers pale in comparison to the ten million who take the Gaokao every year. For many ordinary people, the big test remains sacred.

The Sacredness of Book Learning Despite All Dashed Hopes

In contrast the avoidance of the Gaokao by many elites, rural and working-class parents tend to continue to see the exam as the best route to improved status and a better life. But as China's economic growth slows and its number of graduates increases, finding a white-collar job in the city is becoming increasingly difficult. Commenting on this trend, many parents say it is better to have guanxi than to have a college education. After spending their whole lives in the monomaniacal pursuit of a college degree, jobless grads worry that they have sacrificed their childhood for false hopes.

Observing these developments, some ordinary rural and working-class parents have begun encouraging their children to look beyond orthodox paths to mobility. As one Xiamen migrant mother told me, "I tell my son that it doesn't matter what he does as long as he can find a stable occupation and support his family." Such parents comfort their children with the old proverb, "There are 360 trades, and each one of them has an examination champion." Others no longer see college as a way to change fate but encourage children to pursue higher education so that they will have a credential to fall back on if they fail as entrepreneurs. In their words the Gaokao is not the way out, but a way out.

Among the majority of parents, however, the view endures that orthodox mobility provides the best route to the good life (Kipnis 2011). These perceptions persist despite that fact that skilled laborers now make more money than many college graduates. A construction worker responded in the following terms when I asked him why he did not encourage his son to follow in his footsteps:

> Chinese people look down on those without credentials. In China, if you are an ordinary worker, it doesn't matter how much money you make, people will still consider you inferior. Any kind of manual labor is inferior to office work. . . . In the old times, any scrap of paper with writing on it was considered sacred—it wasn't to be burned or trampled underfoot. Despite all the changes that history has brought about, it's still like that. As the saying goes, "The worth of other pursuits is small, the study of books excels them all" (*wànbān jiē xiàpǐn, wéiyǒu dúshū gāo*).

Unorthodox Mobility, Place, and Dispersal

Conventional Views of Mobility versus the Reality on the Ground: Patterns of Family Sojourning

Official documents—such as state identity cards, household registrations, and passports—represent persons as statically centered in one or two places (generally place of residence and place of birth). Since the early 2000s, the Chinese state has been moving away from a rigid administrative dichotomization of registration into rural and urban types. In practice, however, a de facto two-tier system persists, with people from rural areas and small towns receiving different treatment than their counterparts in developed urban areas (Wallace 2014; B. Li 2015). This division reflects an urban bias, serving the metropolitan interests to which the Chinese state largely caters. Many well-established metropolitan elites in places like Shanghai and Beijing may desire to go overseas, but they have little need of maintaining strong personal connections to the countryside. In contrast, such elites have a strong interest in limiting and controlling the mobility of people from rural areas, whom they perceive as both cheap labor and dangerous competition (H. Yan 2008).

But the reality is far more complex than this rural-urban dichotomization would suggest. The majority of people in China do not fit easily into either category. People do not simply transplant themselves when they move up the hierarchy; rather, they extend their spheres of self-efficacy. To improve their status and life chances, they establish platforms for fortune—temporary or permanent—in the cities. But they maintain close ties with the countryside. Even many long-term urban residents return to their native places for holidays or important life events, such as marriages or funerals. Vast numbers in China move regularly up and down the hierarchy of places, pursuing a variety of sojourning strategies (Skinner 1976).

Many types of sojourners exist. The catch-all term "migrant" poorly captures this variation. In the reform era beginning in the 1980s, farmers began seeking wage labor in urban factories or other venues—a practice that people call going out to work (*dǎgōng*). People refer to such laborers as the mobile or floating population (*liúdòng rénkǒu*) or, informally, as farmer-workers (*nóngmíngōng*). Those who regularly return home are known as migrant birds (*hòuniǎo*) because they work in the city during the growing season and migrate back to the countryside to help out at harvest.

But most farmer-workers no longer farm. Many people in their twenties and thirties are second-generation farmer-workers. For the most part, this generation has known nothing but the floating life. In multi-generational families of farmer-workers, each person may be pursuing different kinds of work or entrepreneurial activity in different urban centers, convening only once a year in their native place for Chinese New Year. In many villages, nearly everyone has gone out to work. Such villages are called "empty husk villages" (*kōngkécūn*) because only old people remain year round to watch over the left-behind children of parents working in the cities. Other parents take their children with them to the city, where they must navigate the many difficulties of attempting to secure access to good education without an urban household registration.

Other types of sojourners are also common. Now as in imperial times, certain villages or towns specialize in producing products for market in big cities (Skinner 1976). In family-operated manufacturing operations, each part of the family may be responsible for a different section of the supply chain, some staying in their native villages to oversee assembly while others travel to various urban areas to purchase parts and conduct sales. Even many ordinary white-collar urban professionals maintain strong connections with their rural native places. Conversely, professionals based in the countryside, such as factory managers or party officials, often commute regularly to the city, where their children go to school.

In many families, people pursue a mix of orthodox and unorthodox mobility strategies. For example, some members go out to work while others pursue college education and a white-collar job. Large families with four or five children are common in the countryside, where the one-child policy was less strictly enforced.

In large families, it is normal for an older sibling, particularly a girl, to go out for work to pay for a younger sibling's education. When these donees graduate, they are expected to return the favor by contributing financially to their sponsors.

The lives of most people in China crisscross or traverse multiple levels of the rural-urban hierarchy. As Myron Cohen (1970) observes, Chinese families are, in many cases, dispersed, though they may nevertheless (and frequently do) strategize mobility as a unit. Skeptics might object that Chinese families are increasingly emphasizing conjugal relations over filial ones (Y. Yan 2003). Most couples now choose to live in their own homes rather than with the groom's family (a neolo-cal rather than virilocal pattern of residence). But parents, particularly on the groom's side, continue to be closely involved in the lives of their children and grandchildren. Thus many families display a virilocal character and might be labeled "viricentric" (Kipnis 2017). More broadly, families tend to operate as aggregates, maintaining close economic cooperation even after siblings divide into more than one household (Judd 1996, xiv). These dispersed yet aggregate families intentionally cultivate multiple centers, or platforms for fortune, at dif-ferent points along the central-place hierarchy.

Dispersal is nothing new. It has characterized Chinese families since impe-rial times. But contemporary regimes of citizenship—passports, IDs, and household residency books—add a new twist. Families coordinate their activi-ties to acquire citizenship in multiple places. Many extend this strategy to for-eign locations by migrating overseas. Coastal southeastern China—and Fujian Province in particular—is famous for being a source of international migra-tion. Generations of Fujianese, Cantonese, and others—known as overseas Chinese—have sought their fortunes in Southeast Asia and the West (Chu 2010; Kuhn 2008). Many employ unorthodox strategies to get abroad, such as hiring human smugglers. As the study-abroad fever demonstrates, however, increas-ing numbers are using education to migrate. And as with domestic migration, many families combine orthodox and unorthodox strategies to change fate. For example, one Fujianese father described how he put his daughter through Columbia University while working menial jobs as an undocumented immi-grant in the United States.

By pursuing such mobility strategies, migrants aspire to achieve citizenship and belonging in more than one state (Chu 2010; Fong 2011). For instance, Chinese immigrants to the United States may acquire a US green card even as they fight to maintain an advantageous household registration in China. Thus people's attitude toward citizenship is flexible, based more on economic rationale than political identification (Ong 1999). But whereas flexible citizen-ship conventionally refers to international mobility, most ordinary people in

China pursue a more modest form of flexible citizenship—the establishment of multiple platforms within China.

Household Residency, Ant Cities, and Prestige

In theory, people's household registration ties them to one locale. But tens of millions survive without household residency in their places of work, even though equal access to social benefits—including welfare, healthcare, and public education—requires official residency.

Urban household registrations are not created equal. Backwater places like Mountain Town or Ningzhou have long encouraged immigration by allowing outsiders to obtain local residency if they buy a home. Starting in the late 2010s, cities with populations under three million have started scrapping registration requirements altogether to attract residents (Z.Y. Zhang 2019). But such places hold little allure in comparison to developed megacities, which have vastly superior schools, living conditions, and social welfare. It can be extremely difficult to acquire residency in China's most desirable urban places. One Beijinger, married to a woman from Ningzhou, quipped that becoming a Beijing resident was harder than becoming a US citizen. Although their son was an official resident, his wife would have to be married to him for ten years before she could apply for residency in the capital city.

Following the abolishment of the work-assignment system and the liberalization of the employment market in the 1990s, college graduates started having to find an employer of suitable size and prestige to sponsor permanent residency. Some cities implemented points-based migration schemes that rewarded prospective migrants based on employer reputation, postgraduate education, entrepreneurship, and other desired characteristics (L. Zhang 2012). Many ordinary graduates fall through the cracks. Without official residency, they join a precarious new class of low-wage, underemployed urban white-collar workers who cluster in low-rent districts. This group is known as the "ant tribe" (yǐzú), a designation that alludes both to their great number and their limited social power. But even for these ants, who fail to parlay a college degree into urban residency, a college diploma often translates into a significant increase in status.

Rising rents and a crackdown on the illegal subdivision of apartments have prompted many provincial graduates to move away from megacities, even as graduate unemployment continues to be a growing problem.[8] More recently, the central state has attempted to rectify these imbalances by relaxing the registration policy (Z.Y. Zhang 2019). The policy for cities with populations over five million remains restrictive. There are thirteen such cities, which include Beijing and Shanghai but also less well-known places like Tianjin, Chongqing, and Hangzhou.

As of 2018, however, mid-sized cities with a population of between three and five million have started making it easier for college graduates to acquire residency. This policy is intended to accelerate urbanization, stimulate economic growth, and alleviate some of the population and housing pressure in China's largest cities. In Xiamen, college graduates under the age of forty-five who have stable white-collar employment can apply for permanent residency, and the policy is even more lenient for new graduates (*Xinhua Net* 2018). Although the long-term effects of this shift are still unclear, guarantees of registration are likely to raise the value of a college education, further consolidating the Gaokao system.

Success on the entrance examination remains the best hope of ordinary people to obtain the status and security that a desirable urban household registration confers. For those who already reside in urban places, the Gaokao provides a means of moving further up the hierarchy of places. By the same token, a college education provides access to important social connections or guanxi, including the most important form of guanxi—desirable marriage partners. For example, the Ningzhou woman who married the Beijinger met her future husband while attending college in the capital. Although her family complained that the man "had no culture," his Beijing residency made up for this deficit by improving the life chances of their offspring. Especially for women, but also for men, the Gaokao creates a platform for fortune in this sense—an opportunity for meeting a desirable life partner.

For these reasons, a great number continue to see college education as a worthy goal. As one rural teacher put it, "The objective after which rural high-school students are struggling [*fèndòu de mùbiāo*] is very clear—get out of the countryside, change themselves, change their [social] environment, [and] give their own future children a better opportunity."

The Countryside in the City, the City in the Countryside

China's rapid urbanization has muddied any clear distinction between urban and rural. During my fieldwork, I became acutely aware of this phenomenon while working at Dragon Gate—a peripherally located high school in Xiamen. Like many of China's urbanites, the majority of Dragon Gate teachers belonged to highly dispersed families with strong roots in the countryside.

Like many cities in China, Xiamen has grown rapidly in the reform era. Growth began accelerating in the 1990s, and during the first decade of the twenty-first century, Xiamen's population doubled from two million to nearly four million. As schools expanded to keep pace, the demand for teachers skyrocketed. The municipal government responded by implementing special tests to attract qualified and ambitious teachers from the countryside. They came from far and wide, eager to acquire household residency in the big city. But even the Dragon Gate teachers who had arrived at the school through the standard routes—the Gaokao and the ordinary teacher's recruitment examination—did not primarily identify as urbanites. Many were of rural background, having used these exams to get out of the countryside. Also, the school itself had only become urban in the 2000s. Only ten years earlier, Dragon Gate had been surrounded by farmland. Now it faced high rises and an eight-lane highway. Some sections of the old village to the school's south—composed of squat structures tucked into labyrinthine lanes— had not yet been demolished. But these "villages in the city" (*chéngzhōngcūn*) were now home mostly to migrants, many of whose children studied at Dragon Gate. Thus Dragon Gate teachers personified Xiamen's urbanization. Either they had watched the farmlands transform into a city around them or they had arrived in the city just in time to see it swallow up its rural periphery.

Some teachers privately grumbled about the talent-attraction program, saying that it had increased competition for promotion. But this complaint did not reflect an urban/rural schism. Nearly all teachers proudly claimed rural roots. Even the older Dragon Gate teachers, who had been assigned their jobs at the school, did not primarily think of themselves as urbanites. As a vice principal said to me, "You look around yourself and see a city, but we're really all just villagers."

Nearly all Dragon Gate teachers have immediate and extended family in their native counties, mostly within a day's drive of Xiamen. They commute regularly to the countryside for family gatherings and important events. Using dispersal to their best advantage, these urbanites of rural origin have enjoyed the benefits of urban residence while using their rural connections to circumvent some of its alienating constraints, including population controls, which tend to be more strictly enforced in urban areas.

Such a high degree of dispersal—the intermixing of rural and urban identities within a single family—is the natural result of the mobility strategies that people pursue. A single example will suffice to illustrate this point. A thirty-something head teacher at Dragon Gate, Ms. Yang, of Hakka origin, hailed from a small town in Longyan Prefecture, about ninety miles from Xiamen, where her father had risen from a worker to a contractor in the highway-construction business. Achieving business success through good guanxi with the local government, the elder Mr. Yang moved his family to the prefectural capital, where he arranged for his daughter to study in the best public schools. Following a good performance on the Gaokao, she move up the central-place hierarchy to Xiamen when she secured her teaching job at Dragon Gate. Unfortunately, Ms. Yang's father died in his fifties from liver cancer, which the family attributed to the large quantities of alcohol that he had consumed to lubricate government deals. After Mr. Yang's death, Ms. Yang's mother joined her daughter in Xiamen, followed by her sister and brother. But Ms. Yang's grandparents remained in the countryside, where the family gathered during Chinese New Year. Ms. Yang's ne'er-do-well brother commuted frequently to his hometown, where he was involved in a struggling shrimp-farming business. Ms. Yang's sister married another Longyan contractor, who had just returned from a construction project in Libya but did most of his business in his home prefecture. Ms. Yang's husband, Mr. He, a physical education teacher at Dragon Gate, was the only member of the family who could claim Xiamen heritage, although his status as an urbanite was dubious. He had grown up in a rural district of Xiamen, Tong'an, which had only been incorporated into the city in 1997. Like many of my interlocutors, Ms. Yang defined countryside (*nóngcūn*) not simply as a physical location but also as a way of doing things. Despite her husband's ostensibly urban origin, Ms. Yang complained that her husband was "a real hick—the most countryside of us all."

Guanxi and Rules: Transforming Guanxi into Quality

As they migrate up the central-place hierarchy, people strive to transform guanxi (which they associate with traditional, rural, feudalistic practices) into quality (which they associate with modernity and urbanity).

In Ms. Yang's case, her late father had used his connections in Longyan to secure every educational advantage for her. Through much added hard work, Ms. Yang transformed these advantages into the meritocratically earned prestige of a government job as a public-school teacher in Xiamen. By the same token, many Dragon Gate teachers, including Ms. Yang, employ their new-found urban connections to help the children of rural relatives. It is common, for example, to help nieces and nephews "go through the backdoor" (a euphemism for corruption) to attend Xiamen schools, where they will have a better chance to succeed on the Gaokao.

Indeed, little gets done in China without at least an added dash of guanxi. Even many rural teachers who meritocratically earned a place in Xiamen through talent-attraction programs had to "go through guanxi" to avail themselves of the opportunity. Such was the case for Ms. Ma, the head teacher of the garbage collector's son (see chapter 1). In 2014, she won a prestigious Xiamen teaching competition that enabled her to move from Ningzhou to the big city. But the Ningzhou municipal authorities, loathe to lose teacher resources (*shīyuán*), would not approve her transfer. To make the move possible, Ms. Ma's father had to seek out connections to a retired Ningzhou education minister, a distant relative who shared the family's surname and native place.

As these examples illustrate, migrating to the city—even by orthodox means—often requires connections. Ironically, however, people say that they migrate to cities, among other reasons, precisely because connections are *less* important there. In the city, people say, it is possible to achieve success even without guanxi. In metropolitan areas, large numbers of individuals, businesses, and institutions compete with one another; moreover, the state more strictly supervises compliance with rules and regulations. For these reasons, life in the city more closely approximates the modern ideal of universalistic or rules-based competition. By the same token, people believe, with some justification, that this modern ideal of meritocratic rules-based competition is even more fully realized in the West—another reason that they send their children abroad. By contrast, they say, connections are everything in China. This is especially true in the countryside, where local patronage trumps meritocratic competition.

These realities are even reflected in the language that people speak. In rural places, such as Mountain County, where outsiders are few, not speaking the local dialect instantly marks one as a stranger. But in big cities like Xiamen, where migrants come from all over the province and country, Mandarin is the lingua franca, reflecting a more established ethos of open, anonymous competition. In short, the rural-urban hierarchy is also a sociolinguistic hierarchy. With more schooling, people acquire simultaneously greater literacy and greater facility in spoken Mandarin, which enables them to move around freely and compete at higher levels of the central-place and social hierarchies (Kipnis 2016, 3).

Nostalgia and the Ambivalence of Progress

Even in China's cities, however, many complain that modernity remains largely a façade. They say that the modern appearance of urban centers masks the realities of corruption, mistrust, exploitation, and environmental degradation.

During my commutes between Xiamen and Mountain County, I found myself in frequent conversation with fellow travelers about the disconnect between the ideal and the reality of urbanization. Far from being a journey into a utopian future, driving into the city felt like descent into an increasingly polluted lowland industrial hell. This apocalyptic landscape was only finally shrouded upon entering the Xiamen city center—a mirage of modernity. In this idyllic scene, office buildings and Western-style hotels and cafes surround a man-made lake populated by a government-supplied flock of snow-white egrets. The tourist who never ventures away from this downtown dream world can imagine that China has catapulted itself into a gleaming, albeit smoggy, future. But ordinary migrants know that this veneer is belied by the relative squalor of their living conditions, the crumbling infrastructure in poor neighborhoods, and the gulf of inequality that looms between the countryside and the city. As one migrant poignantly observed, the city resembles a "gilded turd" (*dùjīn de dàbiàn*).

Citing such disparities, people say that urbanization is largely staged, and modernization fake, false, or empty. They complain that rule of law, regulation, and public morality form superficial appearances that have not "penetrated into people's hearts." As many say, the software (*ruǎnjiàn*) of people's minds has not caught up with the hardware (*yìngjiàn*) of modern infrastructure. But even this infrastructure is suspect. In particular, people disparage the prevalence of "face projects" (*miànzi gōngchéng*)—projects that look good but possess shoddy construction and do little to improve people's lives. Citing such phenomena, some say that modernity is largely a show that officials put on to secure promotion.

In the countryside, by contrast, "heaven is high and the emperor is far away" (*tiān gāo huángdì yuǎn*). People feel less need to embrace the performance of modern ideals, and rules are less strictly enforced. For these reasons, people in the countryside consider themselves to be less hypocritical (*xūwěi*) and more down-to-earth (*shízài*) than their urban counterparts. People of all backgrounds, urban and rural, believe that life in the countryside is cleaner, quieter, and safer; the food healthier; and the people simpler (*pǔshí*) and more honest (*zhēnchéng*). They concede that rural existence may be poor and precarious. It can also be violent. In peripheral areas, there are relatively few police and other supervising authorities; thus, people are more prone to settle matters of honor through fisticuffs. In contrast to cities, however, where people say that interpersonal relationships are dominated by cold instrumentality (*gōnglìxìng*), life in the countryside is suffused with genuine human feeling (*rénqíng*). In rural areas, everyone knows each other. But in cities people act outside these webs of particularistic relationships; thus, city people are perceived to be slick (*huá*), sly (*jiǎo*), and untrustworthy (*bù kě xìnrèn de*).

Note how these perceptions reverse the common urban bias—which is particularly prevalent in metropolitan centers like Shanghai and Beijing—that China's countryside is a lawless, immoral place. One Mountain County High School student—the daughter of a teacher—expressed her concern about moving to the city for college in the following terms: "My parents say that I am very childlike; they worry about me getting cheated. . . . The city is chaotic [*luàn*]."

In the 2010s, nostalgia for an idealized rural past has increased, leading some urban middle-class parents to go back to the countryside to raise their children in rural areas—a phenomenon that bucks the trend of rural-to-urban movement. But people in rural areas still largely see the city as the future. Many who remain behind have to fight the perception that they are losers who could not make it out.

In sum, migrants often agree that life "in itself" (*běnshēn*) is better in the countryside. But jobs are scarce, wages low, and education inferior. Working in the city—with or without a household registration—can seem like the only way of fulfilling their duties of intergenerational care. As they say of this responsibility, "Above are the elders, below are the children" (*shàng yǒu lǎo, xià yǒu xiǎo*). Children loom especially large in this equation. As many parents say, "All my sacrifices are for my kids." Of course, raising children is also a way of providing for one's own future. And for many families, raising successful sons to continue the lineage remains an important goal. As a former cotton farmer from Shandong said, summarizing these trends, "If I stayed in the countryside, how would I pay for my son's education and marriage? And who would marry a poor, uneducated farmer's son? Finally, who would take care of *me* when I am old?"

Overpopulation or Underdevelopment?

Despite people's ambivalence about urbanization, many trace social problems to overpopulation rather than to development. But China's urbanization turns overpopulation into a self-fulfilling prophecy. By drawing crowds of migrants into the city from the countryside, urbanization actually causes the high levels of population density that people associate with overpopulation and underdevelopment—overcrowded public transportation, congested streets, environmental degradation, and an overloaded, hypercompetitive education system. Rapid urbanization reinforces the perception of overpopulation, thus encouraging people to accept and pursue even more drastic forms of urbanization.

China's largest cities, however, seem to suffer less from the problems of overpopulation than its second- and third-tier ones. A Ningzhou teacher of rural origin, Ms. Ma, reacted with surprise on her first visit to Shanghai, China's largest city—a trip on which I accompanied her and her husband. "It's so quiet!" she exclaimed. At hours of the evening when Ningzhou's buses would be packed with people and its streets lined with ad hoc marketplaces that bustled with boisterous, "hot and noisy" (*rènao*) activity, largely suburban Shanghai seemed quiet and empty.

My Shanghainese friends contested Ms. Ma's observation. "Have you visited Nanjing Road, the main shopping street?" they asked. "Have you taken the subway during rush hour?" Out of politeness, Ms. Ma yielded to these objections. But later she confided in me that she did not feel persuaded:

> Your friends think I am a country bumpkin who is not world-wise. . . .
> Of course, any big city has a shopping street, or rush hour. And tourist attractions anywhere will be busy. But they should see Ningzhou at 10 p.m. You can't even find a seat on the bus. Shanghai just feels empty most of the day. Everything is just so well organized and well regulated (*guīfànhuà*)—you don't see the people. . . . Even the air here is better than it is in Ningzhou. It makes me seriously wonder if China is really overpopulated at all. I think it is just not developed enough.

After returning to Fujian, I shared Ms. Ma's thoughts with other friends and colleagues in Xiamen and Ningzhou. But few had traveled to such far-flung places as Shanghai or Beijing. For most, the notion that China might not be overpopulated, only underdeveloped, evoked extreme skepticism. In the face of such resignation and the tangible evidence of overpopulation around them, Ms. Ma's theory seemed like a frivolous challenge to scientific fact. As one of her colleagues said, "Overpopulation is just the reality [xiànshí]."

In the preceding sections, I have shown how people view the central-place hierarchy through the lens of linear time, which is based on a Western-impact view of history. In circular fashion, their perceptions, which include the following, both reflect and become objectified in the hierarchy:

1. People tend to experience peripheral places as chaotic and backward, whereas they see central places as relatively "regulated" and "advanced."
2. People see modernity as largely staged; thus, they experience central places as empty, fake, and counterfeit and peripheral ones as relatively true, genuine, or down-to-earth.
3. People see urban areas as possessing higher quality and value, whereas they perceive rural ones as embodying greater sincerity and humanity.

Such hierarchical effects contain both subjective and objective dimensions. To use the anthropological nomenclature, they are both emic (that is, reflective of cultural perceptions) and etic (indicative of underlying objective realities). In other words, even as they contain a subjective element, people's perceptions refer to systematic variations in social patterns along the central-place hierarchy, which I term hierarchical effects. Examples include the score-value hierarchy (the more central the place, the higher the Gaokao score), sociolinguistic differences (the more central the place, the greater the use of Mandarin), and many other aspects of culture. For instance, the perception that rural people are more genuine implies that people at different points of the central-place hierarchy have different cultural practices, different notions of reciprocity, and, in a phenomenological sense, inhabit different worlds.

Perceptions of the hierarchy also vary along the hierarchy. For example, people of rural origin may contest the view that they possess lower quality than their urban counterparts. As one migrant said, "I think it's just untrue that people from the city have higher quality. Urbanites are much ruder than people in the countryside. Many of them are downright mean. They don't know how to behave [zuòrén]. And the more educational credentials they have, the more arrogant they are."

Finally, because people lead a highly dispersed existence, they move up and down the hierarchy, encountering and adopting different perceptions of it as they do. Intriguingly, people report that moving between places affects how they think. They say that mobility opens their minds (*kāifàng sīxiǎng*). When they arrive somewhere new, they become strangers to those around them. But the world (including their own cultural backgrounds) also becomes strange to them. The normally taken-for-granted (the emic) becomes for a while unfamiliar (the etic). In other words, mobility draws people out of their subjective immersion in the everyday, forcing them to see themselves and their surroundings in a new way—as objects. In this sense, migrants become anthropologists of their own society. Crossing social and cultural boundaries, they reflect on their ordinary assumptions. For this reason, people who move around a lot develop a critical awareness of society that their less mobile counterparts lack. Migrants have a language to describe this experience of gaining knowledge through mobility. They call it "broadening one's horizons" and "becoming world-wise."

Becoming world-wise can cause people to perceive their normal assumptions in a new way. Consider how Ms. Ma's visit to Shanghai caused her to question her assumption that China is overpopulated. In the domain of education, students and teachers who have moved between the countryside and the city tend to possess a relatively high level of awareness of educational inequality. Because the state actively suppresses objective information about inequality (see chapter 3), mobility provides one of the only ways that people can acquire such knowledge. And as many people of rural origin say of the post-Mao era more generally, "In the past, we were stuck in the villages. We thought everyone was poor, and in fact everyone was more equal then. Thus we were relatively satisfied with life. But now society has opened up and become wealthy. As we move around, we can see the great inequalities with our own eyes."[9]

This relationship between mobility and social critique accords with a long-standing pattern in Chinese popular culture. Going back to the imperial era, an immensely popular genre of story—transmitted through folktales, vernacular literature, operas, and more recently in movies—recounts the exploits of itinerant martial arts heroes, known as *xiá*. These Robin Hood–like figures—most famously celebrated in the Ming-era novel *The Water Margin*—wander from place to place, righting the injustices of local bullies and corrupted officials. Meeting each other on the road, they share what they have seen and heard during their travels—a floating life that the genre describes as "wandering the rivers and lakes" (*zǒu jiānghú*).

In my journeys to and from the countryside, I encountered many sojourners—taxi drivers, construction workers, traveling salesmen, ritual specialists, temporary laborers, and even some teachers and students—who described themselves as "wandering the rivers and lakes." Like the itinerant strangers of the popular tradition, they shared what they had seen and heard with other travelers, including me. My own analysis of hierarchical effects represents an attempt to synthesize their insights. Thus I see mobility not only as an object of theorization but also as method for collecting data and critiquing society—a method that I learned from my fellow travelers.

But if mobility has the capacity to inspire critique, how is it that the Gaokao, which ostensibly produces mobility, nevertheless functions as a cultural gyroscope, helping to stabilize the Chinese social order? The answer to this question is complex, involving at least three factors.

First, it is important to distinguish between orthodox and unorthodox mobility. Orthodox mobility is less likely to give rise to trenchant critique of the state, given that this form of mobility is predicated on recognition by the state (see chapter 1). Those who achieve mobility through orthodox means, such as the Gaokao, may sometimes be critical of social inequality; however, they tend to accept the status quo because their status and identity depend on it. By contrast, people who identify with the trope of wandering the rivers and lakes tend to be migrants who are pursuing less orthodox strategies of mobility. But mobility of any kind has a socially cohering effect that counteracts to some degree its destabilizing potential. People who move up the central-place hierarchy become members of more expansive, inclusive social collectivities (for example, Ningzhou instead of Mountain County). They tend to learn and use Mandarin, the national language, and identify more closely with the national collective. This pattern of identification is especially true of people who pursue orthodox mobility.

Second, people in China often see overpopulation and underdevelopment as a commonsense reality that is objectified in the world around them. As I note above, these national conditions function similarly to the notion of fate to reinforce the inevitability of current social arrangements—rapid development led by an authoritarian state. As a result of these perceptions, people see the rural-urban hierarchy as a score-value hierarchy—a hierarchy of talent that everyone should naturally strive to ascend. As the saying goes, "Water flows downward and people move upward."

Third, and perhaps most important, mobility is not as great as people think. The score-value hierarchy is highly stratified. Students from low-ranking schools go to low-ranking colleges in peripheral places, whereas students from high-ranking schools go to high-ranking colleges in centrally located places. In other words, the examination system creates just enough controlled mobility to reinforce the myth of meritocracy while limiting types of mobility that would lead to either widespread critical consciousness or large-scale redistribution of social resources. But the way that the system accomplishes this feat involves not so much an organized conspiracy as an intersection of myriad sometimes overlapping, sometimes competing interests—a hegemonic negotiation.

For these reasons, the examination is an extremely effective tool for channeling people's dissatisfaction with their lot in life into the pursuit of orthodox goals. As I elaborate in the next chapter, however, the ostensible goals of the examination system—modernization and urbanization—are themselves undermining the perception of the examination's fairness. As resources and human capital flow up the score-value hierarchy into the ever-widening cities, people in rural areas are experiencing the examination as more determined and thus less fair. In response, state actors at various levels of the central-place hierarchy strive to maintain a frontstage semblance of fairness while they struggle with each other backstage for scarce human resources.

COUNTERFEIT FAIRNESS

State Secrets and the False Confidence of Test Takers

My generation was raised on poison milk.

—Mingfeng, Mountain County Number One student

"Are high schools in the United States like high schools in China? Do they use the pretense of treating every student fairly to do things that are utterly unfair?"

This question was posed to me by a Mountain County Number One student, Chunxiao, in a message that she sent me after I visited her class. Curious about what lay behind her query, I arranged to meet Chunxiao and her friend Shanshan for dinner in the cafeteria. Eating together provided a good opportunity for candid dialog. The ordinariness of the occasion set everyone at ease, and the hubbub of chattering teenagers and clacking aluminum trays foiled unwanted eavesdroppers.

Chunxiao's main complaint concerned the tracking (*fēnbān*) of home-room classes by test score. In rural areas, schools track students into two, three, or even four or more levels of hierarchy. High-ranking classes are termed "fast classes" (*kuàibān*), low-ranking ones "slow classes" (*mànbān*). Officially, these terms designate the relative speed with which classes progress through the high-school curriculum. But people understand the terms metonymically to refer to the quickness of students' minds. By performing well on regular monthly examinations, students can be promoted from slow classes to fast classes. Poor performance results in demotion.

Chunxiao found herself on the bottom rung of the hierarchy in the slowest of slow classes—a "garbage class."

"Students like me—we feel like second-class citizens," Chunxiao said.

Shanshan, whose class was slightly faster, demurred. "It's not so bad being in a slow class," she said. "I think I'd rather be a big fish in a small pond."

As Chunxiao pointed out, however, access to fast classes could be secured through illicit means such as nepotism, bribery, and guanxi. As the schoolyard jingle goes, "You can study math, physics, and chemistry, but nothing beats having good paternity" (*xué hǎo shǔ wù huà, bùrú yǒu gè hǎo bàba*).

The practice of tracking classes varies along the rural-urban hierarchy. People in urban areas tend to frown on aggressive tracking, which they say works against education for quality by overemphasizing test scores. In centrally located cities, generally only two class levels exist. Fast classes are usually referred to as keypoint classes (*zhòngdiǎnbān*) or experimental classes (*shíyànbān*). All other classes are termed parallel classes (*píngxíngbān*).

In contrast to urban schools, rural schools face less scrutiny from central authorities, so rural administrators feel less need to conform to centrally dictated norms. As a result, they are at liberty to pursue a more aggressive strategy of tracking. Like many other rural schools, Mountain County Number One divides students into no fewer than four streams.[1]

For schools in the countryside, aggressive tracking forms an important weapon in the competition for good student resources (*shēngyuán*), that is, high-scoring students. Schools use extra-fast or experimental classes as a recruitment tool to keep the highest-scoring students from leaving for the cities. Administrators tell parents of top scorers that their children will receive more personalized attention in a rural experimental class than they would in an ordinary class at an urban high school. Also, the relative paucity of educational institutions in the countryside means that rural schools must cater to students with widely ranging test scores, a trend that is exacerbated by the flight of good students to urban places. Under such conditions, administrators say that putting all the best students into one or two classes is a way of maximizing test scores by making the best use of limited student and teacher resources.

Teachers explain that in practice, students in slow classes tend to come from farming families whereas students in fast classes are the children of teachers, managers, and officials. Teachers say that slow-class students are relatively unteachable; in addition, many are considered to have disciplinary problems. Unsurprisingly, however, students in slow classes resent such characterizations. Among slow-class students, Chunxiao was not alone in feeling like a second-class citizen. As one student told me, the difference between fast and slow classes is "like the difference between the rich and the poor." Another punned on his class number, B4, which sounds like "despise" in Chinese. "Being in class B4 [*B-sì*] makes people despise [*bǐshì*] you," he said.

But students' resentment of tracking has to do with more than just a name. As a result of tracking, students in different classes almost literally attend different schools. Students vary in their awareness of the use of bribery and guanxi to obtain coveted places in top classes. But all students understand that top classes gain unfair access to various perks, opportunities, and resources. For one thing, quality of instruction differs greatly between fast and slow classes. Fast classes are taught by the best teachers—those with superior experience and a serious (*rènzhēn*) attitude. Slow classes, by contrast, receive unserious, even unskilled instruction. For example, slow-class students complained that their math teachers were sometimes stumped by the problems that they reviewed—a particularly galling index of unpreparedness. In slow classes, English teachers had poor pronunciation, Chinese-literature teachers spoke with a heavy local accent or "sweet-potato tone" (*dìguāqiāng*), and science teachers told stories instead of lecturing.

Slow-class students likewise protested that students in fast classes gained unequal access to other ostensibly merit-based opportunities. For example, only fast-class students receive invitations to compete in special academic contests and "autonomous admission tests" (*zìzhǔzhāoshēng*), which can give students bonus points on the Gaokao. The exclusivity of such invitations can be rationalized by appealing to alleged differences in ability. Much less easy to justify, however, is the imbalance in nominating fast-students for more subjective honors such as "Three Good Student" (*sānhǎoshēng*). Being named a Three Good Student supposedly recognizes all-around development—good study, good physique, and good moral quality. But in practice such awards go only to high-scoring students. Students like Chunxiao resent the implication that they are morally inferior just because their test scores are lower. Similarly, invitations to join the Communist Party, which are subject to strict quotas, are supposed to be distributed to students according to broad criteria of general merit. In practice, however, these invitations are reserved for students in the top fast classes. And only students in fast classes receive scores of excellent in the general merit assessment or "all-around quality assessment" (*zōnghé sùzhì píngjià*). The stated purpose of this assessment is to provide an evaluation that is not based on exam scores alone. But teachers and administrators make all-around quality synonymous with high test scores by guaranteeing that only students in fast classes get top marks.

Of course, university admission is based almost exclusively on test scores. Thus most fast-class perquisites seem at first glance relatively inconsequential. In more centrally located schools, coveted opportunities for direct admission (*bǎosòng*) might be distributed to well-connected students; however, Mountain County Number One possesses little such largesse to distribute. As I explain below, even the varying quality of teachers may be relatively inconsequential to students' educational outcomes, although no one in Mountain County has seriously considered the experiment of assigning good teachers to so-called bad students.

But slow-class students themselves think that they would have a better chance with better teachers. As one student said, "The system is illogical. The students who need the most help get the worst teachers." And as another complained, "Our test scores are low, but we work hard. We deserve a better chance." Such unfair access to accolades and awards contributes to an all-around ethos in which only test scores seem "real" (*xiànshí*). In the face of this focus, the institution's rhetoric of embracing education for quality and all-around moral development seem empty and false.

The problems of aggressive tracking at Mountain County Number One represent a microcosm of more systemic problems of educational fairness in China. State slogans proclaim that "educational fairness is the foundation of social fairness" and that "everyone benefits from a fair education." The ubiquity of such slogans attests to the great emphasis that the state places on equity. Like Chunxiao, however, many in China regard this rhetoric as misleading or hypocritical. They say that such proclamations are belied by the problems of unequal opportunity and guanxi. Moreover, they regard the state's efforts to rectify the situation as insincere and ineffective.

This gap between rhetoric and reality gives rise to a variety of coping mechanisms. Take, for example, the response of another Mountain County slow-class student, Mingfeng, when I asked him how he maintained psychological equilibrium in the face of nepotism and unequal treatment at his school. Alluding to the tainted-milk scandal that rocked China in 2008, he likened his school's assertions of "fair treatment" to a counterfeit product: "If you don't have a good attitude, you're done for. My generation is strong. We were raised on poison milk."

Mingfeng's comparison of this counterfeit fairness to fake milk has great social resonance in China. Since the 2000s, food safety has become a topic of pervasive national concern, symbolizing a general lack of trust in official pronouncements, public morality, and institutional ideals (Oxfeld 2017; Y. Yan 2012). As Ms. Ma, a Ningzhou teacher, remarked of Mingfeng's metaphor, "What really makes you numb [*mámù*] is when you know that something is poison, but have to eat it anyway." This predicament forms the gist, I believe, of Mingfeng's remark. Mingfeng's notion of "good attitude" largely consists in a form of cynical resignation—or, as Ms. Ma calls it, numbness.

In this respect, Mingfeng was a typical student. Most of his schoolmates, including Chunxiao and Shanshan, shared his cynical attitude. Students in rural schools, where test-score stratification is so visible, are generally less deceived about fairness than their counterparts in urban areas, where parallel classes prevail. But even in urban schools, students frequently complained about the unfairness of the education system, including stark provincial disparities. Despite this pervasive cynicism, however, Mingfeng and his contemporaries agreed on another point. They consistently emphasized how the exam gave them hope of getting out of the countryside and transforming their lives. People in China say that guanxi and politics distort the education system. But they believe that the Gaokao—seen as China's only relatively fair competition—has the power to change fate.

This chapter focuses on this contradictory combination of cynicism and hope, suspicion and belief, which is characteristic of participants in the Gaokao. In many ways, China today is a post-belief society (Osburg 2015). Few believe in official socialist rhetoric, which contrasts starkly with the reality of crony capitalism (A. S. Hansen 2017). Cynicism and irony are pervasive (Steinmüller 2011; Steinmüller and Brandtstädter 2015). Since the 1970s, Chinese society has undergone a performative shift—a term that Alexei Yurchak (2006), writing about late Soviet society, uses to describe a growing gap between political slogans and real-life experience. And to some extent, belief is a Western cultural obsession to begin with (Mazzarella 2015; Seligman et al. 2008; Yurchak 2006). People in China tend to put more stress on indirect expression and ritualized performance than they do on sincerity and inner conviction (Blum 2007; Seligman et al. 2008; Steinmüller 2013). But in China as elsewhere, belief nevertheless remains important. People in China believe in fate, in the gods, in family and friends, and in the greatness of their civilization (Boretz 2011; Carrico 2017; Harrell 1987; Jing 1998; Oxfeld 2010; Sangren 2000). They also believe in test scores. In light of revelations in the 2010s about state-sponsored disinformation campaigns—not only in authoritarian countries but also Western democracies—it seems particularly important to emphasize that belief can be cultivated, distorted, and misled (Snyder 2018).

Ideology does not take any one monolithic form—whether misrecognition, false consciousness, cynicism, or performance. Whereas misrecognition and false consciousness refer to distorted beliefs, cynicism and performance describe acting as if something is true even when one does not believe it. In my view, these different concepts represent not competing explanations but different theoretical attentions or optics for capturing different aspects of people's relationship to power (Boyer 2010). This ecumenical approach helpfully emphasizes how people assume "complexly differentiating" attitudes toward power (Yurchak 2006, 29).[2]

People's attitudes vary through space and time. They may be subject to ambivalence or shift as people navigate different contexts or move from place to place. Individuals living under authoritarian regimes—and, indeed, in other political systems—face a continuum of disciplinary-symbolic control that ranges from soft forms of inducement like monetary incentives to hard ones like imprisonment, torture, and violent force (Wedeen 1999, 150). In a world where stronger forms of resistance result in marginalization, ostracism, censure, punishment, or worse, the choice of Mingfeng and others to maintain cynical resignation—"a good attitude"—may seem the lesser of evils.

Given the general cynical attitude about educational fairness in China, why do people like Mingfeng, Chunxiao, and Shanshan maintain sincere belief in the relative fairness of the Gaokao? To explain this contradiction, I differentiate between *structural fairness* and *procedural fairness*. Structural fairness refers to equality of opportunity. The exam is structurally fair to the degree that people's preparation for the exam—which many conceive as starting in kindergarten—gives them an equal opportunity to cultivate the qualities needed to succeed. Procedural fairness refers to the moment of selection itself. The exam is procedurally fair to the degree that its result is determined by individual merit frontstage on test day rather than being predetermined behind the scenes by social factors like cultural capital or guanxi.

People are well aware that the education system—and consequently the examination—is ridden with structural inequalities. They nevertheless have great faith in the procedural fairness of the exam. This faith rests on two assumptions. First, people assume that the exam—in contrast to other competitions—is adjudicated by an objective, national authority. For this reason, they consider the exam relatively impervious to the local distortions of favoritism and guanxi. Second, people do not believe that structural inequalities are so great that they eclipse procedural fairness.

In fact, however, the exam is even less fair than most suspect, and its objectivity more show than reality. Fairness is largely a fabrication. I take my understanding of fabrication from Erving Goffman, who defines it as "the intentional effort of one or more individuals to manage activity so that a party of one or more others will be induced to have a false belief about what it is that is going on" (1974, 83). Fabrication involves an element of deception and collusion. Those deceived by the fabrication are contained by it. They believe—though not always without nagging suspicion or doubt—that a falsification of some part of reality is what it appears to be.

But what precisely is being fabricated and why? The answer to this question lies in the correspondence between fairness and uncertainty. Recall that events are fateful to the degree that their outcome is both consequential and uncertain. As I suggest in chapter 1, uncertainty possesses two dimensions—aleatory and agonistic. The exam is undetermined in this latter, agonistic sense to the degree that it is determined by individual competition on test day. This notion of uncertainty is synonymous with procedural fairness. To maintain the appearance of fairness, therefore, various state actors—teachers, officials, and administrators—fabricate uncertainty. In this way, they lead test takers to believe that the outcome of the exam is more undetermined than it really is. I term this kind of fabricated uncertainty *counterfeit fairness*, hence the title of the chapter. The purpose of fabricating fairness is simple. By so doing, state actors shore up people's perception that the exam is fateful, thus buttressing the myth of meritocracy.

But here one must distinguish between fairness as a reality (whether fabricated or not) and fairness as an abstract ideal. People may still cling to the ideal of meritocratic fairness even when they lose faith that reality conforms to it. In other words, people's belief in fairness as an ideal cannot generally be shaken by revelations of collusion or fabrication. This is because the ideal consists in a deeply held cultural belief in individual merit. But because individual merit is largely the product of social labor, no one can truly be said to go it alone on test day. Thus the belief in individual merit is ideological, to some degree representing a form of misrecognition or false consciousness. For this reason, the distinction between structural fairness and procedural fairness, though heuristically useful, breaks down in practice. The fair procedural adjudication of individual merit is ultimately unachievable, because individual merit always involves structural biases. The myth that such adjudication is desirable and possible, however, constitutes a taken-for-granted— or, as Bourdieu (1990) calls it, doxic—assumption in Chinese high schools. Ironically, therefore, even those who are responsible for fabricating fairness generally reconcile their fabrications with a sincere belief in meritocracy.

Like other collusive practices, the fabrication of fairness requires secrecy. Ordinary people have only a vague inkling of how the exam is designed and graded, how schools and localities compete for student and teacher resources, and how these resources are distributed among classes. To maintain secrecy, authorities tightly control the distribution of test-score data—a form of censorship by omission. Officials justify this censorship by appealing to its importance in maintaining social stability. As several officials and administrators told me, if people understood the true extent of inequality in the education system, they might lose faith in the Gaokao, its culminating rite of passage. Shedding light on structural unfairness would shatter any remaining belief in procedural fairness. But when I suggest to veterans of the Gaokao that they may be unaware of inequality in the exam system, the majority react with incredulity. They tell me, "Actually, we know how unfair the system is, but we participate anyway. However bad the disparities are, the exam is still China's only *relatively* fair competition."

Granted, the Gaokao is relatively fair. No other social competition in China does so much to create the impression of fairness—an impression that contains much truth. In particular, the exam is carefully policed. Although people frequently use connections to get into a good school or class, it is relatively difficult (though not impossible) to cheat on the exam itself or use guanxi to get into university. Nevertheless, such strictures help to reinforce the ideology that the exam measures individual rather than socially produced capacities. Moreover, those who insist that people in China are well aware of the unfairness of the exam will be hard-pressed to account for the great lengths to which administrators and officials go to conceal their fabrications. For this reason, true believers in the Gaokao often feel disappointed when they discover the "real face" (*zhēnxiàng*) of the exam. I agree that people are aware of structural inequality. But most lack an aggregate view of that inequality that would undermine their relative confidence in the system as a whole. They are cynical about fairness, but not cynical enough.

In other words, false beliefs are of more than one type. Ordinary people not only adhere to false consciousness about the ideal of merit but they also succumb to false confidence about their examination chances. This false confidence has two aspects. People are overly confident in their ability to penetrate state assertions of fairness. At the same time, they tend to overestimate their ability to score well in the exam. The two types of false confidence feed into and reinforce each other. In the face of difficult odds, false confidence is an ego-preserving strategy. By allowing people to imagine that they have more insight and power than they actually possess, false confidence protects their self-image as efficacious social actors.

People's awareness of examination unfairness only reinforces their false confidence in their ability to see through (*kàntòu*) the system. Ordinary people are particularly well versed in educational disparities at the national level, which are widely discussed in the news media. For example, everyone knows that students in China's provincial-level cities like Beijing and Shanghai—municipalities that are counted administratively as provinces—have a much better chance on the exam than those in ordinary provinces. For reasons that I explain below, however, this knowledge does little to undermine people's belief in the authority of the exam. People also know about unfair practices within schools, many of which (though not all) are immediately visible to them. But they have little way of obtaining a clear understanding of the depth and extent of these practices. They are even less clear about disparities and unfair practices beyond the school walls at the local and regional levels. Teachers discourage students from reflecting on score inequality, just as administrators and officials keep their subordinates in the dark about their manipulations of the system. And even prominent government-affiliated Gaokao researchers have no direct way of obtaining official test-score data. If anything, however, disparities between schools in the same city or between the city and the countryside are even greater than the disparities between provinces.

To analyze this seemingly paradoxical combination of awareness and unawareness about fairness, I employ Goffman's (1959) distinction between frontstage and backstage. Analyzing everyday interaction as performance, Goffman suggests that people and institutions project an ideal image that is largely a front. This image forms their frontstage persona. However, it may—in fact, usually does—conflict with backstage "realities." I put realities in scare quotes because, of course, backstage interaction also consists in a type of performance. But frontstage and backstage differ in important respects. When people are frontstage, they usually maintain silence about what goes on behind the scenes. They conceal the work—rehearsals, discussions, preparations, and so on—that go into producing the front. This secrecy is particularly important when this work involves collusion (the intention to deceive).

In the pages that follow, I show how the Gaokao system is organized into spatial layers of secrecy. The frontstage of public controversies helps to distract people from the backstage of even greater disparities. And every backstage has its own backstage. Those who are higher on the administrative and geographical hierarchies tend to possess greater access to inside knowledge. At higher levels, authorities are especially concerned with maintaining social stability. In general, however, the fabrication of fairness depends less on any large-scale organized conspiracy than it does on the local politics of loyalty and face giving. In their manipulations of the system, officials and administrators rely on the help of their friends and connections to pursue their various interests. These interests usually involve burnishing the reputation of schools or regions to accumulate "political achievements" (zhèngjì)—a necessity for career advancement.

In some respects, therefore, life in China resembles a confidence game that state actors play with the public. The term "state actors," like the broader term "social actors," calls attention to this dramaturgical dimension of social action—the way in which it always contains an element of confidence and performance. To build confidence, authorities employ the tools of censorship and persuasion. Through false confidence, people routinely overestimate their insight into this con. In this way, they contribute to their own engrossment in the deception. Ironically, people's various efforts to game the system often increase their false confidence. And to complicate matters further, people persist in their belief in the relative fairness of the exam because it does make a difference in their lives, even if that difference is not as large as many suppose it to be.

Frontstage Controversies: Above There Are Policies, below There Are Countermeasures

In 2013, a television exposé of Gaokao unfairness circulated broadly in social media. This report received praise from teachers and students for being particularly real. Among other things, the report told the story of a Jiangsu construction worker who fell into conversation with a construction manager from Beijing. The two had taken the Gaokao the same year. The construction worker had missed the score cutoff for college admission by only a few points. But instead of retaking the exam—a time-consuming and expensive process—he started working to support his family. Although the construction manager had scored lower than the worker, the manager was able to attend a good college because he was born in Beijing, where the score cutoffs are lower.

People cited this report as an example unfair local protectionism in college admissions, which, as many pointed out, relies on the household registration system. Ordinarily, people are required to take the Gaokao in their place of household residency, which prevents the children of many migrants from attending the exam where their parents work. The discussion around the report called attention to a central paradox of the Gaokao system. People are so confident in their assessments of the exam's relative fairness because they possess much knowledge about its unfairness. They are particularly well versed in national disparities—that is, those between provinces.

These disparities are exemplified by two types of state policy, which are publicly debated in the media. On one hand, preferential policies reinforce inequality by working to the benefit of dominant social groups. On the other, positive policies ostensibly aim to rectify inequality by helping socially disadvantaged ones. Both types of policy work by manipulating the examination chances of students by altering score cutoffs, adjusting admission quotas, or providing bonus points. Students in different provinces face radically different higher-education prospects because of such manipulations and educational disparities (figure 6).[3]

The disparities are particularly pronounced in China's richest provincial-level cities—Beijing, Shanghai, and Tianjin. Locals benefit from inflated admission quotas at regional colleges everywhere, but these cities are home to the lion's share of China's top universities. Tantamount to examination gerrymandering, this arrangement helps to explain why the admission rate to first-tier colleges in such provincial-level cities exceeds 20 percent—double or triple that of most ordinary provinces. Disparities in admission to Project 985 universities are similar or even starker. Between 4 and 5 percent of students in these provincial-level cities gain admission to Project 985 universities, whereas the admission rate to Project 985 universities hovers between 1 and 2 percent in ordinary provinces. And regional protectionism is greatest for the nation's top colleges. For example, the combined acceptance rate for China's top two universities, Tsinghua and Peking, both located in Beijing, is around 1 percent for residents of the capital city, whereas around only 1 out of 1,000 students from Shanghai and a mere few out of every 10,000 students from ordinary provinces can attend these universities (Fu 2013).

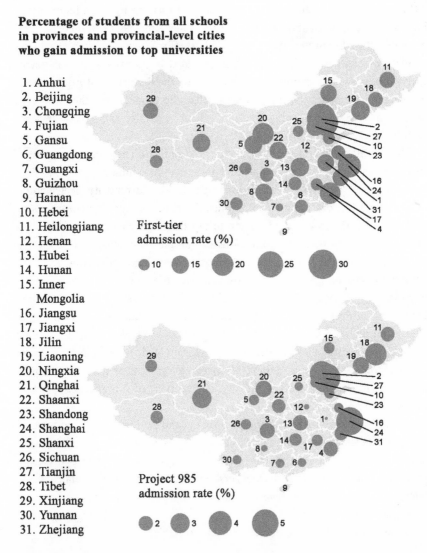

FIGURE 6.   Students in different regions of China have widely varying college admission prospects as a result of educational disparities and the effects of preferential and positive policies.

Source: Chart by Steven Oliver. http://www.sohu.com/a/198431528_507475. Accessed Oct. 12, 2019. Data from 2016. Data unavailable for Hainan Province.

Such preferential policies are difficult to conceal from the public. Cutoff scores and admission rates for each province are a matter of open record. Thus the unfair advantage of metropolitan elites vexes most ordinary families. In the

2010s, the state has attempted to rectify these distortions by encouraging provinces with a disproportionate number of first-tier universities to increase their quotas for the admission of outsiders. But these efforts have produced a backlash. In many places, parents have even demonstrated in the streets, carrying signs with slogans like "Educational Fairness: Oppose the Reduction of Admissions!" Nothing quite arouses the fury of parents like the thought that their children, after so many years of diligent devotion, will face a sudden rise in what they see as unfair competition (Teixeira 2017).

Many families likewise chafe against positive policies. The most prominent of such policies increase the examination chances of ethnic-minority students. People who can certify themselves as belonging to an ethnic minority receive bonus points on the Gaokao. Members of ethnic minorities may also benefit from specially earmarked quotas for admission to top-tier high schools and colleges—a policy known as directional admissions (*dìngxiàng zhāoshēng*). Like preferential policies, positive policies have a regional focus. Most minorities reside in China's underdeveloped western provinces, which also benefit from relatively low score cutoffs overall. But not all positive policies focus on ethnic minorities. Directional admissions exist at the local level across China. In many localities, elite senior high schools reserve spaces for graduates of low-ranking junior high schools, which disproportionately serve disadvantaged students. Both types of positive policy—local and national—provoke allegations of unfairness among those who do not benefit. But the special treatment of minorities in western provinces is especially resented.

The controversies that surround preferential and positive policies underscore the difficulties that state actors face in balancing regional interests with national interests, and individual fairness (*gèrén gōngpíng*) with social justice (*shèhuì gōngzhèng*) (R. Zheng 2011). One person's justice is another's unfairness. In attempting to create an impression of fairness, state actors must play to different audiences and attempt to reconcile competing interests. The resulting negotiated hegemony satisfies few and requires constant tinkering.

Gaokao Migration and Remote Gaokao Reforms

Positive and preferential policies produce similar unintended consequences. They encourage parents to game the system by changing their children's place of schooling. People term this strategy Gaokao migration (*yímín*). Within the borders of China, two types of Gaokao migration exist. In the first type, called "going into the west and down to the south" (*xījìn-nánxià*), parents exploit positive policies by sending children to poor western and southwestern provinces to benefit from the relatively high admission quotas in those places.

In the second, "dashing to the east" (*dōng chuǎng*), parents take advantage of preferential policies by sending children to rich coastal cities. Because students are generally only allowed to take the Gaokao in their place of long-term household residency, both types of Gaokao migration require parents to circumvent residency requirements. Household residency can be changed through various licit, quasi-licit, or illicit measures. But such measures generally require substantial guanxi, sums of money, or both.

Residency restrictions put the children of ordinary migrants at a disadvantage. In the past, such children had little hope of rectifying their situation. They had to return to their official place of residency during their last year of high school, which gave them little time to adapt to the curriculum in their native provinces (Ling 2017). Beginning in 2012, however, the state issued a set of national-level policy guidelines—termed the remote (*yìdì*) Gaokao policies—meant to make it easier for children of migrant workers to take the Gaokao where they live. This policy change was a hard-won accomplishment of the New Citizens' Movement (*Xīngōngmín yùndòng*), a series of grassroots civil-rights campaigns that, among other actions, collected the signatures of more than 100,000 migrant workers who were impacted by Gaokao residency restrictions.[4] But most municipalities have undertaken these reforms only with great caution, because they undermine local interests by increasing competition. These policies also have potentially large knock-on effects on migratory pressures and house prices. Thus it remains difficult for many migrants to attend the exam in their place of schooling.

Increasing international mobility has given rise to a third type of Gaokao migration—international Gaokao migration. This type enjoys less prevalence than its domestic counterparts but is gaining in notoriety as the number of Chinese families with dual citizenship rises. National and provincial authorities have instituted a variety of preferential policies to attract "sea turtles" (*hǎiguī*), or Chinese returning from overseas. Such students take a special, easier form of the Gaokao or receive extra points. International students, moreover, do not face the same household registration requirements as Chinese citizens. Since the 2000s, therefore, some Chinese with dual citizenship have begun abandoning their Chinese passports to gain an advantage on the Gaokao. Many people are vociferously critical of this practice, saying that it produces counterfeit foreigners, but teachers report that it is increasingly widespread. Of course, for international Gaokao migrants themselves, taking the Gaokao is often more than an instrumental means of gaining an advantage in China's college admissions. Migrants often pursue education in China as a culmination of a complex process of transnational identity formation that may involve, among other factors, embracing their cultural heritage, escaping racism and structural disadvantage in their countries of citizenship, rebelling against the transnational ambitions of their migrant parents, or pursuing the adventure and challenge of a college education in China.

Efforts to game the system are common. But the ability to game the system is unequally distributed. People with wealth and power possess a decided advantage. Nevertheless, people persist in their view that the Gaokao is relatively fair. Paradoxically, the tenacity of this belief derives partly from people's admiration of such strategies, which they appreciate as expressions of cleverness and diligence. As people say, "Above there are policies, below there are countermeasures" (*shàng yǒu zhèngcè, xià yǒu duìcè*). This idiom succinctly expresses how bureaucratic power inevitably incites resistance. But the cavalier attitude with which people quote this phrase evinces false confidence in their ability to see through that power.

Positive Policies and National Hegemony

During one of my class observations at Mountain County Number One, a geography teacher posed a provocative question to her class. Was granting extra points to minority students on the Gaokao fair? The class responded with a resounding chorus: "Not fair!" Laughing, the teacher replied, "But we have to make allowances for the fact that their level of development and quality is relatively low."

This anecdote highlights an important difference between affirmative-action policies in countries like the United States and positive policies in China. Both policies engineer social competitions to give disadvantaged groups a greater chance. But unlike affirmative-action policies, positive policies in China do not aim to compensate such groups for discrimination (Yamada 2012). Rather, they follow the logic of developmentalism, with its linear model of time. Policymakers in China see positive policies as ushering minorities—people of low quality—along the path toward development. The concept of reciprocity is different in the two cases. In affirmative action, dominant groups may conceive of themselves as owing disadvantaged ones compensation for a legacy of oppression. In China's positive policies, members of the dominant group, the Han majority, think of minorities as owing *them* for their assistance in development. In China's ethnic southwestern borderlands, for example, slogans abound exhorting minorities to be grateful (*gǎn'ēn*) to the Communist Party. Of course, in contexts of affirmative action, such as those in the United States, members of the majority often also see themselves as benefactors and expect disadvantaged minorities to be grateful. And such policies may likewise have the goal of raising up groups conceived as backward or behind. But it is rare for people in China to see positive policies as a compensation for discriminatory treatment. The logic of civilizing minorities predominates in the Chinese context, where the ideology of developmentalism forms such an important part of the social contract (see chapter 2).

Preferential policies are patently unfair because they benefit elite metropolitan interests to the disadvantage of marginalized groups. But positive policies also serve elite interests, albeit in a less obvious way. In imperial times, state officials employed positive policies to further China's civilizing project of integrating the periphery into the center—a role that such policies still play today (Harrell 1995; Rowe 1994; Zhou 2010).

Without doubt, positive policies provide some assistance to disadvantaged groups. But they do more to alter the optics of college admissions than to address fundamental issues of social justice. Positive policies provide disadvantaged groups with just enough hope to keep them engrossed in the Gaokao. As in the exam more generally, however, the mobility that these policies produce is not great enough to effect significant redistribution of wealth and opportunity. And even when members of these groups achieve admission to college, the education system funnels many of them into low-status institutions and courses of study (see chapter 4). Thus, although positive policies do go some way toward rectifying social inequality, they also contribute to reproducing social segregation and hierarchy.

Frontstage Controversy as a Source of False Confidence

Both preferential and positive policies reinforce elite hegemony in another, more subtle way. Of course, national disparities are an important social issue. But the focus on these disparities distracts people from backstage inequality within regions, places, and individual schools. For that reason, I term national disparities, which are public knowledge, frontstage disparities. In part, people focus on these disparities because protesting them might effect change. But protesters nevertheless overlook deeper layers of inequality that would be relevant to their cause.

People in the provinces know that they are getting a raw deal compared to those who live in provincial-level cities like Beijing or Shanghai. This is just an unfortunate "fact of life" (shìshí). But this fact does not undermine people's confidence in their ability to compete with their neighbors within their province or region. As I elaborate below, however, local disparities are actually greater than many disparities between, say, Shanghai or Beijing and the provinces. Moreover, local disparities derive wholly from fundamental inequalities in access to opportunities rather than from artificial quotas.

In light of local disparities, national inequality constitutes a red herring. As significant as this latter form of inequality is, it sidetracks people from pursuing more granular comparisons and discussions. Because such a fine-grained analysis would turn up even more egregious forms of inequality, the data required to pursue it are censored.

Similarly, the debate over positive policies also functions as a red herring. Those who do not benefit from positive policies see them as adding an extra layer of unfairness to the system. But this unfairness is a front that further diverts people from focusing on backstage local inequalities.

Recentralization of Authority: Xi Jinping's Gaokao Reforms

Of course, if frontstage disparities become too serious, they can seriously damage people's faith in the system. Policymakers have a difficult job. Every effort to balance conflicting interests calls forth angry protests. Every attempt to tighten loopholes incites individuals to discover new, creative ways to game the system. As one prominent Gaokao researcher said, "Making changes to the Gaokao is like a trying to fold a balloon. You twist on one side, and the air pops out on the other side."

In September 2014, China's State Council announced sweeping reforms to the Gaokao (D. Cohen and Beauchamp-Mustafaga 2014; Postiglione 2014). These reforms constitute the most significant nationwide changes to the exam since the radical expansion of higher education starting in 1999. The reforms pursue two goals. On the one hand, they adopt various measures to increase the fairness of the exam. On the other, they make substantial changes to exam design in the name of promoting innovation and quality.

One of the most significant aspects of Xi's new Gaokao reforms is the renationalization of examination design. In the early 2000s, the authority to design exam questions devolved to the provinces. Although people continued to associate the exam with national authority, its structure and content differed significantly from province to province. The original goal of this policy was to promote educational innovation by creating local laboratories for reform. Under this approach, examination questions were created in the provincial capital by high-ranking high-school and college teachers. But this arrangement—no matter how strictly policed—gave rise to opportunities for local corruption and nepotism. Under the new system, which came into effect in 2016, each ordinary province uses one of three national exam papers for the compulsory subjects (Chinese, math, and English), all made in Beijing. This recentralization aims to bolster the exam's authority by reinforcing people's perception of its impartiality and objectivity.

The reforms augment the impression of fairness in several other ways. First, they encourage universities to adopt additional positive policies toward students from rural areas, disadvantaged ethnic groups, and inland and western provinces.

Second, they tighten the loopholes on various quasi-licit ways to game the system, including the payment of "school choice fees" (*zéxiàofèi*) to access good high schools, various schemes for accruing bonus points, advantages given to athletes, and the attendance of special arts tracks in high school. The latter in particular had provided parents and schools with a way of helping students of middling academic ability succeed on the test because arts students had a lower cutoff scores for entrance to first-tier colleges (Chumley 2016). Third, they enable students to take the English section of the exam more than once, allaying the impression that one test determines one's whole life. Finally, the reforms promise to make the Gaokao more transparent through a sunshine policy.

The general tenor of the new policies addresses complaints that the exam can be polluted by guanxi. They broadly conform with Xi Jinping's attempts to shore up Communist Party legitimacy by battling corruption. The reforms were announced by China's top governing body, the State Council, rather than by the Ministry of Education, suggesting the involvement of China's highest levels of political power (D. Cohen and Beauchamp-Mustafaga 2014).

But teachers and administrators express skepticism about the reforms. They say the proposals for ameliorating regional and socioeconomic disparities are modest, vague guidelines rather than vigorous, specific measures. For example, the reforms aim to reduce the gap in college enrollment between rich and poor provinces by only a few percentage points nationally. Moreover, the reforms do little to address more fundamental disparities in the type of college to which students are admitted. Students of rural origin are more likely to attend second- and third-tier institutions and two-year colleges (*zhuānkē*), whereas urban students are more common in first-tier institutions (X. Wang et al. 2013; Yeung 2013). As one teacher said, "At the end of the day, the Gaokao is still the Gaokao. Everything is going to revolve around it, and students are still going to put everything on the line [*pīnmìng*] to conquer the exam." Moreover, despite the state's promise of a sunlight policy, data on educational inequality remain, with few exceptions, difficult to access.

Backstage Knowledge of Fairness: State Secrets and the Chain of Interests

As a quantified and auditable measure of human value, test scores are extraordinarily well suited for ranking people and institutions. One of the main terms for test score in Chinese literally translates as "achievements" (*chéngjì*). Getting high achievements is how students get into college, teachers secure status and bonuses, and administrators achieve promotions. Even educational officials rise through the bureaucracy largely on the basis of raising test scores in their juris-dictions, which make up the most important measure of their "political achieve-ments" (*zhèngjì*). For these reasons, people say of exam-oriented education, with a resigned sigh, that it is just the reality.

One of my Mountain County students, a particularly insightful ninth-grader named Zhiwei, suggested that education in China forms a "chain of interests" (*lìyìliàn*). In Zhiwei's parlance, chain referred to a hierarchy consisting of stu-dents, parents, teachers, administrators, and officials. Drawing from his study of Marxism in school, Zhiwei argued that a relationship of exploitation (*bōxuē*) exists between people at different levels of the chain. Officials claim credit for the achievements of administrators, administrators for the achievements of teachers and parents, and teachers and parents for the achievements of students. Accord-ing to Zhiwei, scores constitute the currency of surplus value that is expropriated from people lower on the chain.

Zhiwei's analysis was insightful but overlooked the part that social labor plays in producing individual merit. Chinese students at all levels of the score-value hierarchy are diligent, but only those at the top of the hierarchy get into top colleges. Certainly, people high on the chain of interests could be said to expropriate the achievements of those lower on it. But Zhiwei misrecognized these achievements as belonging solely to students. Administrators and officials, by contrast, though still subscribing to a belief in individual merit, are relatively aware of the social origins of achievements. They say that by high-school-age children are already more or less fully formed (see chapter 5), and the goal of educational managers lies not only in getting students to study hard but, even more crucially, in securing the right kind of students, or, as they put it, "good student resources."

With this caveat, Zhiwei's notion of a chain of interests provides a useful lens to analyze the relationships of actors at different points on the administrative and geographical hierarchies. These hierarchies tend to overlap. The influence, rank, and power of administrators and officials correspond closely to their position in the central-place hierarchy (see chapter 2). Centrally located schools attract stu-dents from a larger geographical region; accordingly, the administrators of such schools have greater status and rank. Similarly, higher-ranking officials oversee more geographically encompassing regions than their peripherally located coun-terparts. And official promotion is largely synonymous with movement up the rural-urban hierarchy.

In principle, therefore, the interests of centrally located administrators and officials ought to align with those of the more expansive geographical terri-tories they oversee and thus with broader notions of the common good. But people at all levels of the hierarchy generally pursue strategies that maximize student resources for their domain of special control—be it a single student, a class, a school, a city, a prefecture, or a province. In the pursuit of high scores and good student resources, different schools and regions routinely come into conflict with each other.

Knowledge about such conflicts varies contextually and geographically. Even some actors who are relatively low on the chain of interests possess uncommon insight into the functioning of the system. But the average student, parent, and even teacher has little inside knowledge of backstage realities. The efforts of people high on the chain of interest take place largely in secret. And the higher one goes on the chain, the more secret the activities.

Duplicating Data and Dampening Discussion

When I began my field work, I was eager to acquire objective, quantifiable measures of social inequality at my field sites. For example, I wanted to create a comprehensive map of the score-value hierarchy, correlating every school's average Gaokao score with the school's position in the regional system of central places. I also hoped to conduct surveys to examine the relationships between parental occupation, educational history, and college admission outcome. I hoped that such efforts would complement my ethnographic work and contribute to quantitative studies of educational inequality in China. As I stayed longer, however, I learned that schools and government offices themselves gather much of the data that I hoped to collect.

These data-collection efforts form a logical consequence of the importance of test scores in China. The job of every head teacher is to maximize the scores of his or her (usually her) class. Similarly, the job of every section leader is to maximize the scores of his or her (usually his) year. School leaders do the same for the school, and officials for the region. No one leaves these tasks to guesswork. As discussed above, when entering high school, students are already tracked into classes based on their performance in the high-school admission exam. In many schools, head teachers create spreadsheets correlating performance on this exam with detailed data on students' families, including occupation of mother and father, ethnicity, and home address. The subsequent collection of high-school test scores starts immediately. Head teachers work closely with section leaders to produce detailed analyses of every student's test result on every formal examination—monthly exams, mid-terms, and finals (figure 7).

Administrators use the data to strategize the placement of personnel and to make pedagogical decisions. Head teachers use the same data to coordinate the efforts of individual subject teachers and to plan interventions into the lives of individual families and students (see chapter 5). Administrators use back

101多   106多   112多   89多   67多   60多

2012届高三下学期省质检成绩(理科)   高三 (6)班

班次	校次	进退	学号	方名次	姓名	总分	语文	语次	数学	数次	英语	英次	物理	物次	化学	化次	生物	生次
1	3	30	601	7		655	115	18	139	6	131	143	114	8	77	94	79	1
2	6	26	605	11		650	107	112	135	15	139	20	111	22	87	13	79	
3	8	-6	607	19		646	111	40	146	1	137	38	105	76	73	153	74	14
4	11	-7	602	24		642	107	112	121	137	137	38	112	14	88	10	77	4
5	12	6	603	26		641	112	31	124	102	143	4	105	76	86	15	71	35

班次	校次	进退	学号	方名次	总分	语文	语次	数学	数次	英语	英次	物理	物次	化学	化次	生物	生次
19	208	-66	617	953	572	(99)	324	115	222	138	30	93	272	72	176	(55)	381
20	214	68	621	1013	570	109	75	106	354	116	371	98	188	78	86	63	192
20	214	43	624	1013	570	101	263	112	264	131	143	99	176	(62)	317	65	132
22	226	-76	616	1055	568	(87)	497	120	150	129	173	87	337	84	24	61	236
22	226	31	620	1055	568	(99)	324	124	102	128	197	91	296	(65)	285	61	236
24	232	35	606	1083	567	104	181	109	317	128	197	105	76	71	195	(50)	448
25	276	-49	618	1398	557	111	40	120	150	120	327	89	321	(61)	331	(56)	359
25	276	136	627	1398	557	109	75	115	222	(110)	432	94	263	(60)	347	69	60
27	295	90	625	1585	552	(99)	324	114	233	(111)	421	99	176	(64)	295	65	132
28	305	-6	632	1678	550	104	181	106	354	132	123	70	462	74	132	64	159
29	310	45	626	1797	547	108	87	(101)	400	123	287	98	188	74	132	64	159
29	310	109	636	1797	547	110	55	(102)	317	122	302	98	188	(60)	347	(57)	335
31	317	-12	637	1888	544	(99)	324	(99)	417	(111)	421	103	106	72	176	(58)	318
32	321	-84	631	1926	543	(100)	298	(99)	417	117	360	(84)	372	72	176	(57)	335
32	321	108	638	1926	543	103	212	124	102	(80)	513	96	227	70	214	71	35
34	334	-45	628	2059	540	110	55	107	336	128	197	(84)	372	72	176	70	52
35	358	4	639	2449	531	99	324	125	88	92	499	(83)	380	(59)	362	(52)	422
36	370	-31	629	2716	525	112	31	94	452	117	360	67	253	65	132
37	390	-33	634	3012	519	102	241	88	476	124	278	79	413	62	317	61	236
37	390	-14	642	3012	519	108	87	112	264	91	502	85	361	60	347	60	269
9	410	0	635	3568													

FIGURE 7. Head teacher's record of students' practice-test scores. Scores are listed by subject. Individual students' class and school rankings appear on the left, along with their change in rankings vis-à-vis the last practice exam. The head teacher has circled scores that do not meet the cutoff for first-tier universities in each subject. Identifying information has been removed. Photograph by the author.

channels to obtain test data from other schools so they can compare their performance with that of their competitors. In local government, educational officials collect test data to coordinate efforts across the area under their control. Many teachers and administrators can recall meetings in which they were berated by local officials for poor performance on municipal and provincial practice exams. This obsessive analysis of data is characteristic of Chinese audit culture, the history of which stretches back to imperial times (Kipnis 2008).

This data collection forms a culture of expertise that is largely indistinguishable from the efforts of academic educational researchers. High schools and government offices employ scientific methods and approaches to data analysis—quantitative analysis, targeted intervention, control groups, and so on. In many cases, the goals of researchers and those of bureaucrats even overlap. Researchers usually wish to rectify inequality, which generally means finding policy interventions that will raise the test scores of disadvantaged students. By the same token, many teachers work concertedly at the street level to combat the effects of inequality in their classes. In some cases, teachers even participate directly in externally sponsored academic research projects, blurring the division between internal and external research even further (see chapter 5). Granted, most administrators and officials are mainly concerned with raising the test scores of the school or region under their control rather than ameliorating inequality per se. But their efforts work to the benefit of many ordinary families.

The methods and goals of academic researchers and educational bureaucrats overlap in significant ways. Despite this alignment, however, official data are not made available to researchers, much less to the public. In short, official data are top secret. Researchers obtain such data only with great difficulty. I did manage to gain access to some internal high-school data, which sympathetic teachers provided to me on condition of strict confidentiality. I draw from this data in my discussion of educational inequality in this and other chapters. Generally, however, high-school administrators and government officials did not agree to let me conduct large-scale surveys of their students, and even renowned Chinese educational researchers face great challenges in acquiring test-score and admission data.

In theory, making such data publicly available would be fairly straightforward. Like other Chinese government organizations, the Chinese educational bureaucracy is highly centralized. It would be simple for central authorities to ask high schools to report test-score and demographic data up the administrative hierarchy. Central authorities would then be well placed to act as a clearing house for this information. Indeed, central authorities in Fujian Province and elsewhere previously played such a role, albeit for educational institutions internally rather than for the public. Before the late 2000s, provincial authorities circulated the results of the Gaokao, broken down by school, to local education bureaus, which passed these results on to school administrators. But the authorities stopped this practice. By controlling the circulation of test-score data, authorities hoped to lower the fever pitch of Gaokao competition between regions and schools. Around the same time, the government forbade the extravagant feting of municipal and provincial first-place examinees, or champions, who had sometimes even been honored in public municipal ceremonies at local temples to Confucius (see chapter 6). The rationale was the same. Officials hoped to dampen the ferocity of regional rivalry.

In practice, however, little changed after the provincial education authorities stopped disseminating results. Schools and regions found another way to get the data; head teachers now collect Gaokao scores from individual students after the exam. Schools then assemble it and pass it up the administrative hierarchy to local governments. Now as before, local education ministries review and compare the Gaokao scores for different schools. And now as before, regional Gaokao champions are widely celebrated, although not with quite so much public fanfare. From the perspective of individual schools, the new policy has merely resulted in an increased workload. Schools must laboriously collect and collate

Gaokao scores. But this extra work affords school administrators an opportunity that they did not previously possess—the opportunity to massage the data. One head teacher recounted how her superiors had requested that she tweak her students' Gaokao results by a few points. This teacher calculated that if all teachers had been similarity instructed (she was not sure if they had been), the effect would be subtle but profound, making the difference between meeting or missing the exam-score targets that the municipal education bureau had set. The upshot is that competition between schools and regions continues more or less unchecked, but local governments and schools are not as certain of the data as they once were.

In theory, individual schools are allowed to publicize their data, but most schools have no motive to do so. Because only keypoint schools in central places place significant numbers of students into top-ranking colleges, only such schools have any reason to broadcast their test results. By contrast, schools lower on the score-value hierarchy keep their scores a closely guarded secret. Little information can be found about them in the public domain, except vague announcements about improving trends. Government officials are equally circumspect. In general, only large cities like Xiamen publish admission rates for the municipality as a whole. Publicly available data about peripherally located localities are even more sparse.[5]

In light of the frenzied backstage collection of test-score data, the nonpublication of this data is a glaring omission—a loud silence. This censorship not only makes it difficult for the public to gain an objective picture of educational inequality but also makes the work of educational researchers onerous. As one such researcher, Professor Wang, said:

> Some of my colleagues sit on national-level committees advising the government on Gaokao reform. But none of us have any access to detailed government data. Differences in admission rates between schools and regions are really only the tip of the iceberg from a researcher's perspective. We are also on our own in collecting data about which schools have students getting into exactly which kinds of universities, and so on. . . . Without such data it is difficult to provide any objective assessment of policy. . . . I have many former students working in the provincial education ministry, but they are forbidden from helping me to obtain data. They just tell me, "Sorry, teacher, no can do." If I want to do research on educational disparities, I have to send graduate students around to individual schools. In other words, I go through guanxi with administrators at individual high schools to gain access to the data at each individual school, one by one.

Why does the state keep test scores top secret? As Professor Wang observed, "By withholding this information, the government is attempting to dampen [*dànhuà*] discussion of inequity [*bù jūnhéng*]. The government doesn't want people to focus their attention on this problem. Keeping the scores under wraps is a way of putting the whole discussion of inequality on ice [*lěng chǔlǐ*]."

Educational Disparity and Censorship as Fabrication

Shortly after this conversation, Professor Wang included me in his data-collection efforts. He asked me to introduce one of his graduate students to the principal of Dragon Gate. Wang hoped the principal would be willing to provide data on the school's first-tier admissions rates. I felt honored to be assisting a prominent researcher. At the same time, I was alarmed that such measures were necessary. But participating in the project gave me the opportunity to peruse the data of Professor Wang's student, which filled out my picture of inequality in the score-value hierarchy.

These data tell a story of stark regional inequality. Recall that a student from provincial-level cities like Shanghai or Beijing are two or three times as likely to attend a first-tier university as a student in an ordinary province. Within a single province or region, however, a student in a good high school may be more than fifty times more likely to attend a first-tier university than a student in a bad high school. In high-ranking urban schools, nearly all students either attend a first-tier university or study abroad. Top high schools in Xiamen send 95 percent or more of their Gaokao examinees to top-tier colleges. The rates for the best high schools in Ningzhou and Mountain County are lower but still respectable, constituting 80 and 25 percent respectively. But in low-ranking schools in both the countryside and the city, fewer than 2 percent of students attend first-tier universities. In Mountain County, as one administrator said, outside of Number One High School, only a few students managed to test into a first-tier college every year (figure 8).

First-Tier Admissions

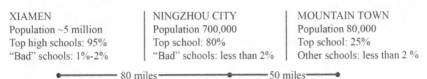

XIAMEN	NINGZHOU CITY	MOUNTAIN TOWN
Population ~5 million	Population 700,000	Population 80,000
Top high schools: 95%	Top school: 80%	Top school: 25%
"Bad" schools: 1%-2%	"Bad" schools: less than 2%	Other schools: less than 2 %

●———— 80 miles ————●———— 50 miles ————●

FIGURE 8.   Student admissions to top universities are skewed in favor of the best high schools in larger cities. Admission percentages are compared here, using good and bad schools and three population examples within the same region. Data from the author.

The disparities between low-ranking and high-ranking schools are so great that high-ranking schools no longer focus on first-tier admissions, emphasizing attendance at Project 985 colleges instead. But the greatest index of prestige is the admission rates at China's two top universities, Tsinghua University and Peking University, which is known as the "Tsinghua-Peking rate" (*qīngbĕilǜ*). Of particular prestige value is the admission rate to elite colleges by "naked score" (*luŏfēn*), which refers to the pure Gaokao score before it is adulterated by various schemes for awarding bonus points.

Students at low-ranking schools complain that students at high-ranking schools possess more opportunities to accrue such bonus points. Furthermore, many students at top-ranking high schools need not take the Gaokao at all, further exacerbating the effects of inequality. A significant number of students at such schools obtain direct admission to top colleges. Education reformers originally intended this program to identify students who possess high quality but not necessarily high test scores. In practice, however, it favors students at top high schools, which receive larger quotas for participation in the scheme. In addition, top high schools in the cities have been sending growing numbers of students abroad since the 2000s. For these reasons, as a Xiamen Foreign Languages High School administrator informed me, only about one-third of students from the best schools in Xiamen obtain admission to top colleges through naked Gaokao scores alone. Another third get admitted through special schemes, and the remainder go to college overseas. But the net effect is that nearly 100 percent attend good colleges.

In sum, the available data paint a stark picture of extreme geographical and social inequality. In the face of such disparities, the suppression of test-score data constitutes a special form of fabrication—censorship by omission. Ordinary people know that their odds of admission to college are bad, but they do not understand the precise degree of their handicap. Just as casino operators keep the house odds secret so gamblers will keep putting money in the slot machines, China's educational officials and high-school administrators restrict the public dissemination of admission rates to protect their reputations and keep families engrossed in examination competition.

Later in my fieldwork, I had an opportunity to ask an official from the provincial ministry of education about this censorship policy. This official had taken an interest in my research, inviting me regularly to discussions over tea or dinner to keep tabs on my work. Comparing the Gaokao to China's imperial examination, he suggested that the test undergirds social stability by "giving ordinary people [*lăobăixìng*] hope." If people knew the true scope of disparities, he said, this knowledge would only "exacerbate the unfair trend." He reasoned as follows: Access to a good high school is determined by test score. But without a good foundation in the compulsory phase of education—primary school and junior high—children cannot do well on the high-school admissions exam. Admission to a good primary school, however, is determined by parents' ability to buy a house in a good school district. As everyone knows, the prices of houses in good school districts have already soared so much that no ordinary family can afford them. So publicizing the real admissions data would only lead to further increases in house prices, further educational competition, and greater potential for social unrest.

The Profanity of Test Design and Grading: Guanxi, Hierarchy, and Objectivity

In large part, people consider the Gaokao objective because of its association with national authority. People say that regional and provincial exams are biased by local interests and guanxi. By contrast, they understand the Gaokao to represent a universalistic, fair, and legitimate national institution.

In this respect, the Gaokao closely resembles the imperial-era civil exam. In the imperial era, higher levels of examination distinction were associated with more centrally located places. The most prestigious examination degree—Advanced Scholar—was conferred by the emperor himself in the capital. Examinees proceeded through a ranked hierarchy of examinations. Each move up the examination ladder corresponded with an ascent of the geographical hierarchy, reinforcing the view that the spatial hierarchy constituted a hierarchy of talent (see chapter 1).

Similarly, Gaokao examinees advance through a series of practice exams, each associated with a progressively more centrally located place. Ordinary weekly and monthly exams are created and administered inside students' schools. At elite schools, mid-term exams may be authored by teachers at sister schools, which generally consist of institutions that occupy a similar place in the score-value hierarchy in neighboring prefectures. In the months before the Gaokao, students take the municipal quality assessment (*shìzhìjiǎn*)—a municipality-wide practice examination. During their final weeks of preparation, they take a provincial quality assessment (*shěngzhìjiǎn*)—a province-wide practice exam. The provincial practice exam is followed by the Gaokao itself—a nationally synchronized ritual.

The role of spatial hierarchy in examinations is similar to its role in bureaucracy and religion. The celestial bureaucracy of gods mirrors the earthly one (see chapter 2). Much as each step up the administrative hierarchy corresponds with control over a more encompassing region, people associate greater magical efficacy (*líng*) with deities who attract pilgrims from a greater geographical area.

In a word, the highest-level officials, gods, and examinations possess a potent charisma that reflects their association with more expansive collectivities.

But students also have practical reasons for supposing that exams form an ascending hierarchy of objectivity and fairness. Appreciating this point requires a detour into the details of how exams are graded and designed.

First, consider the grading process. Examinations contain many multiple-choice questions, to which there are objectively right or wrong answers. But significant sections of the examination incorporate subjective essays and short-answer sections, which must be graded by hand. Local exams are graded at students' schools, the municipal quality assessment in the county seat, and the provincial quality assessment in the prefectural capital. The final examination, the Gaokao itself, is graded in the provincial capital. But most graders are current high-school teachers, who might be liable to various forms of bias. Students and parents reason that graders in the provincial assessment and, especially, the Gaokao are less likely to guess the origin and identity of examinees. They assume these exams to be less polluted by favoritism and guanxi.

A similar logic applies to people's perceptions of the authorship of examinations. Local exams are created by local teachers; thus, they may reflect idiosyncratic biases and methods. By contrast, people assume that prefectural, provincial, and national examinations—crafted in each case by progressively larger teams of teachers working at increasingly higher levels of the central-place hierarchy—are less biased.

But teachers who have personal experience with grading and test design learn to question these assumptions. Gaokao-grading duty is widely considered to be an onerous task. Teachers are asked to volunteer, but few do it willingly. Many teachers can recount their sudden feeling of disillusionment after being initiated into the secrets of grading. Like Dorothy peaking behind the curtain of the Wizard of Oz, they come face-to-face with the reality of the Gaokao's sacred authority. Graders have to work under tight deadlines in factory-like conditions. For two weeks, they cloister themselves in dirty motel rooms and crowded offices, spending long days making split-second decisions that will make or break the fates of students. They are awarded for efficiency and spend a fraction of a minute on essay responses, which generally run to a page or more (800 words) of hand-written text. Unsurprisingly, many graders report feeling like robots.

In addition, graders are usually drawn from top schools in centrally located places. Having themselves attended elite high schools and colleges, many have been isolated their whole lives from the social disparities of China's examination system. Gaokao-grading duty may be the first time they have seen test papers from ordinary schools. One English teacher, who was accustomed to giving her own students sixteen or seventeen points out of twenty on the English essay of the Gaokao, reported being stunned when she first saw essays from schools in the countryside. She had never before witnessed compositions in which, as she put it, the "poor efforts" of students might earn them only a few points or even "goose eggs"—zero scores. Under tremendous time pressure, most graders admit to normalizing their grades. They hesitate to give any score that is too high or too low. Each exam is checked by two teachers, but significant discrepancies must be double-checked, causing delays.

Moreover, corruption reaches its polluting fingers even into this hallowed center of examination power. One grader reported being asked by her supervisor, a vice principal, to be on the lookout for a specific student's examination paper, which she would be able to identify through certain keywords in the essay.

A similar sense of disenchantment accompanies the first exposure of young teachers to the design of examinations. Examinations are created by people, not gods; nevertheless, when teachers begin to create practice examinations themselves, they reflect on the Gaokao in a new way. As one teacher said, "We all look to big cities like Xiamen or Guangzhou or Beijing for model examination questions, but why should we do so? Actually, the designers of those tests are just people, too."

Prior to the renationalization of exam design, teachers complained about test design being predominantly carried out by teachers in centrally located places. They said that this practice gave unfair advantage to elite urban schools. Because high-ranking sister schools routinely share practice examinations, and because the designers of the Gaokao were predominantly drawn from such schools, teachers said that students at those schools were better prepared for the type of question that was likely to appear on the exam. This complaint appears to have been justified. After switching to a national exam paper in 2016, Fujian Province, which previously had performed relatively well on the big test, fell to dead last among the five provinces that shared the same exam paper. Teachers and administrators widely attribute this reversal of fortune to the elimination of corruption from examination design.

Backstage Competition: The Battle for Resources

Self-Fulfilling Prophesy: The Similarity between Schools and Temples

People's attitude toward schools resembles their attitude toward temples. Worshippers prefer temples that they consider to be effective—that is, temples whose patron deities are deemed to be efficacious in responding to worshippers' prayers. Similarly, parents prefer schools they consider to be good—that is, schools that have a good track record of getting children into good colleges. Temples are considered effective if they attract many worshippers, but they attract many worshippers because people consider them effective (Sangren 2000). By the same token, schools are good if they attract top-scoring students, but they attract top-scoring students mainly because they are considered good. The success of both temples and schools relates in a circular fashion to their perceived efficacy. Like the efficacy of deities, the reputation of schools has the character of a self-fulfilling prophesy.

Schools and temples even use similar methods for promoting their reputations. At temples, worshippers typically make a donation as a votive offering to repay (*huányuàn*) the temple's patron deity for fulfilling the worshipper's wish (see chapter 6). To advertise efficacy, temples prominently display the names of donors and the amount of their donations. Similarly, schools prominently post the names of students who have gained admission to top universities. The display of such "joyous announcements" (*xǐbào*; *xǐxùn*) or honor rolls (*guāngróngbǎng*) resembles the display of temple donations. Schools and temples are not the only institutions to employ this advertising strategy. State-sponsored lottery stores likewise display honor rolls, in this case prize-winning lottery tickets (figure 9). Just as temple donations are understood to provide evidence of magical power and high Gaokao scores evidence of educational quality, winning lottery tickets are deemed to provide evidence of divine fortune or good luck (see chapter 6).

Skeptics might suggest that reputation must be understood differently in the context of schools on the one hand and that of temples and lottery stores on the other. Teachers and schools, a critic might say, have real effects on people's lives, whereas deities and divine blessings do not exist. In practice, however, school insiders—administrators and teachers—express more agnosticism with regard to the efficacy of schools than does the average layperson.

Whereas parents ascribe great value to teachers—or at least blame teachers when students fail to achieve high test scores—administrators and officials place more emphasis on student resources. They say that good student resources contribute more to the success of a school than does any other factor. Teacher resources are deemed important, too. But administrators maintain that good teachers derive much of their importance from how they attract good students. As I note above, for example, Mountain County administrators persuaded top-scoring students to stay in Mountain County by offering to put them in special classes taught by only the best teachers.

Of course, good teachers do make some difference in the test performance of students. Ms. Ma at Ningzhou Number One received praise for increasing the average score of her English class by ten points—a significant improvement. Similarly, teachers at Dragon Gate High School in Xiamen earned recognition

FIGURE 9.   Display of merit at a lottery store. Winning lottery tickets are taped inside the window. The characters at the top read "Honor Roll." Schools, temples, and lottery stores all use similar displays to promote their reputations by advertising the success of those who use their services. Photograph by the author.

for raising the school's rank on Xiamen Island from dead last to third-to-bottom among thirteen high schools in only three years. Still, these differences might be described as incremental rather than transformative. The majority of Dragon

Gate teachers hail from high-ranking schools in the countryside where first-tier admission rates hover at 25 percent or higher. But despite their best efforts, Dragon Gate students never exceeded a first-tier admissions rate of 2 percent. Moreover, many of these teachers maintain that whatever improvement they had achieved could be attributed to their effect on motivation and attitude rather than to their pedagogical efficacy per se (see chapter 5). In short, good student resources can make or break the reputation of a school. And the better a school's reputation, the better the student resources it can attract.

For these reasons, administrators and officials see the acquisition of good student resources as a significant, if not the paramount, goal of their work. Their battle for student resources, and the corresponding efforts of parents and families to game the system, dominate the local and regional politics of education. In my field sites, the story of this battle forms a local history of education.

Rural areas are losing. Since the first decade of the twenty-first century, educational disparities have widened as a result of urbanization and the partial privatization of education. But the history of these changes is largely written backstage in the gray areas between official policy and illicit activity.

Public Presentation and Face Giving

Even if ordinary Mountain County Number One students like Chunxiao and Mingfeng are relatively disabused of any illusion that they are treated equally, their school's reputation, and thus its ability to attract good student resources, relies on projecting the best possible public image. For this reason, only fast classes and their teachers have a public existence. Thus any casual observer will receive the false impression that the school is largely made up of good students.

For example, the announcement board in the central quad contains a full roster of all the fast-class teachers, extolling their accomplishments; however, their slow-class colleagues are conspicuously missing. The same announcement board publishes a list of students who have won awards in various prefectural and provincial contests—all of them fast-class students. Similarly, only fast-class students and their teachers have a presence in promotional brochures for the school.

Public rituals exclude slow-class students. Every year in early April around Tomb-Sweeping Day, a festival to honor ancestors, first-year students march to the town's Tomb of the Revolutionary Martyr to be ritually inducted into the Communist Youth League by local political and military leaders. All students must join the league but only fast classes participate in the ceremony. By the same token, school administrators invited only fast-class representatives to give speeches at a mobilization rally (*dòngyuán dàhuì*)—a public event to boost morale for the Gaokao. In this case, however, preferential treatment produced a vocal backlash, causing administrators to take a softer line.

To my dismay, I was recruited more than once into the publicity efforts of the school. On one occasion, a local television station filmed my daily "English corner"—an afternoon English conversation hour that I led. The station reported that the event was open to all students, which was technically true. But slow-class students told me privately that they felt too ashamed to interact with their fast-class peers. On another occasion, a local newspaper observed me teaching, but the class that I taught was cobbled together from a group of the best fast-class students, who were instructed to perform exaggerated enthusiasm for the camera.

In subsequent conversations, students compared such publicity stunts to other empty or fake occasions in which they were asked to perform adherence to the tenants of education for quality, for instance during demonstration lessons and official inspections (see chapter 4). Like the students, I found such public performances uncomfortable. But these events had consequences for the status and reputation of teachers, administrators, and officials—people who had without exception treated me well. Some school leaders had even become my friends, and many addressed me as "brother" during alcohol-lubricated group dinners to which I was occasionally invited. These are gatherings in which, as the clock ticks into the wee hours of the night and empty bottles litter the table, men (the vast majority of leaders are men) "tell the truth," as they say. Naturally, I wanted to help my "brothers"; and naturally, my students wanted to help their teacher. This willing collusion in institutional projects of public impression management forms a basic requirement of the emotional bonds or "human feeling" (*rénqíng*) between students, teacher, and leaders.

Thus public conformity to ideals—even when everyone knows this conformity to be empty—provides an occasion for the sincere expression of sentiment and loyalty between people whose reputations are staked on the maintenance of those ideals. For example, a home-room teacher admonished one of her students for smoking in public: "When people see you smoking, they say that I'm not doing my job. I don't care what you do in private, but when you're at the school, you have to give your teacher face. Giving elders face is a fundamental principle of being a person [*zuòrén*]. How do you expect to survive out there in the world if you can't even do that much?"

Brain Drain and the Privatization of Education: The Principal's Bastard Children

The necessity to put a better face on the school derived in large part from the backstage reality of extreme disparities between fast and slow streams, which had been exacerbated by brain drain and urbanization. As I was to learn, these pressures had gutted the school of its best resources, leading the administration to pursue several secretive coping strategies.

After a few months teaching at Mountain County Number One, administrators asked me to focus my efforts on first-year students to the exclusion of second- and third-year students. Third-year students were off limits because they were in the final stages of preparing for the big test. But I was unsure why senior-two students were removed from my teaching rounds. I only learned the reasons gradually through a series of informal conversations with administrators.

As I discovered, three private high schools had opened in the 2000s in the prefectural capital of Ningzhou. These private schools drew top students away from the countryside by offering them generous scholarships. Parents, after receiving their scholarship checks, joked that "raising a child [was] more lucrative than raising a pig." Experienced teachers were likewise recruited by these private schools, which extended the promise of better salaries and higher bonuses. Publicly, Ningzhou prefectural educational authorities justified privatization as way of improving local educational standards by increasing competition. It was widely rumored, however, that municipal authorities received generous kickbacks from private schools, which earned substantial profits by charging tuition to ordinary, low-scoring students.[6]

In 2008 one of these newly opened schools headhunted the principal of Mountain County Number One, who subsequently used his personal networks to recruit students and teachers away from his old school. This exodus only aggravated the losses that the school was already sustaining as a result of Xiamen's talent-attraction program (see chapter 2). Those who remained in Mountain County resented these developments, complaining that their student and teacher resources were "being stolen" (*bèi qiǎng*).

During my first year in Mountain County, the second-year class, which had been recruited in 2009, continued to be badly impacted by these events. Administrators considered the whole second year to be especially weak— a "garbage year" of "hick" (*tǔ*) students. Administrators reacted by performing triage. They created an exclusive experimental class out of the top-scoring students in the second year. This class received good teacher resources and other forms of special attention. All other resources were diverted to third-year and first-year students.

Meanwhile, school leaders worked with county educational officials to staunch the flow of high-scoring students away from Mountain County. To keep good students in the county, administrators and officials employed the inducement of special new experimental classes for incoming top students. I was enlisted for these recruitment efforts. Administrators asked me to give a special class for potential experimental-class recruits, who were promised that they would be housed with me in my dormitory building—a mostly abandoned structure that I had hitherto occupied by myself. This housing arrangement promised new recruits special access to a foreign English teacher, but also highlighted their relatively sacred position within the school, set apart from ordinary students.

These recruitment efforts were reported to be a success. Many students who had planned to go to Ningzhou or Xiamen stayed in Mountain County. As a result, administrators felt that senior one contained a relatively promising crop of resources. But they considered the second year a lost cause. Accordingly, administrators felt it was a waste of time for me to teach any second-year students outside the experimental class. Of course, this reasoning was not publicized. Students were left to guess why I stopped coming to their classes.

One day in mid-spring, I was eating lunch in the cafeteria with two senior-two boys. My presence prompted a discussion between them about my role in the school. The first boy, Weijun, was studying in one of the higher ranked middle-fast classes. His friend, Lingfu, belonged to a slow class. Normally by this time of year, early March, the whole senior-two year would enter into "graduation mode" (bìyè zhuàngtài). This term refers to a period of intensified instruction, including classes on Saturday and Sunday, in the lead-up to the final battle. Entering graduation mode enables second-year students to hit the ground running in senior three, during which they work in ceaseless diligence seven days a week with few holidays.

But this year's second-year crop of student resources were considered unworthy of such attention, so graduation mode was delayed. Perhaps in other countries students might welcome a lighter-than-expected workload, but not in China. This deprivation of extra instruction prompted second-year students to complain bitterly. As some put it, "Our test scores are not good, it's true. But we are trying hard, and we deserve better." Adding insult to injury, rumor had it that the new principal referred to the second years as his "bastard children"—an apparent reference to how this crop of students was fathered by his now-absent predecessor.

Against this background, Weijun and Lingfu discussed why I was teaching all of the first-year students but only a select few second-year students. Weijun argued his point obliquely. He was one of the top three students in his middle-fast class, he said. But because top classes were already "half-filled" with "students with family connections" (guānxishēng), he could not be promoted to a fast class. "What does that have to do with Mr. Huo?" Lingfu asked, using my Chinese surname. "A lot. They think sending him to our classes is a waste of resources,"

Weijun replied. Lingfu responded with incredulity. His teacher had told him that I would not be visiting his class anymore because their English level was not good enough. As Weijun pointed out, however, this argument did not account for why I would be teaching the slow classes in senior one but not in senior two. This anecdote provides a small but telling example of how state actors—in this case teachers and administrators—conceal awareness of backstage educational practices that might be deemed biased and thus detrimental to the impression of procedural fairness. In this and myriad other everyday ways, street-level bureaucrats collude to maintain a fabrication of fairness that reinforces the false confidence of ordinary students in their examination chances.

Stratification and Awareness of Inequality

In addition to dramatizing the brain drain that the countryside has faced since the 2000s, the experience of students like Lingfu and Weijun sheds light on the relationship between educational stratification and awareness of inequality. Although Mountain County students are highly stratified between different classes, the school as a whole integrates students of many different socioeconomic backgrounds. As I suggest above, Mountain County Number One is like many schools combined into one. Because of this arrangement, students there possess a relatively well-developed awareness of educational inequality. They gain knowledge of inequality merely by observing their counterparts in different classes. Simply the act of going to school creates the awareness-inducing effect that I associate with mobility in chapter 2.

In big cities, by contrast, schools tend to be composed of more homogenous groups of students; in other words, the education system as a whole tends to be more stratified. For this reason, urban students tend not to encounter such vast disparities in educational background and preparation when they attend school. Because they are insulated from exposure to radically different types of student resources, they gain relatively little awareness of educational disparities.

Cross-culturally, survey data corroborate these findings. Students in socioeconomically integrated settings tend to account for differences in educational outcomes by appealing to external, structural factors, such as quality of instruction. By contrast, students in more stratified settings possess a more meritocratic view of success, reporting a comparatively high faith in internal, individual factors, such as effort and intelligence (Mijs 2016).

The above ethnographic observations suggest an explanation for these differences. In homogenous settings, students are relatively insulated from polluting information that would discredit meritocratic narratives of success. But by increasing awareness of inequality, aggressive tracking tarnishes the myth of meritocracy. Students in slow classes begin to see through public projections of fairness. Their general disgruntlement and so-called bad attitude result in large part from this insight.

Stealing, Hoarding, and Manipulating Student Resources

Students differ in their awareness of educational disparities, but few except for the sons and daughters of officials have any real inkling of the backstage politicking that accompanies these inequalities. Summarizing these trends, administrators complain that central places steal or "mine" (*wā*) student resources from peripheral places. In addition to opening private schools in central places, other prominent methods of stealing resources include setting up special autonomous admissions exams (*zìzhǔ kǎoshì*) to recruit top-scoring children directly from the countryside and using moles or plants in rural schools who can receive a fee or kickback for introducing top-scoring prospects to elite high schools in the city. When I queried senior Mountain County Number One administrators about such thefts of student resources, they frequently responded with a sigh of resignation, followed by the idiom that forms the epigraph of chapter 2: "There's nothing to be done. Water flows downward and people move upward." But Mountain County educational administrators and officials are not as resigned to this reality as this reaction would suggest. Educational bureaucrats work hard to staunch the flow of student and teacher resources out of the county and to make the most efficient possible use of those that remain.

Regional protectionism, however, is not the only source of the battle for student resources. Personal ambition also plays a role. And where there is personal ambition, there are guanxi. Guanxi relationships between administrators and officials sometimes lead to relatively dramatic forms of fabrication that involve the hoarding and movement of large amounts of student resources. For example, the principal of Mountain County Number One High School was promoted from the same position at Mountain County Number Two. He achieved this promotion by demonstrating test-score improvement vis-à-vis the better-ranked school. Unbeknownst to many ordinary teachers and students, however, the principal secured these improvements by relying on personal connections with the local education minister, who arranged for his school to receive better student resources.

Students and parents see the Gaokao as a chance to determine fate. In ways that they little suspect, however, their fates may be influenced by backroom negotiations that take place at high levels on the chain of interests. In the pursuit of their personal interests, state actors successfully conceal machinations that affect the examination chances of multitudes. When backstage dealmaking is exposed, it often provokes little surprise from people in China, who have become cynical about state corruption. But ordinary people often have little inkling of backstage maneuvers that directly affect them. The systematic concealment by state actors of these schemes leaves intact people's impression of the relative fairness of the Gaokao. As noted above, people's false confidence in their ability to see through the system often only reinforces the effectiveness of such subterfuge.

Hitting an Edge Ball: Education-Abroad Classes and the Negotiation of Regional Interests

As the draining of student and teacher resources from the countryside became an ever more serious problem, a backlash resulted in several policy shifts. These changes resulted in part from the intervention of provincial authorities, who have greater concern for maintaining the balance of regional interests than do local educational bureaus. Starting around 2006, Xiamen educational authorities greatly curtailed their recruitment of experienced teachers from the countryside. In 2009, authorities prohibited elite urban high schools—top prefectural schools like Ningzhou Number One and Xiamen's triumvirate of elite schools (Foreign Language, Double Ten, and Number One)—from using special autonomous admissions exams to recruit high-scoring examinees from the countryside.

Elite high schools, however, were loath to give up these tests, which had guaranteed a flow of student resources and revenue from the countryside. Many rural parents likewise lamented the suspension of these special exams, which had provided them with a pathway into elite schools. Thus the suspension of autonomous admissions harmed both elite schools and top-scoring rural students but helped ameliorate educational inequalities on a regional level by keeping good students in the countryside. Of course, rural authorities had campaigned for this policy shift not purely to advance educational equity but also to protect their own interests, because the prestige and career advancement of teachers, administrators, and educational officials are so closely linked to test scores.

Various conflicts of interests, however, routinely undercut such policy goals. Educational authorities, schools, and families routinely seek loopholes in the policies to advance their own agendas. In this case, urban schools continued recruiting rural students under the guise of admitting them to special education-abroad classes (guójìbān). Similar to the discontinued practice of admitting high-school students through autonomous exams, admission to these education-abroad classes is predicated on taking a special test, which is open to all. As before, therefore, high-scoring rural students can attend Xiamen high schools as long as their parents can afford the tuition.

As their name suggests, education-abroad classes are nominally intended to prepare students for pursuing college education overseas. Indeed, with China's rising study-abroad fever, an increasing demand for such programs exists (see chapter 2). Moreover, these programs are consonant with the Xiamen municipal government's goal of becoming an international metropolis that can compete on a world stage. During my fieldwork, however, only half or fewer of these education-abroad students actually intended to study abroad. Backstage, these classes were divided into real education-abroad classes and fake education-abroad classes. Only students in the former type of class, who tend to be low-scoring, end up attending foreign universities; those in the latter take the Gaokao.

In Mountain County, local administrators see education-abroad programs as a ploy to steal top rural students. They disparagingly refer to these programs as a cynical guise or as "advertising dog meat with a lamb's head." A particularly descriptive metaphor for such fabrications consists of expression borrowed from ping pong—an "edge ball" (cābiānqiú). An edge ball is one that is legally in bounds but impossible to return. Hence edge-ball policies occupy an intermediary space between the frontstage and the backstage, their nominal conformance with official policy making them difficult to oppose.

In the pursuit of sometimes overlapping, sometimes conflicting interests, various constituencies of families, teachers, administrators, and officials rig and game the system. Fairness and justice are always tainted by self-interest. In practice, these universalistic principles are invariably polluted by the politics of guanxi. The attempts of people to define, redefine, reinforce, fabricate, or undercut fairness do not result in a zero-sum game. Those with greater social and cultural capital dominate the competition. Thus the system works in a way that funnels value, as objectified in test scores, up the central-place and social hierarchies. To accept the legitimacy of the exam, however, people must believe that it is undetermined. For this reason, knowledge about many of the most egregious distortions of fairness is guarded by actors high on the chain of interests, whom these inequalities benefit.

Of course, China is far from the only society where elites limit the flow of information in the interest of social control. In fateful events cross-culturally, ritual specialists often withhold secrets from participants to ensure that they perceive these events as undetermined and thus fateful.[7] In the Gaokao, high-level ritual specialists (administrators and officials) keep back knowledge from low-level ones (ordinary teachers) and from initiates (examinees). As a result, people can believe that the exam is fairer than it actually is. In a world where so much is fake, people see the Gaokao as a rare domain in which performance and substance align.

Nevertheless, most ordinary people possess much knowledge about unfair practices, even if their degree of insight varies. Consequently, attitudes toward fairness are complex, including both misrecognition or false consciousness, on the one hand, and cynicism and false confidence on the other. People widely regard professions of fairness by schools and governments as empty—a view that is symptomatic of widespread cynicism about the Chinese education system. Everywhere, however, they see the Gaokao itself as relatively fair; thus, they believe test scores to be full or real measures of individual merit. Their false confidence in their ability to see through fabrications of fairness prevents their feelings of cynical resignation—numbness—from bubbling over into sharper forms of discontent.

As the philosophical adage goes, however, there is "emptiness in fullness, and fullness in emptiness" (*xū zhōng yǒu shí, shí zhōng yǒu xū*). Remarking on this tension between the empty and the full, the counterfeit and the real, one teacher said, "Chinese people live a very split existence" (*huó de hěn fēnliè*). And as another said, "I am constantly pacing back and forth between ideal and reality." People's sincere belief in test scores represents one effort to bridge this gap. But as another proverb says, "Every medicine contains some poison" (*shì yào sān fēn dú*). Many in China worry that the ascetic, repetitive focus on examinations that they identify as full and real in the Chinese education system renders the system empty and hollow as a whole. Yet from Shanghai, Beijing, and other frontstage places, China broadcasts a picture of educational success to an outside world that is seemingly eager to consume such images (Loveless 2014).

By contrast, people at my field sites often felt disillusioned with this overwhelming emphasis on tests and memorization. Such feelings were given vivid expression by my rural principal friend, Mr. Jian, who had sent his own daughter to study in the United States. Evoking the specter of a nation growing anemic from the emptiness of its youth, he compared Chinese educational practices to the techniques of profit-hungry farmers who grow chemical-laced produce for consumption in the cities: "Our children are like beansprouts grown with hydroponic techniques and artificial nutrients. They grow very quickly, but are poisonous."

But most ordinary students, who do not have the option of studying abroad, can only hope to grow numb about the necessity of consuming another kind of poison—the poison milk of counterfeit fairness. This image serves as a potent metaphor for the great anxiety that ordinary people feel about the exam. Parents worry constantly about the enormous outlay of time and money necessary to raise a successful examinee, as well as the role that guanxi plays in securing educational advantages. Many say that they are "losing on the starting line" (*shū zài qǐpǎoxiàn*). This expression highlights the arbitrariness with which the examination compresses educational competition into one fateful moment even though families have been striving for success since before their children were born.

Nevertheless, the exam largely succeeds in persuading people that it is a legitimate measure of individual merit. The fabrication of fairness helps to explain why. But another important reason lies in how people identify examination success with exemplary moral character. Despite their ambivalence about the exam, people tend to see success in it as a sign of superior virtue, as the next chapter discusses.

DILIGENCE VERSUS QUALITY

Merit, Inequality, and Urban Hegemony

**The way of Heaven is to reward hard work;
without toil there is no harvest.**

—Chinese proverb

Diligence has long been the cornerstone of examination preparation in China. In the imperial era, aspiring examinees typically memorized the whole Confucian canon, the Four Books and Five Classics, which comprise 431,286 characters of Chinese text (Miyazaki 1981). By devoting most of their time to study, diligent students could achieve this feat by age fifteen. Women were not allowed to participate in the exam, but competition was open to men of broad social backgrounds. Thus academic diligence formed a widely admired social ideal.

In contemporary times, test takers—now consisting of boys and girls—see their preparation for the Gaokao as a continuation of this tradition of diligence. The virtue is particularly prized in rural areas, where people say it accords with an agrarian spirit of hard work. In praise of diligence, people cite the old saying— "ten years by the cold window" (*shínián-hánchuāng*). This phrase, which dates to imperial times, evokes the dreary discipline of the examination life and alludes to the modest backgrounds from which many examinees seek to rise. But as my students quipped, they study for twelve years, not just ten.

Diligent (*nǔlì de*) students spend most of their waking minutes preparing for the exam. In Mountain County Number One, which has a fairly typical schedule, I was roused every day at 5:50 a.m. along with the school's approximately 1,500 boarding students (about half the school's student population) by music blaring over the dormitory loud speakers. The young scholars are awakened not by reveille or patriotic songs, as one might expect, but by upbeat Western popular music. During my fieldwork, Taylor Swift was especially well-liked for this purpose.

Students rise to find their most diligent classmates already hard at work. Holding their textbooks in front of them, they amble around the school track, through the halls, or around the courtyard. A preferred method of study consists of memorization (*bèisòng*) or, literally, "back recitation." In imperial times, a student demonstrated mastery of a text by reciting it from memory with his back turned. To this day, to "back" (*bèi*) something means to learn it by rote. Walking in small circuits or rocking to and fro, the young scholars mumble through their books as if in a trance.

In the daybreak hour, growing numbers join this murmuring throng of recitation. The chanting creates an eerie effect in the early morning fog, which wraps its misty fingertips around the school grounds and obscures the surrounding mountains. Observers may easily imagine themselves transported to an earlier era, when previous generations of diligent scholars recited the words of Confucius and Mencius.

At 6 a.m., the canteen opens and the most diligent students—the majority of them girls—obtain a coveted seat. Breakfast is not served until 6:50, but the eager scholars greedily consume every minute in diligent study just as later throngs of breakfasters scrape down every drop of rice porridge from their bowls. Most of the boarders hail from the countryside. Their classmates from town arrive by bicycle, parking their conveyances in neat rows. The new arrivals join the others in the canteen or in the classrooms. According to the official timetable, 6:05 to 6:15 a.m. is reserved for morning physical exercise, but the school encourages students to devote this time to their homework, which they continue to pore over throughout morning study, from 6:20 to 6:50.

At 7:20 students convene in their classrooms for guided morning reading. Two days per week, they recite English or listen to English tapes; two days per week, they memorize passages from their Chinese textbooks; and Fridays alternate between Chinese and English. Classes last from 7:45 a.m. to 5:10 p.m., divided into seven forty-five minute periods—four in the morning and three in the afternoon.

Students perform two types of synchronized physical exercise to aid them in their diligence. For thirty minutes every morning from 9:25 to 9:55, they gather on the sports field for group calisthenics—a practice that is thought to help bind (*shùfù*) them in coordinated discipline. Then, at the beginning of the forth and the sixth periods, they perform eye health maintenance (*yǎnbǎojiàn*). This activity consists in a series of self-massage exercises, which the state instituted in the 1980s to protect students against the alleged ravages of prolonged study, widely thought to include nearsightedness. Once a week on Tuesdays, morning calisthenics give way to the flag-raising ceremony, on which occasion school leaders and selected scholars—paragons of diligence—hold forth on students' moral duty of diligent study in the service of family, school, and country.

Morning and afternoon are separated by a two-hour midday siesta, which gives students living in town the opportunity to return home for lunch. Even during this rest period, however, scholars can be found studying in the canteen. The period between 5:10 and 5:40 p.m. is nominally reserved for extracurricular activities, but few such activities are organized. Boarders use this time to relax or study, whereas townies may go home early for dinner, which officially starts at 5:40 and lasts for an hour. After dinner, students reconvene in their classrooms for supervised evening study hall from 6:40 to 10:00 p.m. Evening study is divided into three periods, each separated by a ten-minute break. When the final study hall bell rings, townies return to their houses while boarders hurriedly shower or buy some snacks from the school store; then the dormitory lights are switched off at 10:30. But many students continue to study late into the night by the light of small lamps. According to a popular saying, "If you sleep four hours, you will pass; if you sleep five, you will fail" (*sìdāng-wǔluò*).

Students are not uniformly diligent. In the morning, late risers straggle into class after the bell. In the evening, small groups of boys from slow classes skip study hall. On my evening jog, I would sometimes see them chatting in inconspicuous groups on the sports field, where the darkness conceals their antics. These students say that the teachers do not really care about them. The priests and priestesses of the exam are resigned to abandoning such hopeless charges to the grim fate of their laziness.

Non-boarding students have an edge on the examination because they can study extra hours in the quiet of their own homes. Dormitories have no desks and are noisy and crowded, with eight students to a room. In their senior-three year, those who can afford the luxury rent a room near the school so that they can study more efficiently.

Students rarely take a day off. Classes in the fast streams receive instruction six days a week during senior one and senior two. In the spring semester of their senior-two year, as the Gaokao begins to draw near, students enter graduation mode—six days of class per week with tests on Sunday. Outside big cities, summer holiday is short—often only two or three weeks. Although this schedule may strike readers as ascetic, students and teachers in Mountain County Number One see discipline as relatively lax there. Far more draconian regimens prevail in private test-prep factories and notorious super high schools (*chāojízhōngxué*), which are said to enforce military-style (*jūnshìhuà*) discipline. On the internet, videos circulate of students at such schools reciting slogans while jogging in formation during morning physical education, or reciting textbooks while they stand in line at the canteen.

In general, however, schools differ only in their enforcement of diligence, not in their evaluation of its importance. This virtue is universally extolled, even if not everyone can be expected to live up to the model of the best schools or the hardest-working students. Without exception, students and teachers agree that great diligence is required to succeed on the exam. As they often repeat, "Twelve years of diligence are all for the Gaokao."

This valorization of diligence rests on the common belief that hard work will be repaid with success. This belief is vividly expressed in the proverb that forms the epigraph of this chapter: "The way of Heaven is to reward hard work; without toil there is no harvest" (*Tiān dào chóu qín, bù láo wú huò*). This message—which could also be translated as "no pain, no gain"—appears in a Dragon Gate High School classroom above the chalkboard in large red characters. Used as an exam slogan, this proverb highlights the agrarian ethos of diligence. Students and teachers frequently compare study to work in the fields and success to the harvest. (I return to people's conceptions of Heaven, the supreme Chinese deity, in chapter 6.)

Many in China conceive of diligence as a characteristically rural virtue. They say that people in the countryside, accustomed to sweat and toil, are better at "eating bitterness" (*chīkǔ*). But people in rural areas have no monopoly on the belief in hard work. Devotion to diligence pervades Chinese society. Indeed, the ubiquity of this virtue has prompted the anthropologist Stevan Harrell (1985) to ask why Chinese work so hard. As he suggests, one answer may lie in the importance of the family to Chinese economic life (Harrell 1985). By some estimates, 90 percent of Chinese businesses are family firms, where diligence, along with the associated values of thriftiness and entrepreneurship, are seen as forming the moral foundation of economic success.[1] The great value that individuals place on caring for parents (that is, being filial) and having successful offspring (that is, extending the lineage) motivates diligence in other spheres. In other words, the particularistic demands of the family inspire universalistic achievements—accomplishments measured against the common yardstick of objective authorities such as the market or the Gaokao. But the Gaokao does more than measure diligence; it also inculcates this virtue. The examination—to which students devote their formative years—reinforces a general faith in assiduous striving.

Even dropouts and examination failures leave school with a belief in the value of diligence. Students, both good and bad, widely praise this value. Those who succeed in life ascribe their success to its presence; those who fail blame their downfall on its lack. Given the high level of social inequality in China, however, it seems paradoxical that diligence should be so widely embraced. People of relatively privileged backgrounds tend to do better in meritocratic competitions; their cultural and social capital gives them a decided advantage. But true believers in diligence hail from across the socioeconomic spectrum;

indeed, people of marginalized social backgrounds tend to express special veneration for hard work. Why should the underprivileged in particular place so much faith in this trait?

There are at two least factors to consider. First, people's faith in diligence is not blind. They consider hard work a necessary rather than sufficient condition of success. Luck is also deemed indispensable (see chapter 6). In fact, a precise formula exists for identifying the ratio of diligence to fortune that people suppose success to require. As many say, "Thirty percent is luck, 70 percent hard work" (*Sān fēn Tiān zhùdìng, qī fēn kào dǎpīn*). This prescription, which even forms the title of a popular song in the local Minnan dialect, is a common refrain around exam time. Some students place even more weight on diligence, claiming that success is 80 percent hard work.

Given the long odds that most students face, however, either ratio would seem to suggest false confidence in the power of diligence (see chapter 3). But without doubt, succeeding on the exam requires prodigious preparation. For this reason, many—particularly those from relatively privileged backgrounds—bristle at any suggestion that their victory owes too much to good fortune. As one Gaokao veteran, the daughter of a high-ranking university administrator, told me, "We work damned hard for our success; no one gives it to us!" And everyone can point to examples of wealthy but lazy classmates who bomb the exam.

Second, and more crucially, people regard diligence as a weapon of the weak. They say that diligence is the only means for those without guanxi to overcome their disadvantage. Thus people see hard work, determination, and grit as constituting true expressions of individual merit. According to this view, the emphasis on diligence in the Gaokao gives ordinary people an opportunity to compete with those who possess inherited social advantages. As a popular exam slogan asks, "Without the Gaokao, can you outcompete [*pīn dé guò*] the second-generation rich [*fùèrdài*]?" Of course, parents and teachers acknowledge the importance of cultural and social conditions (*tiáojiàn*) or environment (*huánjìng*) in cultivating diligence (see chapter 5). But few students like to think of themselves as privileged or lazy. It is always possible to point to someone who has more advantages than oneself. Thus resentment of privilege, corruption, and guanxi is widespread in China, even among the relatively well off. The Gaokao harnesses these feelings of resentment, channeling them toward the orthodox social goal of meritocratic competition.

For all these reasons, diligence has broad appeal. It is a shared value that unites students.

But the decades since the 1990s have witnessed a backlash against this overwhelming focus on hard work. Critics of China's "examination-based education" (*yìngshì jiàoyù*), who tend to come from urban areas, say that rote memorization, which they disparagingly refer to as "goose-fattening-style pedagogy" (*tiányāshì jiàoyù*), poorly prepares students for the innovation economy of the twenty-first century. In response, reformers since the 1990s have promoted "education for quality" (*sùzhì jiàoyù*). This term refers to a range of educational practices that people believe inculcate the capacities for creativity and critical thinking. Quality is associated with sophisticated manners and superior moral personhood. The search for quality reflects the desire to be modern and to compete in a rapidly globalizing employment market.

As a result of education-for-quality reforms, skills that people deem to represent high quality—such as participation in academic olympiads or mastery of a musical instrument—have begun playing an increasingly important role in admission to schools and colleges. But this new emphasis on quality disadvantages rural students. The cultivation of quality requires access to cultural capital and opportunities that well-heeled people in urban areas can more easily gain. When school and college admissions emphasize quality, they dilute the only advantage that rural students possess—their capacity for eating bitterness.

But the diligence versus quality debate presents a great irony. The cultivation of quality requires no less diligence than the memorization of textbooks. Since quality started assuming an important role in admissions, parents and schools have found ways to regiment its instruction. As a result, the decades since the 1990s have witnessed a litany of new examinations, contests, and competitions that purport to measure and certify this virtue. Students now toil diligently not only to "back" their books but also to display creativity and talent. But this regimentation defeats the original purpose of the reforms, which was to provide an antidote to examination-based education.

Thus the middle-class focus on quality does not exclude diligence. Rather, those who emphasize quality merely disdain certain expressions of diligence—in particular, rote memorization. They see such manifestations of diligence, which they regard as backward, as characteristic of China's rural, low-quality past, which they desire to transcend (Anagnost 1997). Urban parents say of successful rural examinees that they "only know how to be diligent." They possess "high scores but low ability" (*gāofēn-dīnéng*). But nearly everyone values hard work. Thus I differentiate between diligence as a rural character ideal and diligence as a widespread social value that even those who stress quality embrace.

Despite a shared focus on hard work, therefore, the ideals of quality and diligence reflect conflicting social interests. The former corresponds to a mostly urban, middle-class interest; the latter to a rural one. This chapter argues that the negotiation between these interests produces an unequal (and potentially unstable) status quo—a form of negotiated hegemony (see chapter 1). Urban interests reign supreme but must maintain rural acquiescence by paying lip service to fairness (see chapter 3). In various ways, the Gaokao has been increasing its focus on quality. But if the test abandoned all rote memorization, then people of rural origin would feel left out of the competition.

Many scholars point out how the discourse of quality reinforces urban hegemony (Anagnost 2004; Kipnis 2001; Woronov 2008; Wu 2016; H. Yan 2008; L. Yi 2011). Others explore the contradictions between education for quality and exam-oriented education (Fong 2006; M. H. Hansen 2015; Kuan 2015; Kipnis 2011; R. Zheng 2011). My contribution lies in investigating the cultural logics that link diligence and quality. To this end, I compare how people vary their strategies of self-cultivation across the rural-urban hierarchy. Even though diligence and quality represent conflicting social interests, they occupy a shared moral universe. But this commonality is easily obscured by the eagerness of middle-class parents to differentiate themselves from people of rural origin. In what follows, I also examine gendered differences in diligence. In particular, I attempt to account for what people refer to as the peculiar diligence of girls. Women in China, as elsewhere, outperform boys in school. Paradoxically, however, their diligence forms a pretense for their relegation to stereotypically feminine disciplines and professions. Ethnic minorities also face a similar form of gendered marginalization, finding themselves frequently shuttled into professions regarded as women's work, like teaching and translation.

Despite the different ways in which diligence is experienced across gender, ethnic, and rural/urban lines, this value provides a moral glue for society, uniting even dropouts and examination failures in a common belief in discipline and hard work. People of all backgrounds strive to change fate through hard work. In many cases, people even succeed in this goal. At the same time, however, their diligent self-cultivation also reinforces social hierarchies and confers legitimacy on national institutions. People's nearly universal faith in diligence reinforces their tendency to blame the moral constitution of individuals for the effects of social inequality.

I do not mean to suggest that people of "high quality" do not display real merit; rather, my concern in this chapter, as in the book more broadly, is with equity (see chapter 1). Who is and who is not able to transform diligence into social power, and why?

Diligence, Quality, and Social Inequality

One of the first things that a visitor to a rural Chinese high school notices is the ubiquitous valorization of diligence. Paeans to hard work are emblazoned everywhere in large red characters on school buildings and classroom walls. These slogans present the good consequences of diligent study and the bad consequences of its absence. Consider a sampling from Mountain County Number One:

> For this thing called study, it is not that we lack time but that we lack diligence.
>
> —on the outside wall of the boys' dormitory

> The pain (*kǔtòng*) of studying is temporary; the suffering (*tòngkǔ*) of not having learned lasts a lifetime.
>
> —on a school building

> If you nap during this moment, in the future you will dream (*zuòmèng*); if you study in this moment, in the future you will fulfill your dreams (*yuánmèng*).
>
> —on the wall in front of the teachers' dormitory

> It is only by getting up earlier than others, by being harder working than them, by being more diligent, that one can taste the sweet flavor of success.
>
> —on the outside of the girls' dormitory

These slogans suggest that hard work has no limit or, as teachers say, no bottom (*méiyǒu dǐ*). Lack of time is no excuse for lack of diligence. With strict self-discipline and good life habits, every precious second can be squeezed from the day and dedicated to examination preparation. Studying diligently is mastering the body through mastering its habits. Study may be painful (*kǔtòng*) or hard (*xīnkǔ*), but this pain—temporary and bodily in nature—pales in comparison to the suffering (*tòngkǔ*) of failure. The latter type of pain lasts a lifetime. It is existential. The ultimate objective of diligent study consists in wish fulfillment. Those who spend their time napping will merely dream about a good life in the future; only those who study hard will fulfill their dreams. But this process involves fierce competition. Not everyone will succeed. Only by exercising supreme self-mastery—only by getting up earlier than others, by being more hard-working—can one achieve the sweet flavor of success.

In rural schools, diligence reigns supreme. The importance and durability of diligence as a value can be demonstrated by comparing the treatment of these mottos with that of political slogans. The latter—such as Hu Jintao's Harmonious Society or Xi Jinping's Chinese Dream—change with each new leader and political season; thus, they tend to be presented in less permanent media, such as posters, banners, scrolling LED message panels, chalkboards, or placards. By contrast, the virtues of diligence are painted directly onto the sides of buildings and walls (figure 10). This treatment reflects how students and teachers see such

FIGURE 10.   A slogan celebrating diligence painted directly on the side of a school building: "The pain of studying is temporary; the suffering of not having learned lasts a lifetime." Photograph by the author.

slogans as relatively true and real in comparison to political rhetoric, which they deem to be relatively empty and false. Diligence is eternal, as people say. It transcends the ephemerality of politics and fads.

In the examination life, the prominent display of diligence slogans forms the tip of a discursive iceberg. Leaders and administrators expatiate on the importance of hard work. Student representatives, who are selected for their ardor and enthusiasm, lead their schoolmates in public devotions to diligence during mobilization rallies. Head teachers continually admonish students to greater assiduousness. Following the big exam, students endlessly debate who earned success through hard work versus who was merely lucky. As teachers and students constantly repeat, diligent study has the power to change fate.

The capacity of the Gaokao to create social mobility is widely overestimated (see 2 and 3). Nevertheless, there is much objective basis to the belief that an emphasis on diligent memorization is advantageous to people of rural origin. In all educational settings, children with superior cultural capital—that is, cultural capital that conforms to the dominant or hegemonic norms of what a cultured person should be—tend to outperform those with inferior cultural capital (see chapter 1). Cultural capital can be acquired implicitly (that is, in an incidental manner without awareness that it has been learned) or it can be taught explicitly (that is, in a regimented fashion) (Bourdieu and Passeron 1977). But most discussions of cultural capital focus on the former. As people in China say, children acquire basic habits and knowledge through osmosis (*xūntáo*) from their cultural environment (*huánjìng*)—the home, the peer group, and the classroom. Those without access to a good environment "lose on the starting line" (*shū zài qǐpǎoxiàn*).

For this reason, many progressive education theorists argue that children of all backgrounds should be explicitly taught the knowledge that they need to succeed in school and society (Bourdieu and Passeron 1977; Gramsci 1971; Guillory 1993). From this perspective, the traditional focus on memorization in the Gaokao is relatively progressive. When the contents of an examination are learned by rote in school, any diligent student has an opportunity to succeed, regardless of family or social background.

Education for Quality

Since at least the late 1990s, education in China has been perceived by many to be in a state of crisis. Reformers argue that China's emphasis on diligent exam preparation prevents students from acquiring the prerequisites for success in the globalizing economy, which are thought to include creativity, innovativeness, adaptability, and practical competency. These critics complain that "if it isn't tested, it isn't taught." They regard the overproduction of students who have "high scores but low abilities" as a marker of China's backwardness. To combat this perceived lack of quality, educational authorities have implemented a raft of reforms, which are commonly referred to as education for quality. The overall goal of these reforms lies in increasing the comprehensive quality (*zōnghé sùzhì*) of China's human capital, thereby improving both individual prospects and the national fortune.

Quality is not the buzzword that it once was (Woronov 2015). In many schools, one is more likely to hear the close synonym "attainment" (*sùyǎng*). The rise of this term as an alternative to quality seems to reflect some popular discomfort with the latter, which combines the logograms for "essence" (*sù*) and "nature" (*zhì*). Many teachers and students resist the implication that one's overall ability and character might be essential to one's nature. By contrast, attainment combines "essence" with "cultivation" (*yǎng*), thus suggesting that one's nature can be intentionally cultivated. Despite this shift in terminology, the term "quality" remains common in everyday talk outside of schools. Moreover, the education-for-quality reforms and the problems that prompted them remain central issues of China's educational policy.

Although these reforms share a single keyword, they are widely divergent in their approaches, contents, and even goals (Kipnis 2006). A summary of the most notable pedagogical initiatives promoting quality includes the following:

1. Various approaches fostering innovation and creativity, such as participation in robotics competitions or opportunities to participate in scientific research
2. Cultivation of special abilities (*tècháng*), such as music, martial arts, or artistic techniques
3. Communicative methods in language-learning classes (focusing on the exchange of information instead of drilling and memorization)
4. Various programs of patriotic education (*àiguó jiàoyù*) to foster nationalism
5. Extracurricular activities such as foreign-language clubs, sports competitions, or debate groups
6. Programs to introduce students to menial work so they can practice life skills
7. Expanded emphasis on physical education
8. Education to cultivate morality (moral quality)
9. De-emphasizing exam scores while emphasizing the whole person
10. Fostering composure or "good attitude" and "psychological quality" (see chapter 5)

As the reader can glean from this list, education for quality is a multifarious concept. Quality means different things to different people. But some clear patterns stand out. In particular, possession of quality is strongly associated with residence in urban areas. The more centrally people are located on the rural-urban continuum, the more quality they are generally construed to possess; moreover, people see the West as a transcendental locus of quality—a perception that contributes to the desire of many Chinese to send their children abroad to be educated (see chapter 2).

In short, people in China associate quality with urbanity, modernity, and development. From a sociological point of view, this character ideal indexes forms of cultural capital that people in urban places can more easily acquire.

Spatial Variation in Attitudes toward Education for Quality

People of all backgrounds tend to feel genuine admiration for accomplishments that they associate with high quality. But attitudes toward education for quality vary widely between rural and urban places. In particular, rural people tend to regard quality reforms as well intentioned but empty. From their perspective, education for quality is a lamentable distraction from examination preparation, and they are inclined to fabricate compliance with quality-boosting policies rather than to implement them. In cities, by contrast, administrators and teachers are more likely to embrace or "throw themselves into" (*tóurù*) campaigns to increase quality. In urban places, even critics tend to see education for quality as constituting a worthwhile if sometimes futile mission.

To some degree, central-place and school-ranking hierarchies are interchangeable in their exhibition of these trends. In attitudes toward quality, the highest-ranking school in the backwater prefectural capital Ningzhou resembles schools in metropolitan Xiamen, whereas lower-ranking schools in Ningzhou resemble schools in the rural hinterlands. As a general rule, moreover, centrally dictated policies are less rigidly enforced in the countryside, where heaven is high and the emperor is far away (see chapter 2).

Some representative variations between my three field sites can be cited in support of these observations. In both low-scoring and high-scoring Xiamen high schools, English-language teachers generally emphasize education for quality during the first two years of high-school instruction, turning only to full-time drilling during the last year. For example, English teachers at Dragon Gate employ communicative methods during senior one and senior two. In this approach, they speak to students only in English and encourage students to speak to one another in English. These methods receive official endorsement from school leaders and inspecting officials, who stress compliance with education for quality. But Dragon Gate teachers, most of whom hail from rural schools where traditional methods are preferred, profess great ambivalence about this focus on communication. They say that it poorly serves many of their students, particularly those of poor migrant backgrounds. In contrast to students at higher-ranking schools, students at Dragon Gate are rarely exposed to English at home, nor are many of them enrolled in after-school English classes from a young age. By de-emphasizing rote memorization, communicative methods subvert the main compensation strategy that such students employ.[2]

In Ningzhou's highest-ranking school, by contrast, quality-oriented English education only finds frequent use in special "public demonstration lessons" (*gōngkāikè*). The manifest purpose of such occasions is to give teachers a forum in which to showcase advanced methods for colleagues from other schools. But these events usually only serve to give face to school leaders and municipal educational authorities by demonstrating that schools pay adequate lip service to education for quality. Students play along, but privately see such lessons as empty (see chapter 3). And few Ningzhou teachers would dream of applying any new-fangled pedagogy to the serious task of preparing students for the examination. Such imported methods, they say, do not suit China's national circumstances.

Farther down the urban-rural hierarchy, no demonstration lessons exist. The few schools in Mountain County are too far apart from each other to create convenient opportunities for intercommunication. As a result, adherence to education for quality must be demonstrated only to outsiders—inspecting municipal and provincial authorities. In 2009, for example, Mountain County Number One instituted extracurricular activities and elective courses to qualify for accreditation as a first-tier school (*yījí dábiāo xuéxiào*), an important index of the school's modernization; however, shortly after provincial inspectors had approved this accreditation, school administrators canceled all extracurricular activities to give students more time to prepare for exams.

Disburdened of any need to teach quality, schools in rural areas focus solely on exam preparation. Pedagogy consists almost entirely in the time-tested method of drilling. Teachers who provide students with opportunities to develop their all-around quality often do so in secret. In one class I observed, a Chinese teacher allowed a student, the daughter of farmers, to organize and lead an end-of-the-year class party. But this teacher was afraid that I would inadvertently divulge his deviation from exam-oriented education to the school administration. Pledging me to secrecy, he said:

> Whatever you do, don't tell the section leader. School leaders don't want me to do anything that is not for the examination. But I still give the kids a break sometimes. These student-organized activities can be a psychological breakthrough (*tūpòdiǎn*) for farm kids. In the city, children have many opportunities for public speech. But when kids from the countryside get up to speak in front of other people, their whole bodies shake. . . . I am just trying to give them experience that will be useful later in life.

As this teacher suggests, the rural aversion to education for quality probably reinforces modes of socialization that cause rural children to be branded as simple and shy—labels that create a disadvantage for them in the job market. But rural teachers and administrators justifiably consider education for quality to be a distraction. They say that only diligent study can prepare students for success in the final battle.

Reducing the Burdens and Purchasing Diligence

Other examples of spatial variation in education for quality are worth considering. Starting in the late 1990s and early 2000s, the state implemented various reforms to reduce the burdens (*jiǎnfù*) of students. The object of these initiatives was, as reformers said, "to give children back their childhoods" by reducing the amount of time that they spent on study. This policy affected high schools most directly by reducing the hours of school instruction, and in particular by banning Saturday classes. But schools resist this reform because they see examination scores as correlated with diligence. Resistance is pronounced in rural areas where, despite official bans, schools continue to hold classes six or even seven days a week (Kipnis 2001).

Mountain County Number One is a typical example of such resistance. While students are in graduation mode, they generally get only one day off a month. Far from complaining about studying too much, however, Mountain County students resent not being able to study more (see chapter 3). And because officials rarely visit, the school makes little effort to hide the intensity of its instruction.

In Ningzhou, by contrast, schools are more careful about how they flout the policy. Ningzhou Number One will hold classes on Saturdays only after slightly higher-ranking schools in neighboring prefectural capitals lead the way. If anyone asks, teachers are instructed to respond in the guise of volunteers—students have voluntarily come to class, and teachers are voluntarily teaching them.

In Xiamen, all mid- and low-ranking schools conform carefully to the ban on Saturday instruction, because defying it can result in steep penalties. Occasionally, however, high-ranking schools may carefully employ variations of the volunteer guise to provide students with limited Saturday instruction. Such ruses are hardly necessary in the city, where private companies—the shadow-education sector—can make up for shortfalls in instruction; students regularly attend supplemental study classes (*bǔxíbān*) outside of school, which are sometimes termed cram schools. As a result, diligent urbanites probably receive as much instruction as their rural counterparts. Of course, if families lack the funds to pay for this extra tuition, their children miss out. Remarking on this phenomenon, one Mountain County student told me that the diligence of urban children is emptier because it has to be bought; rather than "coming from inside," it is facilitated by a monetary transaction.

Private schools, which are increasingly common in my field sites, give parents another way of purchasing diligence (see chapter 3). Even in the countryside, well-heeled parents may commit undiligent children to such schools, which famously run a tight ship (*zhuā de hěn yán*). Under their military discipline, so-called bad students sometimes see dramatic score increases, though teachers report that these increases often disappear overnight when students leave this environment.

Rural students may look down their noses at the empty diligence of urbanites, which they regard as paid for by others. But this critique does little to salve an unpleasant reality. The reduction of study burdens, as with quality reforms more generally, has diluted the power of pure diligence as a weapon of the weak.

The Peculiar Diligence of Girls

For both men and women, diligence is a way of getting ahead in a world that is ruled by guanxi. But for women, whom teachers widely consider to be superior in this trait, diligence has special significance. China, like the vast majority of human societies, is a patriarchy (Ortner 1972; Sangren 2000). In the world of work, the nepotistic domain of alcohol-lubricated banquets and backstage meetings, where many consequential decisions are made, is a milieu controlled by men. Inside most families, women are subordinate to men, and the majority of people in leadership positions—in public or private spheres—are male.

Of course, China is far from unusual in having gender disparities. In no country on earth do women receive equal pay for similar work.[3] Indeed, according to some measures, China is relatively egalitarian. On the United Nations gender equality index, it ranks near the middle, eighty-fifth among 188 states.[4] China's modern history is one of relatively steady improvement in the status of women, and measured against the norms of the imperial era, the strides are enormous. Before the twentieth century, few women received an education and none could take the civil exams (Ko 1994; Mann 1997). Many girls bound their feet, which was considered a marker of beauty and elite status— and formed its own rite of passage—but left women with a lifelong crippling disability (Ko 2005).

By contrast, women today compete directly with men in most domains and are considered their formal equals. Without doubt, women of rural origin continue to be underrepresented in higher education (Cherng and Hannum 2013; Hannum and Adams 2007; X. Wang et al. 2013), but overall, women now outnumber men in college and postgraduate programs.[5] Women's educational gains have been particularly rapid since China's massive expansion of higher education beginning in the late 1990s. The proportion of women in college rose from around 25 percent prior to 1990 to over 50 percent in 2009 and has continued to rise, reaching 52.5 percent in 2016 (Xu 2018). This accomplishment is especially impressive in light of how women, far from being the recipients of affirmative action, are subject to strict quotas in many degrees and programs. Citing the national interest, university administrators, at the behest of the central government, protect certain majors from admitting too many women. Programs that are subject to such restrictions mainly belong to stereotypically masculine fields, such as law enforcement and military science; but women sometimes also face quotas in other majors, such as foreign languages, in which, officials say, without such measures they would make up the vast majority of students.

Since the 1980s, population controls, despite often grievously impinging on reproductive rights, have paradoxically contributed to women's improving status (Shi 2017). Particularly in urban areas, where the one-child policy was more strictly enforced, parents began investing more resources in girls, who in many cases were singletons (Fong 2002, 2006; Kajanus 2015). In rural areas, by contrast, families could have two children if the first was a girl. In practice, many families flouted even this relatively lenient version of the population-control policy. In my rural field sites, families of four or five children are not uncommon. Because many parents will keep having children until they give birth to a boy, large families often consist of several older sisters with one younger brother. This trend is one indication of how the countryside tends to lag behind the city in gender equality. But women's status has risen everywhere, and even in some rural areas, such as parts of northeastern Liaoning Province, singleton daughters have become common (Shi 2017).

Women have achieved this improved status in spite of the persistence of patriarchal attitudes. The area of my fieldwork, the Minnan region of Fujian, is widely regarded as a particularly patriarchal part of China (Friedman 2006). Especially in rural places, it is common for families to "favor boys and look down on girls" (*zhòngnán-qīngnǚ*). Because girls marry out of the patriline, people say they are like "scattered water" (*jià chūqù de nǚér, pō chūqù de shuǐ*), that is, a resource unworthy of investment. Several academically successful girls in Mountain County told me that their parents and grandparents, despite feeling pride in their accomplishments, repeatedly expressed the desire that they had been born boys. And many teachers believe that a women's proper place is in the home. The principal of a local junior high school said, "If girls don't get into senior high school, they should get married and have children right away." Of course, exceptions to such attitudes are widespread, and opinions are shifting. For example, one farmer, who had four girls and one boy, was ridiculed by his neighbors for educating his daughters. But when two of his daughters were admitted to college, he was elected village head (see chapter 2). Nevertheless, these incremental changes only underscore the underlying status quo of masculine domination.

My field sites are far from having a monopoly on patriarchy. Despite gains in equality, women all over China continue to face pervasive sexism and epidemic levels of domestic violence (R. Zhao and Zhang 2017). For these and other reasons, women—particularly those of rural origin—represent a disproportionate number of suicide victims in China (Kleinman et al. 2011). Gender discrimination and sexual harassment, as in many societies, is endemic; thus, it remains difficult for women to break the glass ceiling. In Chinese high schools, for example, men are promoted into leadership roles, whereas women usually remain teachers until they retire. Even women will express pity for men who are stuck too long in the role of teacher, which is regarded as a feminine occupation. Of the schools that I surveyed, the only ones where women served as senior leaders were located in the city, and those were rare. In Xiamen, a city of five million with thirteen senior high schools, only one recruited a woman as principal.

In many ways, the Mao era (1949–76) was a period of relatively rapid strides in equality between the genders, which resulted from the state's muscular intervention in people's private affairs (Santos and Harrell 2017). Marriages had to be approved by one's work unit, for example. Women were encouraged to work, and men were prohibited from engaging in polygamous relationships. But the gains of women have slowed in the post-Mao era and, in some domains, even reversed (Fincher 2016). The party-state has largely withdrawn from its close supervision of marriage. This privatization of marriage gives individuals greater scope for personal choice but has resulted in the partial resurgence of gender norms of the presocialist decades of the 1920s and 1930s, when it was common for men to take multiple wives and for a woman's parents-in-law to have say over conjugal property (Davis 2014). With the end of the one-child policy in 2015, the Chinese state has begun to encourage women to marry younger, produce more offspring, and exemplify traditional virtuous femininity. In general, women welcome the opportunity to have more children if they wish. But many fear being subjugated to husbands or getting relegated to traditional roles as the sole caregivers of children and elders. In a backlash to persisting patriarchal attitudes, growing numbers of women—pejoratively termed "leftover women" (*shèngnǚ*)—are delaying marriage (Fincher 2016; Gaetano 2014; Howlett 2020; Ji 2015).

In this context, academic diligence takes on special significance for women. For many, it is a way of pushing back against patriarchal norms. In school, girls explicitly see diligence in this light. When I asked one student at Mountain County, Chunxiao, why girls work harder than boys, she replied, "I think it's a kind of disobedient attitude [*bùfú xīnlǐ*]. China is a patriarchal society [*nánquánzhǔyì shèhuì*], so women want to prove their ability." In my interviews and discussions with other women, I found Chunxiao's sentiment to be widely shared. In the past, they said, women saw marriage as the second chance to change fate, after the Gaokao. Now, by contrast, many see education as a path toward mobility, as well as a way of finding their true selves and increasing their power of choice in life. This trend includes not only women of urban origin but also a growing contingent of rural-to-urban migrant women. For this group in particular, pursuing higher education in the big city is a way to not only achieve social mobility but also escape the patriarchal ethos of rural places. Many of these women feel torn between their dream of pursuing personal development in the cities and the need to perform virtuous femininity for their parents and relatives back home. Despite their ambivalence, they are pursuing higher education in unprecedented numbers.

Diligence is not the only traditionally masculine virtue in which women surpass men. As an important idiom in which devotion to parents is expressed, superior academic diligence also marks women as more filial. At the same time, more and more women are assuming a dominant role in supporting elderly parents financially (Fong 2006; T. Zheng 2009). Observing these trends, parents increasingly regard women as surpassing men in filial piety overall. For this reason, rising numbers of parents would rather have a daughter than a son, further contributing to women's status (Shi 2017).

Skeptics might object that filial piety merely places women in a subordinate role. But the expression of this virtue also contains a demand for recognition. On one level, filial devotion centers on recognizing the authority of the patriarch, but on another level, children use their devotion to achieve moral agency. Through being filial, they position themselves as potent actors who themselves are worthy of social recognition (Sangren 2000). By surpassing men in filial piety, women are demanding acknowledgment as the moral equals of men.

Gendered Divisions of Labor and the Rich, Han, Urban Male Club

The above observations have comparative relevance. Women outperform men academically in many contexts cross-culturally; worldwide, they complete college at greater rates (Buchmann and DiPrete 2006; Inhorn 2020). But in China as elsewhere, women's expanded participation in education and labor markets tends to come in the form of gender-differentiated roles (Bourdieu 2001; Charles 2011). Rather than being entrusted with the duties of decisionmaking and management, women often find themselves in lower-paying fields or in relatively junior, frontstage positions, such as bank teller or secretary.

The causes of this gender differentiation are complex, but certainly involve the many sexist stereotypes that hamper women in their school careers (Harding 1998). Girls in China, as elsewhere, must grapple with the widespread view that they are innately inferior in mathematical and scientific reasoning. In this respect, they are said to exhibit an intrinsic lack of quality. Confronted with such stereotypes from a very young age, many girls internalize them. For example, in the same breath in which she told me about her disobedient attitude toward the patriarchy, Chunxiao insisted that boys possess better logical reasoning.

Because of such sexist attitudes, women's superior diligence paradoxically forms a pretense for their relegation to marginalized social roles. Because girls are widely considered (by teachers, parents, and themselves) to be deficient in logical reasoning, they find themselves funneled into the humanities (*wénkē*). In the Gaokao, the humanities—Chinese, history, politics, foreign languages, and geography—are mainly tested through multiple-choice and short-answer questions, the responses to which can be "backed." Thus the humanities are considered relatively empty, suitable only for frontstage performance. People apply this judgment to all the humanities but pronounce it with particular fervor against propaganda-infused subjects like history and, especially, politics. As one student who had just failed a politics quiz told me, "It's all socialist brainwashing." By contrast, the sciences (*lǐkē*)—mathematics, physics, chemistry, and biology—require students to "do problems" (*zuòtí*). Because people believe that the sciences have a real effect and require real skill, they see these subjects as relatively practical, down-to-earth, and true. They say that boys, with their alleged superior logical reasoning and strong cognitive ability, have an advantage in such subjects, which require problem-solving skills rather than mere memorization.

Until the mid-2010s, most senior high-school students in China had to choose between a humanities stream and a sciences stream. In the new system, they may select subjects of specialization from both the humanities and the sciences. In practice, however, students still tend to concentrate in one domain or the other. Those who consider themselves to have the ability to study the sciences usually do, even if they enjoy the humanities. The sciences promise students a wider choice of majors and greater future earning potential. As the saying goes, "Study math, physics, and chemistry, and you can go anywhere under heaven without fear!" (*xué shù lǐ huà, zǒu biàn tiānxià dōu bú pà*).

Women outnumber men in the humanities (Ma et al. 2016). Many women say they wish that they could focus on the sciences but lack the ability. As Chunxiao said of her own decision to quit studying science, "The spirit is willing but the flesh is weak." Because women tend to gravitate toward the humanities in high school, they are overrepresented in so-called softer college majors such as languages or social work; by contrast, men are relatively dominant in science, technology, engineering, and math (STEM) fields. Men are particularly overrepresented in areas of the hard sciences that have practical applications and greater earning potential (Guo, Tsang, and Ding 2010).

These arrangements perpetuate the stereotype that men use talent to succeed, whereas women rely on the empty skill of regurgitating memorized facts. People regard it as natural that women serve in such frontstage roles as teller, secretary, translator, or speech writer, while men get on with the backstage work of management, invention, authorship, and leadership. Given that China is a technocracy, in which engineers and scientists occupy the majority of state leadership positions (Andreas 2009), women's underrepresentation in these fields has far-reaching ramifications for their ability to exercise power in society.

Women are not the only group to suffer from such stereotypes. Ethnic minorities are likewise widely considered deficient in scientific reasoning. Many people of minority background report that the education system—through negative stereotypes and quota systems—tends to track them into marginalized, feminized kinds of work, such as teaching and translating minority languages. Consequently, minorities, like women, are underrepresented in science and engineering (Wan and Jiang 2016). To some degree, this phenomenon reflects a rural-urban disparity, given that many minority populations are concentrated in rural areas and people of rural origin more generally tend to underperform urbanites in the sciences (Wan and Jiang 2016; J. Li and Yang 2015). But whereas ethnic minorities are often described as stupid and lazy, people of rural origin are said to exhibit an excessive form of low-quality diligence, like women. Thus, within many rural settings, women, and especially ethnic-minority women, are doubly disadvantaged. Given such trends, it is unsurprising that colleges tend to be a rich, Han, urban, male club (X. Wang et al. 2013). Within this elite club, the exclusive domain of STEM fields is even more likely to conform to this demographic.

These various forms of marginalization do not form disparate social phenomena. Rather, they operate according to a coherent if oppressive cultural logic. At one level, this logic is based on ideologies (for example, on the belief that it is natural for women and minorities to be bad at science or for people of rural origin to have low quality). But at a more fundamental level, this logic relies on a series of fundamental assumptions about nature and society. Taken together, they form what anthropologists term a cosmology—a way of making sense of the world. The cosmology implied by the above arrangements can be analyzed as an interconnected series of structural homologies (science and humanities, masculine and feminine, urban and rural, civilized and uncivilized, Han and minority, high and low quality). The Gaokao plays an important role in reproducing this cosmology, reinforcing the hegemony of an urban, male, Han elite.

The Regimentation of Quality

Ironically, the widespread concern with raising quality, which began as resistance to exam-oriented education, has progressively transformed into what the proponents of quality oppose—a focus on formal assessment and teaching to the test. An increasing focus on quality is even being written into the exam itself. I term this process the *regimentation of quality*.

The reasons for this trend are complex. At the most basic level, people desire the legitimacy that examinations confer, and without formal assessment, quality is nebulous. It has become a widely desired object, forming a major idiom for personal and national development (see chapter 2). But those who lack cultural capital or, as they say, a good home environment can only hope to acquire it through hard work. Moreover, many of the capacities that people associate with high quality—say, for example, the mastery of a musical instrument—can only be learned through years of dedicated discipline under the tutelage of a careful coach. Certainly, some forms of cultural knowledge are transmitted implicitly without much conscious effort—for instance, artistic taste (Bourdieu 1984). But focusing on such conventional examples of cultural capital may lead to overemphasizing how other forms of distinction are absorbed through osmosis as opposed to conscious effort. In a culture in which people believe in the capacity to change fate through hard work, it is perhaps unsurprising to find them cultivating qualities that many regard as attributes of admired social classes or groups.

The difference between diligence and quality as character ideals lies not in how one emphasizes hard work while the other does not. Rather, the main difference is that competing for quality requires a much higher economic and social bar. Those with the greatest advantage in this competition are urbanites with access to cultural, economic, and social resources. Displays of quality occur in the rarefied world of extracurricular opportunities, academic competitions, and talent shows, among other activities, to which people of rural origin have little access.

Subjective Questions and Cultural Capital

Teachers are quite sensitive to how some parts of the examination are more amenable to the method of diligent memorization than others. For example, they observe that students of rural origin do much better on objective questions (*kèguāntí*) than they do on subjective questions (*zhǔguāntí*).

Objective questions are those that have only one right answer, such as multiple-choice questions. In the humanities, such answers can be backed, learned by rote. In the sciences, they are determined by methods that students learn through explicit instruction and diligent study. By contrast, subjective questions are open ended and their answers cannot be simply memorized.

The most prominent subjective questions on the exam are essay questions in the Chinese and English sections. Essays require linguistic and cultural competencies not easily acquired through drilling. Students from better environments—that is, those with greater cultural capital—generally perform better. For this reason, teachers consider the Chinese and English sections to be easier for urban children, who are exposed to a good cultural environment from a young age.

The disparities in cultural environment between rural and urban areas can be shocking to the uninitiated. Ms. Ma, my Ningzhou English-teacher friend, remarked on her first trip to Shanghai that the city had English-language newspapers, English-language advertisements, and even English-language TV channels. Foreigners, whom she had never seen in large numbers, were abundant. This environment, she said, not only offered students constant opportunities to practice their English but also gave them the sense that learning it might be of practical value.

There are many other ways in which urban children have a better environment for learning English. Urban parents send their children to English-language summer camps, sometimes overseas. In Xiamen, well-off parents may hire Filipina maids to speak English to their children. Even those who cannot afford such luxuries benefit from easy access to the shadow-education industry. Finally, students in the city start learning foreign languages from an earlier age and focus on communicative competency when it can make a meaningful difference to their foundation.

English is not the only subject in which rural students face a cultural capital deficit. Chinese, in particular, is another discipline in which they tend to underperform. But the latter disadvantage comes as a surprise to many rural parents. In contrast to English, which they realize that their children must learn, they assume that it is natural for their children to be able to speak their native language. Why should they need to devote extra effort to this subject? Many children of rural origin, however, have little exposure outside of school to the formal and literary types of language that appear on the Gaokao.

Although the subjective sections of the exam put people of marginalized backgrounds at a disadvantage, proponents of quality argue that such questions provide a superior measure of talent. Still, many teachers object to this claim, saying that it would have more weight if subjective questions were graded according to open-ended criteria rather than a point system. In reality, though, the subjective sections are graded in factory-like conditions under great time pressure; moreover, the goal of grading is to resolve fine distinctions in point score between candidates (see chapter 3). As skeptics argue, these distinctions probably mean little in terms of assessing quality but can have a great impact on exam outcome.

Despite the dubious merit of using subjective questions under such conditions, this type of question has increased in importance since the 1990s. Test designers have expanded the proportion of short-answer questions and increasingly created essay questions that force students to think outside the box. Not surprisingly, people of rural origin react with ambivalence and even frustration. In response, instructors try to teach rural students shortcuts and tricks for coping with subjective questions, though with limited effectiveness.

Cultural Bias

The increasing emphasis on subjective test questions demonstrates how the regimentation of quality introduces an urban cultural bias into the structure of the examination. The contents of the exam are also prone to such bias. Test designers strive to create questions that assume a high-quality background, and this practice represents a way in which quality becomes doubly regimented.

Researchers in the United States and elsewhere have extensively studied cultural bias in examinations (Hanson 1993). Inspired by such studies, scholars in China have called for bias investigations regarding the Gaokao (D. Yang 2006; R. Zheng 2011). Discussions of bias even receive public attention, and every year people debate the essay questions in the Chinese-language section of the exam. Past questions have asked students to respond to lyrics of popular songs or discuss cultural buzzwords. Critics argue that students of rural origin may have little to say about such topics. Although ethnic-minority students receive comparatively little public attention, the same is a fortiori even more true of them, because many are relatively unfamiliar with mainstream Han culture.

Such problems are probably more pervasive and insidious than critics imagine, and even well-intentioned teachers routinely introduce bias into the exam. This problem became apparent to me when I had an opportunity to observe Ms. Ma, who is herself of rural origin, drafting examination questions. The leadership of Ms. Ma's school, Ningzhou Number One, had asked her to create the English section of a mid-term exam that would be shared with a sister school in another city. At a time when Gaokao questions were still designed at the provincial level (see chapter 3), Ms. Ma considered this task to be an honor. Her direct supervisor, a vice principal, would be entrusted the same year with helping to design the English section of the Gaokao. Thus Ms. Ma's own exam questions might have an influence on those that appeared on the big test.

She asked me to look at her draft examination questions. They required students to read an advertisement for a touch-screen phone, and I suggested that many students of rural origin would possess neither the vocabulary nor the context to perform this task. In 2013, many students in Mountain County still used the payphone in the school courtyard to call home. Even if students knew about the existence of touch screens, many had never owned a smartphone or even a cell phone themselves.

After some consideration, Ms. Ma acknowledged that rural students might find themselves at a disadvantage. "You know," she explained, "the problem is much bigger than this one example. The reason that I chose the smartphone is that we are encouraged to include the most advanced and up-to-date things in our test questions. But you're right that people in the countryside might struggle with this kind of question. We're just too backward. We haven't yet caught up with the cities."

The Admixture of Quality and Guanxi: Bonus Points and Direct Admission

The regimentation of quality also affects college admission in direct ways. The most blatant uses of quality in the admission process are probably the highly controversial practices of direct admission (*bǎosòng*) and Gaokao bonus points (*jiāfēn*). A wide variety of schemes exist for awarding bonus points. In the past, such schemes varied greatly from province to province. Under current reforms, however, they are being nationally unified and greatly curtailed. But bonus points continue to be awarded for a range of accomplishments associated with high quality, such as participating in high-level athletic competitions, placing in national academic olympiads, or winning contests that aim to identify future innovators. Students may also acquire extra bonus points for specific universities by taking special autonomous admissions exams. These bonus-point schemes ostensibly award students for their personal accomplishments; however, they generally work to the advantage of high-quality students in urban areas (L. Liu et al. 2014; D. Yang 2006). Further, critics complain that nepotism influences the distribution of opportunities to compete for bonus points (R. Zheng 2011).

Direct admission similarly tends to advantage urban children. This program enables high-ranking administrators to distribute a small number of places at elite colleges directly to a select group of hand-picked students. Direct admission was originally intended to identify students who possess high quality but not necessarily high scores. But schools in the countryside are generally awarded small quotas or no quotas for direct admission, and, as critics complain, the process is easily contaminated by guanxi. To avoid the impression of corruption, administrators often use test scores to screen students for the program even though this approach contradicts its original intention.

The Cultivation of Special Abilities

The regimentation of quality is not just a matter of the form and content of the examination alone. Rather, it is institutionalized throughout the education system, particularly in urban areas. Cultivating special abilities (*tècháng péiyǎng*) is a significant manifestation of this trend of acquiring skills not normally emphasized in Chinese schools, such as art, music, and sports. In theory, these forms of quality cannot be learned through exam-oriented education; still, families take a highly regimented approach to their cultivation. For instance, children who learn to play a musical instrument undergo frequent examinations as they advance through a graded hierarchy of ability levels.

At first glance, such demonstrations of quality would seem to be of little consequence for college admission, which overwhelmingly depends on Gaokao scores. But as critics point out, special abilities exert a strong, albeit subterranean influence on the admission process. As part of education-for-quality reforms, authorities banned schools from using examinations to screen and select students during the compulsory phase of education (which, during my fieldwork, included the six years of elementary and three years of junior high school). Only some special schools, such as foreign-language schools, retained official permission to examine potential candidates. As before, however, the success of students, teachers, schools, and regions was judged by examination scores, so schools and officials began casting around for suitable guises under which to circumvent the ban. In the absence of examinations, schools started employing various indexes of quality—such as the cultivation of special abilities—to recruit talented, high-scoring students (and, as a consequence, exclude many poor or working-class students) without openly defying the regulations. Students with highly cultivated special abilities tend to come from families with the resources to place a premium on education and thus tend to produce high-scoring children. The regimentation of special abilities into graded examinations provides schools with objective verification of talent. By emphasizing special abilities, administrators and officials can have their cake and eat it too. They pay lip service to education for quality while recruiting top students. For these reasons, many parents and teachers consider the fad for special abilities to be hollow. As one critic said, "If the time comes when raising pigs is considered to be a special ability, we will see more kids from the countryside going to top colleges."

Many other methods exist for circumventing the ban on the improper use of examinations to screen students. One such influential method, which recent reforms have curtailed, was participation in the International Mathematics Olympiad, an extracurricular mathematics contest. Another method is to hold examinations under the guise of quality assessments. In all cases, such recruitment mechanisms give an advantage to the wealthy, urban, and highly educated. The best elementary and junior high schools recruit the highest quality students, who go on to the best senior high schools. The focus on education for quality provides well-heeled urban parents with an additional advantage in the competition for scarce educational resources—a means of gaming the system.

Quality in Diligence and Diligence in Quality

The above trends highlight an important contradiction of quality. Demonstrating this virtue requires hard work but imbues its possessors with a mark of distinction that differentiates them from people who rely on mere diligence alone. Urbanites paradoxically both embrace and reject diligence.

This paradox can be explained by considering some important differences between diligence and quality as character ideals. Quality is primarily associated with the home rather than with the school—that is, as sociologists say, with primary socialization rather than with secondary socialization (Bourdieu and Passeron 1977). Granted, the cultivation of quality requires great diligence and explicit instruction. But this cultivation takes place outside the formal framework of schooling. Students develop quality in extracurricular activities, after-school classes, and at-home practice. From the perspective of the school, therefore, quality appears to be the product of a good environment and good families. Teachers acknowledge that the cultivation of quality requires hard work, but they simultaneously perceive quality as something that comes naturally to children of good family background. Thus, quality provides not so much an alternative to diligence as a supplement to it. Just as test scores mystify the social labor that produces them by transforming that labor into a measure of individual merit (see chapter 1), the perceived naturalness of quality further mystifies test scores, adding luster to their charisma.

Teachers are not immune to this allure of quality, which can be hard to resist. Ms. Fu, a psychological counselor at Dragon Gate High School, once visited Xiamen Foreign Languages High School, one of the most prestigious high schools in the city. After observing a student-organized world cultures fair, she was greatly impressed with the quality of the students. "They have quality to die for!" she exclaimed. Shortly thereafter, she led a motivational assembly for Dragon Gate students in preparation for the Gaokao. With only one hundred days to go before the big test, they were eager to learn ways to improve their performance. Inspired by her visit to the Foreign Languages High School, Ms. Fu encouraged Dragon Gate students, many of whom came from poor migrant families, to cultivate special abilities. She explained that top scholars at the elite school, many of whom were accomplished musicians and athletes, emphasized the importance of balance between study and hobbies. This balance, she said, was a secret of their examination success.

Without doubt, maintaining a good attitude is important to test performance (see chapter 5). But stressing the importance of extracurricular activities to students in a low-ranking school three months before the final examination mystifies the examination system. Ms. Fu's logic puts the cart of quality before the horse of test performance. Top-scoring students in top high schools do not achieve superior test results merely as a result of pursuing high-quality hobbies; rather, they outperform their low-quality peers because their cultivation of quality from early childhood indexes a good home environment and facilitates access to the best schools.

Do examinations select people of merit? Many teachers agonize over this question, including Ms. Fu, who, on her bus ride back to Dragon Gate from the world cultures fair, encountered a troubling lapse of public spirit (*gōngdéxīn*). Foreign-language students, she said, had not yielded their bus seats to older passengers. When I asked how she reconciled the "quality to die for" of these students with their apparent lack of public spiritedness, she offered the following explanation: "They may have high all-around quality, but some of them are certainly lacking in *moral* quality!"

Many critics of the examination system complain that it does not teach young people how to "be a human being" (*zuòrén*) and conform to basic standards of morality. Voicing such a complaint, one of Ms. Fu's senior colleagues, Ms. Wang, used the analogy of production: "Students who neither know how to study *nor* how to be human beings are inferior goods [*lièpǐn*]. Students who know how to study *and* how to be human beings are superior goods [*yōuděngpǐn*]. And students who know how to study but *not* how to be human beings—well, they are *dangerous* goods [*wēixiǎnpǐn*]."

Expressing nostalgia for the era before economic marketization, Ms. Wang suggested that the examination system was producing more dangerous goods than ever before. She accounted for this fact by suggesting that schools naturally form microcosms of wider society, which she deemed to have become dominated in the post-Mao era by a general atmosphere of corruption and selfishness. Although she herself placed morality before test scores, she lamented that the moral dimension of education for quality had become disconnected from society at large. As she put it, "The kids don't believe what teachers tell them anymore. They think what we say is not realistic [*xiànshí*]. They look around society and see that the bad kids adapt best."

Ms. Wang's critique centered more on the widening social gap between rhetoric and reality, or performative shift (see chapter 3), than it did on the examination itself. Defenders of the test argue that no matter what the explicit contents of the exam or the general state of society, diligence itself constitutes an important index of moral quality. People speak of successful examinees in reverential terms, even as examination heroes and champions (see chapter 1). Teachers and administrators presume that students of the highest moral quality—the most filial and obedient—tend also to be the students who do best on the Gaokao. They reason, despite some dissenting voices, that those who cultivate the extreme level of self-mastery that success on the exam requires are likely to also be the most considerate and modest.

Cross-culturally and throughout history, examinations have engendered similar debates. In the United States, for example, controversies have long raged over whether college admission tests such as the SAT select students of good character or, similarly, whether or not the Medical College Admissions Test (MCAT) chooses worthy future doctors. Much as quality has been employed to deny people of rural origin access to elite colleges in China, character has been used to exclude members of undesirable groups from US colleges. In the 1960s and 1970s, when the SAT started gaining dominance, administrators used character as a criterion of admission in part to reduce the proportion of successful Jewish applicants, who excelled in standardized exams (Karabel 2006). Asian Americans, fighting what many term a bamboo ceiling, contend that they face similar discrimination today.[6] Yet selecting students of good character can also be used as a method for increasing the diversity of college classes (Stevens 2009). Much depends on how this nebulous term is defined.

Comparable debates abound in China's own long history of examinations. Conversations that took place hundreds of years ago may strike contemporary readers as startlingly modern. Perhaps the most famous example is the controversy surrounding Neo-Confucianism, or Way Learning. This intellectual current became fixed as the canon of the imperial exams in the thirteenth century CE, remaining the orthodoxy for nearly six hundred years (see chapter 1). Ironically, however, Way Learning started its life as an anti-examination philosophy. Its founder, Zhu Xi (1130–1200 CE), complained that the exams of his era, which called for test takers to compose original verse, elevated unctuous performance over the cultivation of virtue (Bol 1989). By contrast, other critics of the day argued that examinations did not do enough to capture the expression of creative, spontaneous individuality. As polymath and statesmen Su Shi (1037–1101 CE) wrote, "The learning of [examination candidates] is exactly like striking prints; they come out according to the block; there is no need to decorate them into rare and precious instruments" (Bol 1989, 175).

As such debates attest, the contemporary tension between exam-oriented education and education for quality echoes age-old controversies about whether examinations select people of high moral virtue. These debates reflect not only differing ideals of merit, and thus personhood, but also conflicting social interests.

Competing social groups negotiate to secure canonical status for examination contents that will be advantageous to their own interests (Bourdieu and Passeron 1977; De Weerdt 2007; Guillory 1993). For these reasons, intellectual currents and pedagogical approaches that are initially identified with moral reservations about examinations can eventually become incorporated into the examination orthodoxy.

In short, examination systems inevitably reflect an internally contradictory compromise between many different interests—a negotiated hegemony. In contemporary China, this negotiated hegemony is dominated by an urban, Han, male elite. In this negotiation, diligence forms a common denominator—a shared cultural value. The desire to change fate through diligent self-cultivation is widespread in China. Even the cultivation of quality requires great diligence. But the discourses surrounding diligence also provide a pretense for the marginalization of women, people of rural origin, and ethnic minorities. In addition to being regarded as an intrinsic failing, these groups' alleged lack of quality is alternatively attributed to an excess of the wrong kind of diligence or to a lack of this virtue overall. Paradoxically, the cultural logics of diligence reinforce social hierarchies even as they encourage people to transform destiny. The Gaokao's social significance derives in large part from how it inculcates people with a belief in this cultural virtue. But the importance of diligence goes well beyond the big test. People of diverse callings profess great faith in the relationship between hard work and success. Although they grant that this relationship "never reaches a one-to-one ratio" (*yǒngyuǎn bù chéng zhèngbǐ*), they nevertheless regard the fruits of diligence—exam success, wealth, and filial children—as proof of superior moral rectitude.

This meritocratic logic proves surprisingly resistant to critique. Paragons of diligence can always be cited in its support. The same Mountain County student who complained to me about the relative emptiness of urban diligence emphasized that rural-urban inequalities did little to undermine her faith in the fairness of society itself. To make this point, she cited the success of Jack Ma, the internet mogul, who failed the Gaokao twice before finally passing with a modest score. Later, he went on to found his own company, the now world-famous Alibaba Group. For this student, Ma's persistence in the face of failure demonstrated a superiority of character that presaged his later success. Reflecting on this story, this student said, "Actually, it doesn't really matter whether or not the Gaokao is ultimately fair. Society itself will always be fair—success will forever belong to the diligent."

According to this view, just because Jack Ma failed the Gaokao does not mean the Gaokao failed Jack Ma. Thus the lesson that people draw from failure on the Gaokao is rarely that diligence is meaningless. All committed students are diligent, if not uniformly so; moreover, the undiligent have resigned themselves to their grim fate long before examination day. Rather, examination postmortems usually revolve around more nebulous and difficult-to-quantify qualities of character. Students debate which top students choked and which dark horses rose from obscurity to pull off clutch performances (see chapter 5), just as they obsess over whose displays of good or bad luck might imply the presence or lack of divine favor or karmic merit (see chapter 6).

COURAGE UNDER FIRE

The Paradoxical Role of Head Teachers and the Individualizing Moment of Examination

Attitude determines knowledge.

—Ms. Fu, Dragon Gate High School counselor and head teacher

It was late December 2013, six months before the Gaokao. In the Dragon Gate auditorium, Ms. Fu, who is both a school counselor and a head teacher, led an assembly of senior-three students. Pacing back and forth, microphone in hand, she presented coping strategies for managing the psychological pressure of the final battle. Her talk incorporated corporate-style motivational training, including a PowerPoint presentation on the four secrets of successful people. She concluded by teaching students a "magic spell" (*zhòuyǔ*)—a mantra of self-affirmation—which she promised would boost their confidence by improving their attitude (*xīntài*). Stressing the importance of attitude, she asked the following rhetorical question:

> What is more important to examination success: knowledge or attitude? Let me tell you, on test day, it is attitude that determines everything. . . . If the test lasted a few weeks, then knowledge would be the only imperative. But because the Gaokao lasts only two days, attitude determines knowledge (*xīntài juédìng zhīshi*). You can study all you like, but if your attitude is bad on test day, you will choke (*kǎozá*).

Her speech encapsulated a sentiment shared by students and teachers: Success on the exam requires knowledge, acquired through years of diligent study, but what makes or breaks test-day performance is psychological state, or attitude. In the heat of the fateful event, students' own bodies—hearts racing, hands shaking—confront them as alien powers that must be faced down and mastered through heroic acts of composure.

This chapter considers the relationship between knowledge and attitude. If knowledge is generally subject to the kinds of effects that Bourdieu (1977, 1984, 1986) glosses under the rubric of cultural capital, how do we account for the capriciousness of attitude? As Gaokao observers commonly remark, top students can choke on the exam, whereas dark horses can tap into their latent potential (*qiánlì*) to surge (*bàofā*) from behind. In other words, the examination assesses not merely the diligent accumulation of knowledge but also less tangible aspects of character. In particular, it tests the ability of students to maintain composure and mental flexibility in the face of high pressure—attitude or psychological quality. These qualities may be tied to cultural capital but also seem to exceed its analytical grasp.

As Ms. Fu's speech suggests, teachers are highly aware of these dynamics. Head teachers in particular obsess over the relationship between attitude and knowledge. But by combining the roles of teacher, counselor, and surrogate parent, they have a contradictory effect on students and their families. On one hand, they constantly analyze the test performance and family life of individual students to make pedagogical interventions in their study habits and to correct perceived deficits in their home environment. To be sure, teachers generally focus on the students whom they deem to have the greatest potential. But particularly at schools like Dragon Gate, where many students come from relatively unprivileged backgrounds, their efforts can help to reduce educational inequality. On the other hand, teachers emphasize that students and families should focus on what they can control rather than on aspects of fate that lie beyond their power to change. Encouraging students to take personal responsibility for their scores is an important part of coaching them to have a good attitude. Paradoxically, this emphasis on good attitude, although it helps students improve their performance, strengthens the myth of meritocracy. Hence head teachers ameliorate social disparities while reinforcing them. Performing both analytical and affective labor, they help individuals both to transcend and to come to terms with their circumstances—to change and recognize fate. The work that head teachers do thus complicates conventional accounts of cultural capital and the reproduction of inequality, which tend to emphasize the importance of objective factors, such as social hierarchy, in determining individual subjectivity (see chapter 1).

A few days after her talk, Ms. Fu sat across from her colleague, Ms. Yang, in a Xiamen shopping mall over bowls of spaghetti. The two head teachers discussed the performance of their students. Ms. Fu was teaching junior high school, where the stakes were lower, whereas Ms. Yang was teaching senior three—the all-important year before the Gaokao. Ms. Yang's class, Class 4, was an underdog that had surged from behind to advance dramatically in the school rankings since the beginning of the year. She had taken over the class from another head teacher, who had been relieved of her duties because of her class's poor scores.

At first glance, it was difficult to account for the sudden improvement of Class 4. Ms. Yang's predecessor—an experienced senior colleague—could hardly be faulted for pedagogical incompetence. And Ms. Yang had only led the class for a few months, giving her insufficient time to make substantial changes in long-standing habits. But Ms. Yang had expended tremendous energy refining the class's study approach. Among other things, she adjusted students' seating arrangements, gave them pep talks, convened parent-teacher conferences (*jiāzhǎnghuì*), and made frequent home visits (*jiāfǎng*).

In explaining the class's sudden change of fortunes, her colleagues said that Ms. Yang's effectiveness lay in these efforts to show concern (*guānxīn*) for her students and attend to their educational discipline (*jiàoxué jìlù*). They credited her with successfully adjusting (*tiáozhěng*) various environments (*huánjìng*), including those of individual families and that of the classroom as a whole. Ms. Yang's labors had unleashed the latent potential of the students of Class 4, who had outperformed all the other senior-three classes except for one—the senior-three fast class—on the latest monthly exams.

In recent weeks, however, Ms. Yang had sensed her students slacking off. They seemed to be growing weary, becoming complacent. Ms. Fu termed this condition a high-altitude reaction. "The challenge," said Ms. Fu, "is to keep the students in shape [*bǎochí zhuàngtài*] but let them relax a little so that they peak right before the Gaokao."

"Right," Ms. Yang replied, "but that's easier said than done."

As the exam grows nearer, these themes of attitude, motivation, and timing begin to dominate the attention of head teachers. They say that students are like professional athletes, who must neither relax too much nor burn out through overtraining. During my fieldwork, I came to think of head teachers as resembling baseball coaches. As a sport, baseball epitomizes the combination of three seemingly incongruous tendencies—an obsession with performance statistics, a heavy interest in team dynamics, and a fascination with individual character, composure, and grit. Baseball coaches must be at once statisticians, strategists, psychologists, and leaders. Like baseball coaches, head teachers pore over numbers. They meticulously comb through the results of weekly, monthly, and yearly examinations, analyzing this data to plan interventions in students' study habits. Coordinating the efforts of individual subject teachers, head teachers strive to ensure that students develop evenly in all subjects rather than displaying "bias" toward one discipline or another (*piānkē*). And although only some schools have official school counselors like Ms. Fu, every head teacher assumes a counseling role. Through frequent personal conversations, teachers attempt to intervene in the attitudes and psyches of students.

Many of these tasks are common to head teachers in other countries, but in China they have an additional responsibility outside the purview of many of their international counterparts. In China, head teachers routinely extend their influence deep into students' families, much as top-level coaches pay attention to the personal lives of their athletes. During home visits, head teachers provide parents with advice on family governance. They may act as surrogate parents, and in rural places teachers may foster the children of absent migrant parents. In these ways, they insert themselves directly into the minutiae of family life to a degree that many parents in Western contexts would find offensive. But parents in China are usually grateful for this help.

People in China perceive the work of head teachers as quintessentially Chinese. As a provincial educational official told me, head teachers combine paternal and pedagogical authority in a way that hearkens back to the teacher ideal of the imperial era. By integrating these different forms of authority, head teachers form a pivot between school, society, family, and students. In this intermediary position, they face pressure both from above (from school leaders and society) and from below (from parents and students). A Ningzhou head teacher compared the role to being like "the chicken in a Kentucky Fried Chicken sandwich"—a thin slice of meat squeezed from both sides. Senior Dragon Gate head teacher Ms. Wang said, "The head teacher is a coach, a maid, and a counselor. She has to pay attention to students' study and to their psychology, among many other things. She has to adjust [*tiáozhěng*] the relationship between school and society and that between student and parent."

Playing this adjusting role, the head teacher labors at the threshold of what many in China term the external (*wàijiè*) and internal or "personal" (*zìshēn*) factors of success. People generally associate the former with circumstances outside of the individual's control, including place of birth, gender, and background. They discuss these external factors in the same breath as supposedly innate (*xiāntiān*) characteristics, such as intelligence, sometimes glossing both as fate. By contrast, people consider personal factors, including attitude and composure, to be within the individual's control. Like baseball coaches, head teachers incorporate individual character into their game plan.

All boundaries between the internal and external, the innate and the acquired, and even between school, family, and society, are arbitrary in the sense that they are institutionally produced and culturally constructed. Indeed, the work that head teachers do relies on the ultimate incoherence of those boundaries; the head teacher in a sense personifies their porousness. As one of their main tasks, head teachers help anxious parents compensate for their so-called poor home environment, or perceived lack of conditions—that is, their shortfalls in social, cultural, and economic capital. In particular, a good head teacher makes parents and students conscious of their cultural deficits relative to the orthodox examination curriculum, and then works to help them correct the shortfalls. Parents, intent on artfully disposing the lives of their children to give them the best possible conditions for success (Kuan 2015), eagerly accept this help. In their view, no one is better positioned than head teachers—the high priests and priestesses of the exam—to help them achieve the best use of available resources.

Much justifies parent's faith in the judgment of head teachers. In a way, head teachers are social researchers. Visiting student's homes and observing them in class, they produce knowledge of the type that anthropologists call para-ethnographic. This term refers to research by non-anthropologists that closely resembles the ethnographic work that anthropologists do. Unlike most anthropologists, however, head teachers consciously employ their knowledge to intervene in the lives of their subjects. In fact, some head teachers—particularly in urban areas—are even involved in university-sponsored research that aims to ameliorate social inequality, even as they employ every means possible to maximize the latent potential of their students.

Head teachers often have an appreciable effect on students' test scores, and parents bend over backward to secure a good head teacher for their children. But the quality of head teachers varies greatly along the score-value hierarchy. And even good head teachers must confront the intractable paradox of their profession: they cannot help students compensate for cultural-capital deficits and cope with examination pressure without encouraging them to take individual responsibility for their examination performance.

In short, the positive influence that teachers have on mobility is achieved at the expense of reinforcing the individualizing effect of the exam. By the same token, even as the labor of head teachers relies on the porousness of the boundaries between the external and personal factors of success, it reconstitutes and recoheres these boundaries, especially in the psychic life of the individual examinee.

Internalizing the Environment: Pressure and Models

Peer Pressure and Class Rankings

Teachers say one of their key challenges is establishing influence over children after their habits are already largely formed. Head teachers feel that they can still have a direct effect on students of junior-high age or younger, but by senior high school, children are less plastic and more resistant. As one teacher noted,

"Senior-high students are like trees that have already taken on a fixed shape." As a result of this rigidness, teachers devise indirect methods of influencing students. In particular, because senior-high students are susceptible to peer pressure, head teachers seek various ways, as they say, "to use the class to influence individual students."

One of the strongest forms of peer pressure that a teacher can wield derives from rankings (*míngcì*). Based on test scores, students receive a precise ranking within their class and year, and though teachers have been encouraged to de-emphasize scores in their search for quality, they remain focused on this all-important metric to induce peer pressure. They incite students to constant comparison with each other. As one student put it, "You're always thinking about how you're doing in relation to someone else, whether or not you study as well as him or her. The pressure is huge. It's a terrible feeling."

In the past, rankings were posted publicly on a board in the classroom. Under education-for-quality reforms, however, this practice was outlawed. But as with many such reforms, the new policy was "not implemented in reality" (*méiyǒu luòshí dào shíchù*). At any given moment in the academic year, most students are still painfully aware of their precise standing within the class.

This awareness has several sources. Because quality reforms encourage teachers to use positive feedback, they commonly name and praise students at the top of the rankings. At Dragon Gate, public billboards list the top and most-improved students in each subject. Meanwhile, those with bad rankings may learn of them directly from teachers, sometimes in front of the whole class. But teachers have a simpler and more efficient method for communicating rankings. In many schools, the seating arrangement for monthly examinations is based on the rankings of students in their previous month's exam. The ingeniousness of this method is that it creates enormous pressure while leaving no lasting trace. It thus evades the gaze of inspecting officials, who must certify that schools are maintaining compliance (or at least the appearance of compliance) with the principles of education for quality.

Now as before, the constant drumbeat of rankings assumes enormous significance in students' lives. The consequences of rankings are both practical and emotional. High-scoring students can earn promotion to a better class—a fast or keypoint class. Low-scoring ones are threatened with demotion. Unsurprisingly, bad students report feeling ashamed and humiliated, whereas the high-ranking are said to feel superior (see chapter 3).

The peer pressure induced by rankings extends to parents, who are periodically convened by head teachers for parent-teacher conferences. Unlike in many countries, however, where teachers meet in private with the parents of individual children, teachers in China generally call together the parents of every child in a class for a public group meeting. Speaking to the whole gathering, head teachers praise and shame individual parents by detailing their children's successes and failures, improvements and setbacks, and exemplary behaviors and disciplinary problems.

This emphasis on rankings results in an ironic contradiction. In other contexts, teachers discourage students from comparing themselves with their peers. In particular, they disparage the tendency of relatively privileged students to "compare daddies" (*pīndiē*), that is, to brag about the social connections, accomplishments, and wealth of their parents. But to a significant degree, exam scores are a proxy for these other forms of capital.

The Importance of Environment

If the modus operandi of peer pressure is comparison of test scores, the scope in which the comparison achieves its effect is the class environment (*bānjí huánjìng*). Environments come in many shapes and sizes. In addition to the class environment, people also refer to the school environment. Families and places, too, have environments. People also refer to environment with such expressions as "atmosphere" (*fēnwéi*) or "mood" (*qìfēn*)—terms that might be translated as "ethos."

The influence of the environment plays a crucial role in Chinese pedagogical discourse. Ms. Wang, describing its significance, said, "In China, people have always been concerned with the environment. Do you know the expression 'One who stays near vermilion gets stained red, and one who stays near ink gets stained black'? It's like that. People, especially children, are highly impressionable. They take on the color [*sècǎi*] of the people around them." This way of thinking accords with Confucian thought, which emphasizes individual plasticity and the effects of cultural milieu (Munro 2001). According to this way of thinking, people are born good, but their goodness is easily corruptible and requires constant cultivation. To cultivate goodness, students must acquire good habits through the emulation of good models.

The significance that people in China ascribe to exemplary models is widely reflected in Chinese social and educational practices (Bakken 2000). Although environment has material aspects (equipment, buildings, books), people conceive of the environment—whether class, school, family, or place—as largely consisting of behavioral models. People come under the influence of an environment by forming relationships with these models—peers and authority figures. Borrowing from psychological discourse, teachers sometimes explicitly refer to such relationships in terms of identification (*rèntóng*).

In Chinese high schools, teachers consider indoctrination and punishment to have a place; however, they see such forceful methods as relatively empty because they can be resisted. By contrast, they say that the establishment of good models (*shùlì hǎo bǎngyàng*) has a subliminal effect (*qiányí-mòhuà*), which is relatively real. Teachers' conception of subliminal influences parallels sociologists' analysis of the implicit effects of cultural capital (Bourdieu and Passeron 1977). Teachers say that subliminal effects occur through osmosis (*xūntáo*), a word that evokes the image of ambient social forces that, like smoke (*xūn*), gradually shape (*táo*) individuals by permeating them. Teachers generally use osmosis to refer to influences that they consider positive and healthy. But they also believe that a bad environment can undo students.

For these reasons, teachers devote great energy to adjusting minute aspects of students' environments. For example, they think deeply about how to arrange classroom seating. This apparently straightforward question involves a host of intricate considerations, including whether or not to put strong students next to weak students, seat girls next to boys, or reward high-scoring students with desks at the front of the class. The goal is to create an environment of mutually reinforcing role models in which students have a positive reciprocal influence on each other through emulation and competition.

This supposition of mutual influence through the environment forms another important rationale for the aggressive tracking practices that many schools adopt. Such procedures are justified by the widespread perception that high test scores reflect moral superiority. Although education for quality discourages teachers from drawing a direct correlation between score and quality, many teachers believe that the most obedient and filial students congregate in the best classes. Following this line of thinking, teachers usually strive to group good students together while minimizing the influence of those they perceive as bad elements.

Fosterage Arrangements

Of course, teachers are not alone in giving careful consideration to children's environment. Parents also obsess over this question. Creating good conditions is a main goal of their various efforts to game the system, which frequently involve scouring their social networks for potential ways to establish a better environment. To a degree that many parents in North America might find alarming, parents in China are willing to cede control over their children to achieve this goal. For example, many rural teachers operate boarding houses, serving as surrogate parents for children whose birth parents are working as migrant laborers in urban areas. In the countryside, even very young children may live with their teachers. Reasoning that teachers possess a superior cultural level, many migrants prefer such arrangements to leaving their children behind with grandparents, whom they see as lacking culture.

Migrants are not alone in wanting to improve their children's environment through various foster relationships. With the transformation of China's economic fortunes in the post-Mao era, generations of entrepreneurs have risen from modest backgrounds to amass great fortunes; however, such parvenus (*bàofāhù*) often consider themselves, like migrant workers, to suffer from a deficit of culture (Osburg 2013), and it has become common for them to hire a live-in tutor—for example, a recent college graduate—to help them raise their children.

Less well-to-do parents may rely on a less expensive strategy. Many seek well-placed relatives in the city or even in a foreign country who can be persuaded through some debt of guanxi to act as surrogates. Particularly in rural areas where it is common for families to have more than one child, examples of children being raised by non-nuclear relatives are commonplace. Sometimes such surrogacy arrangements even take place over great separations of time and space. During my fieldwork, a bestselling how-to book, *Fangyang de Nühai Shang Hafo* (How a free-range daughter got into Harvard), described a father's clever utilization of his social network to find a series of foster parents in foreign countries for his child (Qiuye 2015). As this father proudly proclaimed, from the age of four his daughter had attended fifteen different schools in twelve different countries, eventually securing admission to Harvard University.

Many parents in China send their children to boarding schools, although this does not fall within the category of fosterage as conventionally conceived. It is common for children to board during senior high school, but many begin boarding at junior-high age or even younger. In rural areas, the closure of local schools means that sending children away from home may be the only option that parents have. But even those with other choices will often embrace the opportunity to hand their children over to a boarding school if doing so will improve their educational prospects. Given that educational quality and opportunity generally increase as one moves up the hierarchy of central places, parents usually try to send their children to centrally located places. A similar logic applies to the explosion of interest in overseas study since the 2000s, because people see developed countries as a superior or transcendental locus of quality (see chapter 2).

These various efforts to secure a good environment may strike some Westerners as extreme. Many middle-class white Americans, for instance, would consider fostering or boarding young children an abdication of parental duties, and even in China many people object to such arrangements. Some teachers express frustration with parents' alleged unwillingness to take responsibility for their offspring. As one teacher told me, "A lot of parents just see kids as pets. Parents think that all they need to do is feed them, clothe them, and send them to school. If they could, they would just give their children to teachers and be done with it."

And, indeed, fosterage relationships enable parents to do almost exactly that. But from the perspective of many parents, fosterage constitutes not an abdication of moral duty but rather its fulfillment.

Cultural Differences in Conceptions of Hierarchy

The cultural particularities of the Chinese context can be brought into relief by comparing it with the US context, which people in China regard as constituting a quintessential cultural Other. In many other respects, Chinese and US cultures of meritocracy are strikingly similar. Thus the prevalence of fosterage in China represents a cultural difference. What accounts for this difference, and what is its significance?

One approach to answering this question lies in considering people's differing attitudes toward social hierarchy. People in China often openly discuss how they possess cultural deficits vis-à-vis others with more privileged backgrounds. In many middle-class US contexts, however, such a statement would seem strange. In the United States, people are unlikely to discuss their lack of culture in relation to one another, just as they would rarely ask strangers how much money they make. The open discussion of social hierarchy is generally considered impolite or taboo. Given that everyone in the United States is supposedly equal, at least in principle, it is distasteful to draw too much attention to inequality. As a result, people in the United States generally tend to assume more social-class equality than really exists (Frank 2016; Kraus and Tan 2015; McNamee 2009).

In China, by contrast, people possess a relatively high level of awareness of socioeconomic hierarchy, which they consider a natural part of social life (Whyte 2010). Whereas in the United States and many other Western countries, wealthy people tend to dissimulate or conceal their social status, in China they generally take steps to make their status maximally legible (Osburg 2013). The discussion and display of cultural level, wealth, and other markers of hierarchy is relatively commonplace, and usually open. "How much money do you make?" is a common question, even among total strangers.

Different cultural ideals of mobility account for these cultural differences. In both Chinese and US cultures of meritocracy, people strive to transform themselves by changing their place in the social hierarchy. For people in China, however, the explicit purpose of this self-transformation consists in repaying one's filial debt and in nourishing and expanding one's outward radiating network of guanxi connections, which centers on one's native place (or, given the dispersed quality of most Chinese families, on several places) (Fei [1947] 1992). Following this way of thinking, people in China tend to conceive of all people as being ranked within a single social-geographical civilizational hierarchy, with its center in the national capital (see chapter 2). The expansion of one's social network is synonymous with one's rising status in this universal civilizational hierarchy, in which everyone is differently situated. It seems natural for people to have different levels of culture and unequal cultural environments.

In US conceptions of merit, by contrast, the importance of affective ties to parents and relatives is relatively muted; instead, people tend to emphasize self-sufficiency and independence. Individuals have the moral imperative not only to transform themselves but to reinvent themselves, which often involves obscuring or sometimes even disavowing one's social origins. And the notion that everyone should be measured against a single cultural-geographical hierarchy would seem ludicrous to many Americans.

For these reasons, people in China are generally less resistant than people in the United States to acknowledging differences of cultural and social capital. The American ideals of equality, independence, and self-reinvention tend to conceal the effects of these forms of capital from Americans more completely. Of course, such comparisons are at best indicative and heuristic. Many exceptions to the general trend exist, and one would expect to find contextual, geographical, and socioeconomic variation. As I note in the introduction, moreover, the cultures of meritocracy in China and the United States appear to be converging. Since the 1980s, inequality has increased within countries throughout the world, including in the United States (Milanović 2016). As a consequence, the middle classes everywhere are becoming more anxious about maintaining their social status. And in the United States as in many Western countries, it is not even clear if a middle class still exists in any meaningful sense (Temin 2017). Thus people in the United States may be becoming more accustomed to the inevitability of social hierarchy.

Nevertheless, the above discussion helps to explain the predilection of parents in China for pursuing fosterage relationships and boarding arrangements that would be intolerable to many Americans. People in the United States tend to emphasize the unique contribution of parents to cultivating a child's individual personality, which has equal value to those of other children no matter what that child's social position. By contrast, if parents in China believe that fostering a child away will help improve his or her eventual position in the civilizational hierarchy, many will consider it highly irresponsible not to pursue such arrangements. Most people in China can recite the story of how the mother of Mencius, the famous disciple of Confucius, moved three times to find a suitable neighborhood for her son to grow up in. In this story, the mother of the future sage relocates her family from two neighborhoods (the first next to a cemetery and the second next to a marketplace) before finding the ideal environment in which to cultivate his goodness: a neighborhood next to a school. Many read this tale as a parable of the importance of environment. Dutiful parents go to great lengths, even sacrificing their emotional connection with children, to give them good conditions for study.

Intelligence versus Latent Potential

The sensitivity of many people in China to the importance of cultural capital and environment accompanies a relative de-emphasis on factors considered to be predominantly innate, such as intelligence. People in China are less likely to interpret the results of standardized examinations as a measure of intelligence than are their US counterparts.

The most common standardized college entrance examination in the United States, the SAT, is descended from an IQ test (Lemann 1999). Americans still commonly conceive of the SAT as measuring smarts. But admissions officers at elite US colleges resist overreliance on the SAT, saying that the test, though perhaps to some degree a measure of cognitive dexterity, cannot really assess character. At different times, elite colleges have used character to both exclude socially marginalized groups and to increase diversity (see chapter 4).

Without doubt, it is important to attend to the social interests that different conceptions of character advance, but these debates overlook the moral dimension of the examination. As a fateful event, the SAT, similar to the Gaokao, is a trial of merit in which people personify high cultural virtues. In the United States, and to a lesser degree in China, these virtues include intelligence. Although intelligence may not appear to be a cultural virtue—that is, as an aspect of character—on closer examination it conforms to our folk conceptions of character.

Remember that character is conceived cross-culturally both as a relatively durable aspect of the self and as something that requires periodic proof (see chapter 1). Similarly, people tend to think of intelligence as something that individuals both have and must show. This folk conception of character even seems to influence scientific understandings of intelligence. Since the 1960s, the distinction between crystallized and fluid intelligence has become commonplace in intelligence research. Crystallized intelligence describes habituated patterns of cognition learned through experience. Fluid intelligence refers to innate cognitive dexterity—the ability to think on one's feet. But note how neatly this distinction maps onto folk notions of character as both involving characteristic qualities and requiring regular demonstration.

From an anthropological point of view, intelligence is not an objectively existing biological capacity of individuals but rather a culturally determined character ideal. For this reason, ideas of intelligence differ from place to place and through time. Mainstream scientific conceptions of intelligence have diffused globally along with intelligence research. Nevertheless, people's notions of intelligence exhibit striking cultural variation.

In the United States, the general tendency is to emphasize the innateness and heritability of intelligence, despite little evidence that this characteristic is primarily or even largely genetic. In fact, research suggests that differences in intelligence can be largely explained by the type of social effects that Chinese summarize under the category of environment. This point can be demonstrated through a discussion of what intelligence researchers term the Flynn effect. This term refers to a puzzling paradox that was first systematically formulated by intelligence researcher James Flynn (1987). People seem to do better on IQ tests with each succeeding generation, suggesting that something environmental determines intelligence (for instance, increasing industrialization). At the same time, however, children tend to perform similarly to their parents on IQ tests, suggesting that this trait is heritable. But the correlation is smallest when children are young (around 0.45 in the pre-teen years) and greatest when they are almost adults (about 0.75 by late adolescence) (Dickens and Flynn 2001, 346, 361). Flynn himself suggests that this paradox can be resolved by analyzing how children are influenced by their environments, on the one hand, and learn to create their own environments on the other (Dickens and Flynn 2001). In other words, genetics play a role, but their effect is vastly overestimated. Although Flynn writes from the tradition of quantitative psychometric research, his insights correspond closely with those of qualitative sociologists like Bourdieu (Bourdieu and Passeron 1977). They also accord with the Confucian emphasis on human plasticity and environment.

Without doubt, analogs to the North American obsession with IQ exist in China. In a personal conversation, one Chinese researcher suggested to me that a fully scientific administration of the Gaokao would result in an ideal society ruled by people of high IQ. In a further example of IQ fetishism, many in China believe that the world's races can be ranked hierarchically according to intelligence. Moreover, they place great emphasis on the genetic heritability of intelligence in some contexts. For example, many in China exercise great care in selecting an intelligent and allegedly genetically superior spouse in the hopes of having excellent offspring. Because excellence is widely associated with urbanity, Han ethnic origin, and health, these practices reinforce and naturalize discrimination against rural people, ethnic minorities, and people who are disabled. All these views accord with the broadly eugenicist goals of Chinese population-control policies, which aim to increase "excellent births" (see chapter 2).

But people in China consider even such a supposedly heritable characteristic as intelligence to be influenced by the behavior and environment of parents and children (Sleeboom-Faulkner 2010). Take, for example, the widespread practice of fetal education (*tāijiào*), in which mothers sing, read, and play music for their unborn child—a practice that people believe contributes to the intelligence and all-around quality of children. In accounting for success and failure in life, moreover, many in China—including professional educators—will argue that intelligence is overrated. Even if urbanites widely describe people of rural background as stupid or simple, such descriptions—like the commonest expression for intelligence (*cōngming*, often translated as clever)—seem to describe ingrained dispositional attitudes as much as they do innate characteristics.

People rarely use the Chinese term for IQ, *zhìshāng*, in everyday educational contexts. Instead, teachers emphasize differences in disposition that are acquired through good habits, among which diligence and persistence reign supreme. People talk about success as representing not the fruits of intelligence but rather the spoils of a hard-won battle between diligent self-cultivation and the dark forces of antidiligence—guanxi and nepotism. In accordance with the Confucian pedagogical ethics that I describe above, the cultural environments of individuals—including their peers and role models—create the conditions for the cultivation of good habits.

Unleashing Latent Potential: Internal/External versus Innate/Acquired Models of Learning

For the above reasons, teachers in China generally concur that innate intelligence forms a necessary but not sufficient condition of examination success. They understand environment to play the predominant role. The reaction of my colleagues to a Chinese newspaper exposé about super high schools (*chāojízhōngxué*) provides an example. Coming out during the time of my fieldwork, the exposé described in detail the superior educational resources of top-ranking high schools in metropolitan cities, as well as the great sums of money they sometimes charge in illicit fees (Yihai Zhao 2012). Notable student achievements included publication of original scientific research papers and admission to elite Western universities. My response to the article was quite different from that of Dragon Gate head teacher Ms. Yang. Emphasizing intelligence, I reacted with awe over the great social disparities between super high schools and ordinary high schools. I suggested to her that students at super high schools could not possibly be superior to Dragon Gate students in IQ, a capacity that I argued must be equally distributed throughout society. Ms. Yang, however, dismissed my comment. In her view, the issue of intelligence was a non sequitur. "What is amazing to me," she said, "is how these super high schools are able to stimulate children's latent potential" (*jīfā qiánlì*). Whereas I automatically reached for intelligence as an explanation—even if a negative one ("there cannot be such large differences in intelligence")—Ms. Yang's starting position consisted in her notion of latent potential. According to this view, students may differ in their latent potential, but latent potential, unlike innate characteristics like intelligence, is fungible and possessed by all.

This conception of students' educational development in terms of latent potential forms a mainstay of educational discourse all over China. But this concept has a wide cultural life beyond education, structuring people's understandings of finance, history, and medicine, among other domains. In the realm of state-sanctioned psychological discourses and practices, the concept of latent potential is part of a broader shift of social responsibility away from state and collective institutions toward the individual in the post-Mao era (J. Yang 2015). Stocks, nations, and material energy (*qi*) are also described as possessing latent potential. A common structural metaphor guides people's understandings of these disparate domains, between which much conceptual cross-pollination occurs. Like stocks, nations, or *qi*, students have the ability to surge or to underperform. As a primary stakeholder in student's test outcomes, the head teacher hopes that students' latent potential will be fully realized; indeed, he or she actively strives for that eventuality. But such outcomes are subject to factors beyond any single individual's control. Moreover, only students with great latent potential may be worthy of a teacher's investment of time.

In explaining how the super high school unleashed the latent potential of students, Ms. Yang described the school environment as part of what she termed the external world, which forms an overarching term for environmental influence. According to this view, different aspects of students' external worlds activate or unlock their latent potential. In this way, students internalize or incorporate aspects of the external world as personal characteristics.

Such views on personal development have wide currency in China. Chinese educators vastly prefer this external/internal model of explanation to one based on the innate/learned binary that dominates in North American views of intelligence. The difference is subtle. Both types of pedagogical model assume that the individual is to some degree a blank slate. But Western conceptions of innateness evoke the concept of original sin. According to such innatist views, people may be unable to overcome basic inborn failings. By contrast, Ms. Yang's model—which evokes Confucian notions of inherent goodness—tends toward the assumption that all children start out more or less equal but are influenced differently by their external environments. As these environments become internalized through habit, children's quality or level of cultivation gradually becomes fixed, as Ms. Wang would say.

Latent potential is understood differently in different times and places. For example, the current obsession of seeing the stock market in terms of latent potential may be unique to this historical moment. But latent potential also points toward something enduring and fundamental about Chinese conceptions of personhood. Confucian currents of thought going back to the great twelfth century synthesizer of Neo-Confucianism, Zhu Xi, similarly emphasize the per- fectible pattern (*lǐ*) of human beings, which must be intentionally cultivated (Bol 2008; Brokaw 1991)

Of course, people in China also have conceptions of innateness. These concep- tions are generally associated with Heaven. Innate characteristics are described as "before Heaven" (*xiāntiān*) or "Heaven born" (*tiānshēng*); by contrast, learned characteristics are portrayed as "after Heaven" (*hòutiān*). The Chinese word for genius (*tiāncái*) literally means someone who possesses talent (*cái*) that is given by Heaven (*Tiān*). This conception of Heaven-given talent recalls Western notions of giftedness.

In sum, people in China employ models of learning based both on the innate/ learned binary and on the external/internal binary. These different models are structured by different underlying metaphors (Lakoff and Johnson 1981). The innate/learned binary emphasizes time, ascribing traits to before and after birth. By contrast, the external/internal binary foregrounds space, grouping character- istics according to whether they originate outside or inside a person. In China the latter model is generally preferred. Similarly, people in the United States also use both types of explanatory model—temporal and spatial. But in contrast to Chi- nese preferences, they generally prefer to explain ability according to the innate/ learned binary.[1]

Differential Access to Conscientious Head Teachers

To some degree, combating inequality is institutionalized within mainstream educational practices in China, personified by the head teacher. Within Chinese high schools, head teachers are the street-level bureaucrats charged with helping students and parents overcome their cultural deficits. Their effectiveness in this task derives from how they easily traverse domains that people in other places usually consider to be separate. The goal of their analytical and affective labors is to adjust the relationships between students' various environments, particularly the school environment and the home environment. By contrast, teachers in the United States and many other Western countries only infrequently and indirectly intervene in home life.

Head teachers can be a parent's best resource in overcoming cultural- capital deficits. But access to a good head teacher is no given in Chinese schools.

For one thing, high-scoring students receive preferential treatment. Thus head teachers may work to reinforce cultural-capital differences by neglecting students with low test scores or by giving biased advice to parents based on conscious or unconscious prejudices against rural people, ethnic minorities, and women. These tendencies are exacerbated by the gift-giving culture that prevails in Chinese schools. Families that can afford to give expensive gifts to teachers or hold banquets in their honor can expect more individualized treatment.

By the same token, the commitment and skill of head teachers varies widely along the central-place hierarchy. Head teachers in high-ranking or centrally located schools tend to be relatively committed (*tóurù*) to their roles, whereas head teachers in low-ranking and rural schools tend to be less so. The commitment of head teachers in central places like Xiamen is reflected in such practices as visiting students' homes, talking frequently with their parents, holding motivational speeches during class meetings (*bānhuìkè*), and actively monitoring even low-scoring students. In Xiamen, even low-ranking schools like Dragon Gate possess committed head teachers, like Ms. Yang. In Ningzhou, by contrast, only teachers in top high schools display commitment. At lower-ranking schools, students complain about the unserious attitude of their teachers. They say that teachers spend their time smoking and drinking tea instead of working. And further down the rural-urban hierarchy at Mountain County Number One, only fast classes have serious head teachers. Even good head teachers in Mountain County seldom conduct home visits, partly because half or more of their students are boarders.

The Role of Head Teachers in School Choice

Parents know that the commitment and quality of head teachers vary widely. Thus securing access to a good head teacher forms a paramount consideration in their attempts to exercise choice over the school and class that their children attend. In many cases, however, parents struggle with the choices they face. For example, parents may possess the means (guanxi and money) to secure access to a better school for their children. But they may be in doubt about whether or not this investment of social and economic capital will pay dividends that justify the expenditure. Good head teachers can help parents overcome deficits in cultural capital by advising them about how and when to game the system.

When children take the high-school entrance exam, parents commonly consult with their junior-high head teacher about school choice. Shortly after a child commences senior high school, many parents likewise consult with the child's new senior-high head teacher, asking whether it is worth it to spend money on bribes and extra fees to secure access for the child to a better school or class.

In these conversations, teachers will frequently tell parents that students of middling academic achievements may thrive in a lower-ranking school where they receive extra attention, but may languish in a highly ranked school where they will be relegated to the bottom of their class. By providing this kind of advice, head teachers may be of great value to parents. But many parents may be only dimly aware of the complexity of head teachers' considerations in responding to their questions. In deciding how to advise students, head teachers typically consider not only the interest of the child but also that of the class.

One Dragon Gate head teacher, Ms. Wang, said that there were two types of children whose parents she would advise to spend money on changing schools. The first consisted of children who merely had a bad day on the high-school entrance exam. Such children might lack psychological quality or composure but could make large improvements in their mental fortitude by competing with high-scoring students. In any case, the actual ability of such children (as measured by test score) exceeded the average of the class to such a degree that they would need a more challenging environment to unleash their full latent potential. By letting such students go, however, Ms. Wang acted against the school's interest in attracting and maintaining good student resources (see chapter 3).

The second type of students whom Ms. Wang advised to transfer were bad students—bullies, rebels, and other troublemakers. Ms. Wang said that she typically employed academic pretenses to persuade the parents of these bad apples that it was in their interest to switch schools. In doing so, she had the interest of her class at heart. Such students would damage and pollute the class environment, she said, affecting others' test scores and, eventually, Ms. Wang's own reputation.

Shadow Education and Blind Spots Regarding the Environment

Head teachers also help families address cultural-capital deficits by advising parents on how to supplement their children's regular school learning through various forms of shadow education, either by hiring private tutors or by paying for lessons in after-school supplemental study classes. Head teachers commonly advise parents and students on which subjects to supplement and on how best to secure such supplemental instruction given a family's financial constraints.

Although educational disparities are greater than most people usually suspect (see chapter 3), parents and teachers generally understand that supplemental study is necessary to compensate for deficits in what is seen as their children's cultural foundation. But this awareness varies between families and according to academic subject. For example, students of rural origin may have serious deficits in formal, academic Mandarin, but have little awareness of this problem (see chapter 4). One head teacher in Ningzhou explained:

> Parents rarely consider that the process of acquiring the knowledge that is necessary for success in Chinese is one that requires years of accumulation. This lack of awareness is particularly a problem for students from rural areas, who are . . . often weak in Chinese and English. Thus, I advise rural students to start supplementing Chinese lessons as soon as possible.

Although people in China possess a generally high degree of awareness about the effects of cultural capital, this awareness has limits. Ironically, these limits arise from the same cultural logic that helps parents overcome disparities in cultural capital. Parents understand that they suffer from so-called cultural deficits but take comfort in how these shortfalls can be eliminated through diligence. Yet disadvantages that cannot be rectified through this virtue alone fall into a cultural blind spot—one that can be particularly serious among people of rural origin.

The Magic of Educational Research

Conducting paraethnographic work and data-driven analysis, teachers resemble social researchers in their efforts to reflect on and address differences in cultural capital between students. Indeed, the practice of pedagogical research is institutionalized into the high-school bureaucracy. All teachers have to produce research papers, which are a prerequisite for promotion. To support this requirement, high schools produce reams of academic journals that few people ever read. Although many teachers regard such publications as empty, some particularly committed colleagues approach these projects with a sincere attitude. At Dragon Gate, for example, Ms. Fu conducted surveys of students' psychological states and coping mechanisms, using this information to help her craft motivational assemblies. A few of the most dedicated head teachers may get involved in university-sponsored research projects, cooperating with their former college professors to study the effects of various pedagogical innovations on student test outcomes.

Such projects may be of questionable pedagogical benefit but still have significant effects on student morale. For example, Ms. Shen, the head teacher of the Dragon Gate senior-three keypoint class, had affiliated herself with just such a university-sponsored research project, which was aimed at investigating the effects of a novel pedagogical technique—the "long-writing method" (xiěchángfǎ)—on students learning English. The champion of this methodology, a professor at a provincial-level teachers' college, advocated having students take a free-writing approach to their essays; they should write whatever came to mind, length being more important than substance. At the same time, teachers were to refrain from correcting students, because corrections would increase their "rejection of English and feeling of being wronged." The purpose of this approach was to accomplish two admirable but somewhat contradictory goals. The first was to ameliorate social inequality by helping children at low-ranking schools like Dragon Gate improve their test scores. The second was to correct a perceived weakness in the Chinese education system, namely, the focus of foreign-language instruction on raising test scores rather than on improving competency. In these respects, the long-writing method joined a slew of recent pedagogical innovations focused on education for quality. But it was constructed to overcome teachers' frequent criticism of such innovations, namely, that they were disconnected from teachers' real task of improving Gaokao performance.

The long-writing method promised more than it delivered. Privately, Ms. Shen said that she was deeply skeptical of the technique. She did not see how merely requiring children to write longer essays would help them on the test. As she put it, "Kids need to have more English in their heads before they sit down to write." The teachers involved in the study also disagreed with the principal investigator on an important point of research methodology. To the investigator's chagrin, they actively cultivated awareness among students that they were being researched, promising them that their participation in the study would improve their performance on the Gaokao. In direct contravention of the principle of blind research, Ms. Shen billed the long-writing method as an important government research initiative and manufactured evidence to prove to students that it worked. Selecting one of the weakest students in the class, Ms. Shen guided the student through several revisions of his long writing, even though the long-writing method explicitly prohibited correcting students in this way. Following this procedure, she produced a model essay that she attributed to this student's efforts. But Ms. Shen had injected the essay with her own knowledge of how to achieve a high score on the Gaokao. For instance, she emphasized the importance of good handwriting. Because graders spend only a few seconds on each essay, she told her class, an elegant script could help compensate for mediocre contents. Showcasing the evolution of the students' essay in a PowerPoint presentation, she told them that the improvement in his work was a result of the long-writing method that they were learning.

In the end, therefore, the long-writing method became a vehicle for Ms. Shen's own pedagogical theories. But she used her association with the project to imbue her theories with the charisma of objective scientific research. Her students' test scores did improve, but she herself suggested that this improvement resulted less from the long-writing method than from the combined effect of her pedagogical intervention and the morale boost that students received from participating in a state-funded research project. In other words, her performance of pedagogical effectiveness combined, as she said, "subjective and objective factors," or what I have termed affective and analytical labor, in ways that are difficult to disaggregate.

In some respects, the head teacher's art resembles the magic performed by shamanic healers. Like a healer, the effectiveness of Ms. Shen's practice resulted in part from bringing students' experience into harmony with powerful collective cultural symbols—in this case, the objectivity of science (Lévi-Strauss 1963). But the effectiveness of Ms. Shen's practice certainly also resulted from the great energy she devoted to her work. She was widely recognized by her colleagues as deeply ambitious, and many of her colleagues said she associated herself with state-funded research because of the status that it conferred. Indeed, Ms. Shen expressed a deep interest in my own research when I first came to Dragon Gate, but her curiosity quickly attenuated as she determined that my study had no immediate practical application. Nevertheless, she deemed the mere association of her class with a foreign researcher to have a positive effect on its morale in addition to increasing her own prestige. She asked me to visit her class, the keypoint class, much more frequently than I did the others. But her colleagues resented this attempt to monopolize my time. Eventually, a school administrator intervened, resolving the conflict by arranging for me to rotate through all classes on a fixed timetable.

Ms. Shen's behavior epitomized the ideal type of the conscientious head teacher. Combining aspects of coach, counselor, researcher, and parent, she embraced a thoroughgoing pragmatism in her attempts to affect students' educational outcomes. Within the general limits of acceptable behavior, she would do anything to improve the test scores of her students.

Home Visits

Among the most profound ways that committed head teachers can influence educational outcomes is through direct intervention in the home life of families. Head teachers see intervention as an integral and indispensable part of their work, and various methods exist to influence the home environment. Parents frequently consult teachers for parenting advice, and teachers periodically hold parent-teacher conferences, but by far the most direct method is the home visit. On these occasions, teachers travel to the family home to speak with parents and students together.

Pretenses for home visits vary. Sometimes a disciplinary problem, such as a student skipping classes or missing evening study sessions, can provoke a visit. More generally, teachers conduct home visits of specific students at strategic junctures when teachers believe that their involvement might make an appreciable difference in students' study approach or morale. Whatever the explicit rationale, however, the underlying motive almost invariably consists in raising children's test scores.

But teachers also see their visits of individual students as affecting the dynamics of the class as a whole. In other words, home visits are intended to adjust not only individual student performance but also the general academic atmosphere of the class. Ms. Yang largely attributed the remarkable improvements of Class 4, the dark horse class, to extensive home visits.

Different head teachers tend to share the same general objectives for home visits, though their approaches may diverge. Despite the great institutional importance of head teachers, few attempts exist to standardize their practices. Instead, head teachers learn their craft from their mentors and from word of mouth. Within this variation, however, general trends emerge. On home visits, head teachers commonly advise students and their families on the minutiae of life habits, including study approaches, sleep routines, and even personal hygiene. Head teachers appeal to parents to remove various technological distractions like cellphones and TV remote controls. Frequently, head teachers pressure parents to force children to change their personal appearance, for example by cutting their hair to the specified length (standard coiffures exist for both boys and girls). They often urge families to improve students' home environment by making books and magazines available.

Because teachers see examination success as connected with moral quality, their advice for families frequently contains a moralistic dimension. Head teachers may even insert themselves into family disputes about proper filial behavior. For example, Ms. Yang admonished a girl, Jingjing, when her mother, who was taking care of three other children, mentioned that the girl had not been washing her own clothes as she had promised to do. "Don't be so lazy," Ms. Yang scolded Jingjing. "Washing your clothes will only take you fifteen minutes before you go to bed. Having more regular habits will also help you study and sleep." Parents usually express gratitude for such help. As this girl's mother said, "Teacher, it is best that you say it. . . . She doesn't listen to me at all." In their efforts to ensure a good home environment, head teachers will even resort to giving marital advice, imploring parents to reduce family conflict or even delay separation or divorce until after the big test.

In these ways, head teachers get involved in the functioning of families and the lives of students to an extent that would be unthinkable in many Western cultural contexts. A head teacher at a top-ranking Xiamen high school who had spent a year on a Fulbright program serving as a teacher's assistant in the United States summed up this cultural difference succinctly. With a giggle of schadenfreude, she said, speaking in English, "In the States, students have rights. In China, they have no rights." Effective head teachers exert a considerable degree of control over the private lives of students and parents. But far from resenting such visits, Chinese parents—especially those of humble social backgrounds—generally consider them to be an honor. The very fact that the teacher deigns to visit their home can improve the morale of child and family.

Externalizing Inner Potential: Attitude, Composure, and Morale

Motivating Underperforming Students: Finding Pressure Points

During home visits and other interactions with students, an important task of the head teacher consists in providing encouragement to students who possess latent potential but lack motivation. Head teachers invest the most time and energy in such underperforming students—those with great room for improvement. If underperformers can be persuaded to raise their efficiency and throw themselves into their studies, they can contribute significantly to the ranking of the class and, consequently, to the reputation of the head teacher. Head teachers therefore devote extensive thought to the problem of motivating underachievers, frequently consulting close colleagues for advice.

One such consultation occurred during the spaghetti dinner between Ms. Yang and Ms. Fu that I describe above. As the school counselor, Ms. Fu was considered to have special insight into student psychology. Thus Ms. Yang frequently sought her guidance on particularly difficult cases. On this occasion, she inquired about Wangshu, a lazy student who nevertheless possessed great latent potential. "I just don't know what motivates him" Ms. Yang sighed. "He isn't doing as well as he could. It's so frustrating. I don't feel like I am getting through to him."

"There are two kinds of motivations—the motivation to achieve happiness and the motivation to avoid pain," Ms. Fu replied. "For this kind of student," she continued, "it is not enough to give him positive motivation. Find out what he hates most, what he most afraid of. Take a systematic approach. Try surveying his parents, his classmates. Find the right point, then prick him where it hurts."

Ms. Yang's and Ms. Fu's discussion of this problem student demonstrates the pressures that head teachers face. Having already made much progress with her class in a few short months, Ms. Yang was feeling the weight of her success. All her efforts would be for naught if the class failed to live up to the heightened expectations of administrators and teachers. If she could succeed in keeping the class in shape, however, she could enjoy a significant monetary bonus and—more important—the rewards of increased reputation. Of course, she cared about the students and their families too. Helping them achieve their best score was helping them fulfill their dreams.

As one of Xiamen's lowest ranking schools, Dragon Gate had its share of rebels, bullies, and slackers. But Wangshu was none of these. Ms. Yang felt that the boy's potential for development justified special attention. She had already tried to talk with him but had failed to have any effect. In exasperation, she started giving Wangshu the cold shoulder (*lěng chǔlǐ*) to show her dissatisfaction.

But Ms. Fu did not agree with this approach. Expanding on her suggestion to prick him where it hurt, she offered the following advice:

> No, you can't ignore him for too long. After you find his weak spot, try approaching him normally. Let's say you find out that he can't stand it when people look down on him. Then you approach his weakness indirectly, by saying something like, "What kind of person do you hate most?" You'll catch him off guard—he won't know what you are talking about. Then you say something like, "I think you hate most people who look down on you." After you've done it, look at him sternly. He won't be anticipating the prick. But you have to get him when he isn't expecting it, when his defenses are down. That is how you can get into his unconscious (*qiányìshí*) to have a real effect. Then you should just walk away. Let your words sink in. Don't let him question you or follow up. Have the last word. This approach is bound to work.

Many may find this manipulative use of psychology ethically questionable. Such concerns are important, but I wish to focus on another aspect of this anecdote, namely, how it highlights the meticulousness of the affective labor that conscientious head teachers perform. Although they may lack Ms. Fu's official counseling credentials, every head teacher expends considerable effort on thinking about student psychology. Many employ similar tactics even if they do not use psychological jargon to describe them. Various forms of humiliation, subtle and unsubtle, form an important weapon in the head teacher arsenal.

As the above exchange between Ms. Fu and Ms. Yang illustrates, head teachers tailor their speeches to students' individual circumstances.

The home visit that I mention above contained another example of such tailoring. In addressing Jingjing, Ms. Yang employed peer pressure and appealed to the girl's filial duty to save money for her parents, who were experiencing financial hardship:

> This is the most important year of your life. . . . You have lots of latent potential that you are not realizing. With a few exceptions, everyone in

the class has about the same ability, right? So you have to ask yourself, "Why do they manage to get high scores when I do not?" . . . You need to be more diligent. . . . Everyone knows: If you have money, you can go to a two-year college. But you don't want to burden your parents. They are already working very hard (*xīnkǔ*).

Although the contents of such speeches vary, they follow familiar patterns. The filial duties of children form a frequent topic. During home visits, head teachers take advantage of the presence of parents to remind students of their debts to parents and family. Comparison to peers is another recurring theme. In addition, the speeches of teachers often exhibit a strongly gendered dimension. For example, head teachers may tell boys that they have a responsibility to be the man in the family. By contrast, they may tell girls that the Gaokao is important to finding a husband who will help them take care of them and their parents. With higher scores, girls can go to better colleges in more centrally located places, where they will find "bigger fish"—better marriage prospects.

Using Inner Potential to Change the Environment and Master Fate

In addition to illuminating head teachers' use of peer pressure and filial duty to motivate students, Ms. Yang's speech demonstrates how teachers emphasize the basic goodness and inherent plasticity of students. Ms. Yang avoids mention of allegedly intrinsic or innate characteristics, such as intelligence, while focusing on how all students possess similar latent potential, thus foregrounding the value of diligent effort.

But a disconnect exists between teachers' practical interventions in the family—including guidance on study habits and supplemental study—and the rhetoric of diligence that head teachers promulgate. Teachers clearly recognize the significance of environmental factors, and they help families overcome various cultural-capital deficits by encouraging them to adjust aspects at home. But head teachers also emphasize the importance of personal responsibility for diligent study. For example, during a home visit, Ms. Yang responded to the apologies of one parent for having "no culture" (*méi wénhuà*). This mother, a vegetable seller, lamented that she had not provided her son with an adequate cultural environment. "You can't blame yourself," Ms. Yang said. "It is your son's responsibility to do better."

From a head teacher's perspective, however, this apparent contradiction is not so glaring. In a statement that evoked Flynn's theory of intelligence, Ms. Yang reconciled this paradox as follows: "The external world influences personal factors in success, but personal factors can also change the environment." According to this logic, students have a moral responsibility to create good environments for themselves so that they can unlock their full inner potential. Accordingly, teachers emphasize that students must remain positive about their ability to change the outcome of the exam. As Ms. Yang put it, "In the end, you have to encourage students to believe that their fate is in their own hands; you tell them over and over that 'you can master your own fate' [nǐ de mìng nǐ zìjǐ zhǎngwò]."

Indeed, Ms. Yang and other conscientious head teachers, like Ms. Shen and Ms. Wang, are true believers in this principle—for them, attitude really can change fate. They see the effects of attitude every year during the examination when some students give up and others surge at the last minute. As Ms. Yang put it, "Teachers shouldn't amplify unchangeable objective factors. Instead, we focus on what *can* be changed."

Boosting Confidence and Morale: Maintaining the Pace and Getting in the Zone

As the test approaches, what can be changed grows smaller and smaller. For this reason, teachers focus more on morale and attitude than on study strategies and habits. In the final months before the exam, they increasingly emphasize the importance of confidence and determination, admonishing students to persevere and "not to surrender" (bù tóuxiáng). As Ms. Fu said in her motivational speech, the relative importance of attitude and knowledge inverts as the exam grows closer.

One hundred days and thirty days before the Gaokao, most schools organize mobilization rallies or, as they are sometimes called, assemblies to pledge resolution (shìshídàhuì). Evoking the mass rallies of the Mao era, such events form important occasions on which teachers attempt to improve attitude (figure 11). Student leaders from every class join school leaders to direct the senior-three year in chanting slogans like, "Battle the Gaokao with all your strength!" and "Never give up! Never say die!" Students often regard these gatherings as relatively empty, however, citing their formulaic quality. By contrast, the assembly that I described at the beginning of this chapter was relatively well received. Students considered this event meaningful—a fresh and modern alternative to more traditional rallies.[2]

At this assembly, the organizer, Ms. Fu, emphasized the importance of the unconscious in determining test outcomes. She told students that their unconscious perceptions of themselves could make or break their exam performance. The magical spell that she taught students was designed to help them change

FIGURE 11. A pre-Gaokao mobilization rally. School leaders, sitting on the stage, look on as a student gives a speech to the assembled senior-three class. The slogan reads "2012 One Hundred Day Gaokao Sprint: Assembly to Pledge Resolution." The name of the school has been removed. Photograph by the author.

these perceptions. This spell was a self-affirmational mantra. Ms. Fu asked each of the gathered students to praise himself or herself out loud. "Think of your best attribute," Ms. Fu said, "and insert it into this phrase: 'Because I am the most diligent, kind, athletic, considerate, or whatever, I am the most amazing person!' . . . Everyone stand up. I want you to shout out your magical spell."

As a final flourish, Ms. Fu selected volunteers to square off against each other in a magical duel. Standing on opposite sides of the auditorium, students took turns shouting their affirmations into a microphone. In a cacophony of feedback and student laughter, the dueling pairs duked it out, bellowing their best attributes at the top of their lungs. Although perhaps damaging to students' hearing, the assembly was widely reckoned to be good for their confidence.

In addition to such mobilization rallies, weekly class meetings mark another important occasion on which conscientious head teachers give eleventh-hour motivational speeches to students. As the big day looms, head teachers concentrate their efforts on two types of students—top performers and those who might surge late in the game. Particularly conscientious head teachers conduct last-minute home visits. They urge students to keep in shape for the examination and avoid slacking off during the final weeks, as Ms. Ma did with Zeyu, the garbage collector's son, in the anecdote that opens the book (see chapter 1).

Even closer to the exam, Ms. Ma visited Yujian, another underperforming student. During this conversation, Yujian's mother was present and played an active role:

> Ms. MA: I know you don't mean any personal disrespect to me by missing evening study hall, but look at the top students in the class. They really never do anything but study.
>
> YUJIAN'S MOTHER: I have seen it myself. Every day after class, Yujian and his friends all have to get together and hang out, but the top students are always sitting in class and studying.
>
> YUJIAN: I really worked hard for a while during the second semester of senior two, but I couldn't hold out.
>
> Ms. MA: But now you've got little time to make up for slacking off, so you have to increase your efficiency. It is forty days before the Gaokao. If you keep your leisurely attitude, you are just not going to be able to compete with other people.
>
> YUJIAN'S MOTHER: That's why the teacher is visiting today. You probably have some more latent potential that can surge (*yīnggāi yǒu qiánlì kěyǐ bàofā*).
>
> Ms. MA: Yes, this is it. It is really time to really give it a go (*qiāo yīxià*).

Ms. Ma made reference to the exact number of days remaining before the Gaokao. In the final year before the big exam, every student and teacher always knows this number, which is ubiquitously displayed on the school grounds and in every senior-three classroom. As this countdown falls into the double digits, teachers become wary of what Ms. Fu called a high-altitude reaction. Just as athletes taper their conditioning before a race, students must neither peak too early nor slack off too much. Thus, the goal of students' final preparations is to get into what students and teachers call "examination shape" (*kǎoshì zhuàngtài*)—a phrase that literally translates as "examination state." Getting into the state implies a physical and mental discipline that can easily be lost (*shīqù*) and thus must be maintained (*bǎochí*). As with notions of flow or "getting into the zone" cross-culturally, examination shape evokes the ideal of being able to perform under pressure with an effortless unselfconsciousness that one achieves only through diligent preparation and mental focus (Csikszentmihalyi 1991). But few students describe their exam experience in such terms of unstrained engrossment. As in many fateful events cross-culturally, the greatest impediment to achieving such a state during the Gaokao lies not outside but rather inside oneself. As the test grows closer, psychological pressure increases to a fever pitch.

Coping with Pressure

It is more common for students to react to examination pressure by overworking than by slacking off. Teachers, too, become overworked, running themselves ragged in the brutally hot summer weather. Ms. Ma took on a skeletal appearance. Ms. Yang suffered from serious chronic back pain. Ms. Wang, a veteran head teacher in her fifties, fared better, merely complaining of exhaustion. But the suffering of teachers is considered inconsequential, whereas the state of students, under the teachers' auspices, makes or breaks a school's reputation.

During the final weeks, students tend to be accident prone, fall ill, or encounter various other inauspicious (*bù jíxiáng*) occurrences. To curb these tendencies, schools institute special policies, treating students like prize horses before a big race. In the final days before the exam, they are not required to attend classes or evening study hall, although teachers must be available at all times to answer their questions. Some schools make the last practice examination optional. Many teachers tell students to relax their study schedule to a minimal regime that keeps their knowledge "activated." At the same time, they admonish students to maintain normal life habits and sleep routines and they ask parents to spend time with children engaging in relaxing activities. In many schools, parents are instructed to avoid talking about the upcoming exam except to declare their unconditional love no matter what the result. Some students like to let off pressure through physical exercise, but school administrators fear that students will injure themselves or suffer heat exhaustion. Thus examinees are banned from participating in competitive sports or strenuous activities in the weeks leading up to the test.

Methods for coping with pressure include a variety of medically minded interventions, which increase in frequency and number as the exam approaches. Depending on the context, people may assess such measures either as possessing actual effectiveness (*shíjì xiàoguǒ*) or consisting mainly in psychological comfort (*xīnlǐ ānwèi*). Many of these practices for adjusting the body fall broadly under the rubric of traditional Chinese medicine (Farquhar 2002). To help children fortify their health, parents supplement (*bǔ*) the diet of their offspring with various kinds of healthful foods. Some foods—such as fish, walnuts, and eggs—are thought to having brain-boosting powers. Meanwhile, medicine shops everywhere carry expensive herbal products for "supplementing the brain" (*bǔnǎo*). In some schools, teachers have been reported to hand out ginseng tablets to children on test day. Ms. Fu taught the assembled Dragon Gate students a form of acupressure massage for coping with anxiety.

Although Chinese medicine is widely accepted in the context of the exam, biomedicine is not. As of this writing, the use of anxiety-reducing or cognition-boosting pharmaceuticals, such as beta blockers or amphetamines, appears to be rare, although their employment in high-pressure academic environments is well-documented in other cultural contexts.[3] When I asked students and teachers in China about this surprising lack, many expressed disdain for such unnatural interventions.

A significant exception to this rule consists in the practice of using biomedicine to intervene in girls' menstrual cycles. Before the exam, many teachers will advise parents to have their daughters control their cycle through the administration of birth control pills.[4] Other types of medical intervention seem to lie between Western and traditional medicine. In a 2011 case, a Hubei school was discovered to have administered intravenous vitamins to senior-three students en masse, causing a nationwide scandal. The public objected less to the contents of the IV bag, which were regarded as relatively natural, than to the school's forcing students to undergo a medical procedure, no matter how minor.

Additional mechanisms for coping with examination stress include various popular-religious and magical practices, which, like dietary supplements and medical interventions, are ambivalently perceived as both psychological comfort and efficacious intervention (see chapter 6).

Bodily Conditions, Untimely Love, and Unconscious Rebellion

Despite the best efforts of parents and teachers, many students succumb to the pressure. In the final months before the exam, students are closely observed for any type of strange behavior—a new love interest, a sudden illness, bouts of insomnia, or any number of other problems. People usually interpret any deviation from normal routine as a symptom of examination pressure.

Consider, for instance, the love interest of Ms. Ma's highest-scoring student, Yuqing, the daughter of a local police detective. Just a few short weeks before the exam, Yuqing became smitten with one of her classmates. The young couple's romantic involvement was sleuthed out by Ms. Ma when she noticed the pair sharing an umbrella during a squall. Confronted by her teacher, the girl confirmed Ms. Ma's suspicions. Ms. Ma then promptly informed Yuqing's parents, who reacted with great alarm. Although they fretted that the girl's reputation might be damaged by having a boyfriend, Yuqing's mother and father did not object to the match primarily on moral grounds. Rather, they worried more about how the budding relationship might affect her exam score. Yuqing was a top student, ranked number one in Ms. Ma's class and number three in the whole school. She had a chance of testing into Peking University, Tsinghua, or a top university in Hong Kong, which would represent a coup for all concerned—the municipal educational authorities, the school, Ms. Ma, Yuqing's family, and Yuqing herself. Thus the girl's private life became a matter of official concern. School administrators regularly probed Ms. Ma for updates on the girl's emotional state.

To protect Yuqing's rapport with her head teacher, her parents decided to tell their daughter that they found out about her relationship by observing the love-birds on their apartment complex's security cameras, which, given her father's detective skills, seemed plausible to the girl. To avoid adding to her pressure, her parents pretended not to mind about the boy. Backstage, however, a frantic series of consultations between parents and teacher ensued. For a time, Yuqing's mother spent thirty minutes every day on the phone talking with Ms. Ma about her daughter's state of mind.

The general consensus between Ms. Ma and school leaders was that Yuqing's relationship was not likely to have a negative effect on Yuqing's boyfriend, who was not a top student; in fact, it appeared to have provided him with renewed motivation. Yuqing, on the other hand, seemed distracted and listless. Her scores on the final practice exams were unstable—sometimes high, sometimes low. Thus her performance on the Gaokao was anticipated with a mixture of hope and anxiety.

Parents and teacher diagnosed Yuqing's love interest as a form of rebellion. Indeed, when her father eventually confronted her about her boyfriend, a dispute ensued. Yuqing accused him of being a dictator, contrasting him with her boyfriend, who she said was mild and considerate. She told Ms. Ma that her love for the boy had opened her eyes to the meaning of life beyond the narrow world of examinations. As Yuqing later told me, she began to question the significance of the Gaokao. Her budding romance suggested to her that one could be happy without so much pressure and toil. Parents and teacher felt helpless. The more they implored Yuqing to consider the future, the more she protested that they did not understand her.

In the end, Yuqing did indeed perform much worse than expected—an outcome that everyone attributed to her unstable psychological state. Looking back on the incident a few years later, however, Ms. Ma regretted betraying the girl's confidence. Yuqing's class was the first that Ms. Ma had led through the Gaokao, and she had lacked experience in such delicate matters. "Honestly, I should not have made such a big deal of the situation," she said. "Doing so just ratcheted up the pressure on the girl."

Like a love affair, a sudden illness before the Gaokao may likewise be interpreted as a sign of stress or even rebellion—a somatized symptom of examination pressure. As Ms. Fu said of illness, "Getting sick is the unconscious's way of giving students an excuse to do poorly on the exam." Or as another teacher said, "Being sick is a coping mechanism—a way of finding an external reason why you are going to fail the test." For instance, Ms. Ma interpreted Zeyu's stomach illness as a symptom of examination pressure (see chapter 1).[5] But some students resist such theories of somatization, reacting to them with skepticism and even anger. One Mountain County student complained bitterly about the attitude of parents and teachers to illness. She compared this attitude to that of Olympic spectators toward the injury of the star hurdler Liu Xiang who was widely criticized on social media when he hurt himself right before the 2008 Beijing Games: "When Liu Xiang was hurt, people blamed him for his injury even though it wasn't his fault. It was so unjust. Some things are just out of the individual's control. It's the same way with exams. If you don't test well, then parents and teachers couldn't care less about you [bù mǎi nǐ de zhàng—literally, 'won't pay your bill']."

Insomnia is widely regarded to be one of the most pernicious symptoms of pressure. This condition is so disturbing because it resists individual efforts of conscious diligent control. Indeed, the culture of diligence is antithetical to sleep (see chapter 4). To combat insomnia, teachers and administrators encourage good sleep hygiene, emphasizing the importance of regular habits. Nevertheless, insomnia seems to be widespread, and constitutes a prominent cause of under-performance. In candid conversations, few examinees will recount sleeping well in the days before and during the exam. And sleep disturbances can prove long-lived. Some Gaokao veterans report experiencing recurring nightmares about the test for years afterward.

Macho Nonchalance and Examination Composure

In general, however, Chinese students treat all such symptoms of pressure with macho nonchalance. Mental toughness is lionized as a predictor of exam success, and students generally discuss mental frailty only with their closest friends or family. For this reason, it is difficult to estimate the prevalence of examination-induced mental illness, which, because of its stigma, is unlikely to be captured by ordinary surveys. For instance, I only learned about the examination anxiety of my friend Ms. Ma after knowing her for nearly two years.

In the final months of my fieldwork, I joined Ms. Ma and her husband on a trip to their hometown in the countryside, where we met Ms. Ma's little sister. One evening, the four of us were sitting around chatting in the living room of Ms. Ma's family home. Rummaging around in a drawer, her little sister produced a stack photos, report cards, and certificates from Ms. Ma's childhood for me and her husband to admire. Ms. Ma was full of surprises. A placard certified her as a provincial-level athlete. "How on earth did you get one of those?" her husband asked. Her little sister passed around class photos from various years of school, asking if we could pick her out. I tried to imagine how the playful smiling child in Ms. Ma's primary-school photos had transformed into the grim-faced examination warrior in her high-school photos.

As we looked at these materials, Ms. Ma's sister suddenly started talking about the night before Ms. Ma's Gaokao. She remembered staying up all night holding her big sister, who was shaking uncontrollably. "We didn't get a wink of sleep that night, did we?" said Ms. Ma's sister.

Ms. Ma laughed with embarrassment. "I bombed the Chinese section," she said. "Thank God my English score was so high."

Despite having had dozens of conversations with Ms. Ma about her test experience, I had never once heard Ms. Ma describe this emotionally charged moment. As with many of the best, most successful students, a certain affectation of coolness and emotional distance always accompanied her narration of examination success. Among other things, her sister's story left me wondering how well Ms. Ma would have done if she had not been so nervous. Just as her certificates of success were locked away in a dusty drawer, her examination humiliation was carefully excluded from her public persona. Display of the former would signify immodesty, display of the latter a lack of psychological quality.

The strictures on immodesty, however, do not seem to apply to people's boasts of examination composure. Men, in particular, are inclined to brag about this character trait. Many consider examination composure a masculine virtue—a quality that girls can adopt but that does not come naturally to them. A high-level manager of a Shanghai pharmaceutical company, Mr. Zhang, provides a case in point. This man described how Gaokao success catapulted him from a rural Zhejiang village into a good university in the early 1980s, a time when the admission rate for such universities was only 1 or 2 percent. Mr. Zhang boasted that he had subsequently succeeded brilliantly in every exam he had ever taken—the graduate-student entrance exam, the Chinese bar exam, and the notoriously difficult accountant's exam. I asked what was his secret was. He replied:

> I never get nervous. You know why? I just tell myself it doesn't matter. I wasn't nervous about the Gaokao at all. My parents are farmers. I just told myself that it wasn't so bad being a farmer. I didn't care whether I passed or failed. My classmates were all nervous. None of them got into college. Only I did. Afterward, whenever I take an examination, I have never been nervous.

Commenting on this story, another Shanghai manager—also a successful examinee and, as it happened, a committed Zen Buddhist—told me that the secret to success in management was the same as the secret to success in examinations.

It was, he claimed, a lesson that one likewise learns by practicing Zen. "You have to learn to let go [*fàngqì*]," he said. "Let go of your desires, let go of your worries. Let go of what people think of you. Only by letting go can you succeed."

The twelve years of study leading up to the exam represent a team effort, incorporating the help of parents, relatives, teachers, and school. But the moment of examination itself is a profoundly individuating experience. Students train for the test as members of various social constituencies (family, school, place, nation) but take it as individuals.

The examination is carefully policed in a concerted effort to ensure that examinees approach it unaided. In the days preceding, the school may be open for business, but the examination halls themselves—converted classrooms—become sacred ground. Entrance is restricted to high-level administrators and other necessary personnel. On test day, only students and test proctors are allowed into the school. At the gates, security guards check students' identities against their examination admission badges, seeking to prevent any attempt to cheat through the use of "sharpshooters" (*qiāngshǒu*), or substitute examinees (*tìkǎo*). These efforts add to many further anti-cheating measures. Cellphones and other electronic devices are strictly prohibited. Students must carry all writing implements in a clear plastic container, the permissible inventory of which is meticulously prescribed. In many places, students are swept with metal detectors. The examination halls themselves are surveilled in person by proctors and remotely through closed-circuit TV. Other high-tech countermeasures sometimes include signal-jamming devices and even aerial drones.

The net effect of all these efforts is to strip people of every vestige of their social environment so that they face the examination alone.[6] Accordingly, the raw Gaokao score—before any bonus points are added—is termed the naked score (see chapter 3). Whereas people see the award of bonus points as corrupted by guanxi (see chapter 4), they perceive the naked score as a purely personal achievement.

Other policies guarantee that examinees are removed from their guanxi networks. Teachers serve as test proctors but they usually do not invigilate the students at their own schools—a policy that resembles the "rule of avoidance" that prohibited officials from serving on their home turf during imperial times (Miyazaki 1981). In addition, senior-three teachers are forbidden from proctoring the exam, which minimizes the risk that test takers might be supervised by teachers who know them personally. And in contrast to practice exams, which students take at their own school, the Gaokao may require students to travel to neighboring schools. On test day, therefore, students are surrounded by strangers, which heightens their sense of isolation and nakedness.

Surely, however, the greatest source of individualization is the fateful moment of the exam itself. Students confront their test papers on their own, each of them sitting behind a single desk separated from others by a meter—an arrangement that resembles the isolated examination cubicles in imperial-era exam halls. As they open their test papers, their hearts race. All their lives have been leading up to this single moment, which they have been told since early childhood decides fate. What ensues is a dramatic struggle of wills in which the individual examinee approaches every problem with the wary eye of a test veteran. What traps have the designers laid? What surprises lurk in waiting? A bad performance on a single section can rattle even an experienced examinee, making it impossible for him or her to eat or sleep between the first and second day of the exam. In many ways, the Gaokao, like other high-stakes examinations, is a modern version of China's imperial examination hell (Miyazaki 1981)—a hell that each student must face alone.

Thus examinees do not merely engage in a game of wits against the test designers but also in a struggle to maintain control over their own bodies, which oppose them like an alien power. Extreme stories of failed composure are legend. Students regale one another with tails of examinees who faint, wail, lose control of their bowels, or even attempt to commit suicide during the exam. But the sensationalism of such tales overlooks the legion of prosaic individual struggles as hall after hall of isolated examinees face down their individual demons in ghostly silence. One Mountain County student described his examination experience like this:

> Anyone who has been working hard knows how to solve the problems. You think that we encounter a problem that we don't know how to solve [*scoffs*]? Lack of knowledge is not what causes you to fail on test day. Instead, it is your mental state that matters. How fast can you work? Will you be able to stay cool if you encounter a variation of a problem that seems unfamiliar? Will you be too nervous to think straight? Those are the kinds of questions that make or break a test performance.

On test day, as Ms. Fu says, attitude determines knowledge. As a fateful event that every student must face alone, the Gaokao subjects every examinee to an individual trial of merit. Of course, the notion that students are the sovereign producers of their own fates is belied by the massive amount of labor that the external world has expended on educating each child. As one parent put it, "Examination success is not the achievement of children alone but of the whole family"—and, I would add, an accomplishment of their teachers, school, place, and myriad other external social circumstances that make them who they are. Nevertheless, the examination rips students out of this social context, encouraging them to take individual responsibility for the outcome.

The individuating moment of the final examination forms the climax and crux of a long ritual process that transforms the social labor of exam preparation into a charismatic badge of individual merit. The capriciousness of composure, and the epic struggles of character that individuals undergo to master their bodies, provide every examinee with seemingly objective support for this attribution of personal responsibility. By the same token, the concerted efforts of head teachers to strengthen the will of students—a necessary part of exam preparation—further encourage them in their individuality. Despite everyone's awareness of the environmental causes of examination success, teachers and parents join students in seeing their final performance as a measure of personal character. In the days and weeks following the examination, all these stakeholders ruminate about the individual triumphs and failures that make people surge or choke.

As with other aspects of character, much evidence suggests that great inequality surrounds the distribution of attitude or composure. As Mr. Zhang said, it is easier to keep a cool head if one does not care. In many cases, however, the stakes of the examination are higher for students who hail from marginalized social backgrounds. To be sure, relatively privileged students often feel extreme pressure to perform on the exam, and some unprivileged students adopt a lackadaisical attitude toward it. But for many students of modest origin, the Gaokao represents the only way out of the socioeconomic circumstances into which they were born, whereas those with greater resources may choose to study abroad or attend private colleges, or more easily be able to retake the exam.[7]

Few students of any origin will blame society for their failure. Instead, the examination postmortem focuses on social reciprocity. In the days following the exam, students and teachers endlessly debate who deserved and did not deserve success based on their diligence of effort and strength of will. By themselves, however, such rational explanations do not always satisfy people's search for a coherent explanation of exam outcomes. In particular, such orthodox justifications fall short in explaining the many chancy factors that attend the examination. How does one account for a last-minute fever, a correctly or incorrectly guessed answer, a good or bad seat, a hot day, or myriad other accidents that can have fateful consequences for examination performance? To explain such vicissitudes, people are inclined to reach for less tangible explanations—luck, fate, divine intervention, and other forms of cosmic reciprocity—as the next chapter discusses.

MAGIC AND MERITOCRACY
Popular-Religious Responses to
Examination Anxiety

If your faith is sincere, your prayer will be effective.

—saying in China

Early on a Sunday morning just four days before the Gaokao, a group of teachers and administrators gathered inside the school gate of Ningzhou Number One. As they milled around, a tour bus arrived to transport them to a village seventy kilometers south in the mountains of neighboring Fuqiang County. An onlooker might have mistaken the group for tourists, but they had a more serious purpose. They were gathering for a school-sponsored pilgrimage to a prominent Daoist temple, Yongning, to pray for success in the "final battle." Because the state forbids schools from organizing religious activities, the pilgrimage was to be conducted in secret. It was nevertheless mandatory for senior-three head teachers, who were joined by the school's senior leadership, including the senior-three section leader, two of the three vice principals, and the principal himself.

The group had planned to conduct the prayer trip on the following day, Monday, which was an auspicious day, the fifteenth day of the lunar month. They had also intended to include a side trip to the Confucius Temple in Ningzhou. At the last minute, however, government officials requested the principal's attendance at a meeting. Thus the visit to Yongning, which was regarded as having real efficacy (*língyàn*), was rescheduled for Sunday. Then on Monday, while the principal was in his meeting, the teachers would make an unaccompanied trip to the Confucius Temple, which was deemed of secondary importance.

Despite being close to the school, the Confucius Temple receives relatively few visitors. The building lay derelict in the 1980s and 1990s while other temples in the city were being rebuilt. As elsewhere in China, most of the city's religious sites were defaced or destroyed in state-mobilized campaigns to wipe out so-called feudalistic superstition during the Cultural Revolution (1966–76 CE). But interest in popular religion has resurged in the reform era. In many places, temples again occupy an important place in local society (Chau 2006; Jing 1998). Since the 2000s, the central state has even attempted to capitalize on this revival, making tentative moves to resuscitate the status of Confucianism as a quasi-official ideology (Billioud and Thoraval 2015). Government officials have organized public rituals to honor the sage. Some cities, such as Quanzhou, have used Confucian temples to stage celebrations of first-place Gaokao examinees. In deference to official atheism, however, such occasions are framed—in public discourse, at least—as secular. State actors generally present their support of Confucianism as philosophical, even if many ordinary people regard the sage as a deity.

Hence the visit to the Confucius Temple could be interpreted in different ways. When the teachers laid a wreath of flowers at the statue of the sage on Monday, some observers might have seen it as a pious act and others as a nod to central-state ideology. This ambiguity helped to ensure that no accusations of superstition would follow from this relatively public occasion. The teachers themselves played down the significance of the visit.

In stark contrast, they saw their pilgrimage to Yongning as an utterly earnest event, the magical efficacy of which could exert real influence on exam results. Although the pilgrimage flagrantly flouted the official ban on religion in schools, no one worried that it would result in censure or punishment. The trip was conducted with the knowledge of municipal officials. Also, the temple was far from the city and the teachers would be literally lost in the crowd at Yongning, one of the most popular places of worship in the region.

Unlike the cult of Confucius, Yongning receives no central-state endorsement. But the temple attracts pilgrims from far and wide, including Taiwan and Hong Kong. In contrast to the historical neglect of the Confucius Temple, Yongning has remained active throughout living memory. Locals say that Yongning and other remote rural temples continued to receive visitors during the Cultural Revolution. Even if exaggerated, such reports testify to the devotion with which these places are regarded.

Of course, Yongning is not the only temple that people consider efficacious in the matter of exams. For example, the Ningzhou temple to the God of Examinations, Wenchang, bulges with pilgrims around exam time (figure 12). But school administrators favor Yongning. Its patron deity, the Yongning ancestral patriarch, is especially well known for performing miracles. The deity is considered so powerful that uttering the name is taboo. Speaking with reverence and awe, worshippers refer to pilgrimage only in oblique terms as "going to that place in Yongning."

FIGURE 12.   People of all ages praying for examination success. Worshippers gather for a ritual at the temple to the God of Examinations. Photograph by the author.

On the day of the pilgrimage, the weather was hot and humid, approaching one hundred degrees Fahrenheit. The teachers had been instructed to fast, and some felt lightheaded in the heat. Arriving at the base of the temple hill, they hiked up several flights of stone stairs, stopping to burn incense at some of the minor shrines on the path to the main temple.

As they climbed, the group passed evidence of the deity's potency. Row after row of names had been etched into the temple-complex walls, announcing the identity of donors who had given money to the temple to thank the god for answering their prayers. The main temple was old, but it was overtowered by a recently constructed statue of the ancestral patriarch, a giant edifice that dominated the adjacent mountain slope. Over a hundred feet tall, the bright golden edifice contained a large hall that was lined from floor to ceiling with countless rows of hardwood vestibules, each of which was occupied by a gold-leaf statuette purchased by a wealthy donor to repay the deity for answering prayers.

At the top of the last flight of stairs, the teachers approached the main temple, which overlooked the valley below. The space around the altar was packed with worshippers. So close to the Gaokao, many of them were parents, students, and teachers praying for success. Burning incense, they prostrated themselves before the deity's effigy, which was stained black from the smoke. After murmuring some prayers, they deposited the glowing sticks of incense in a giant bronze urn on the altar. Students, some in school uniform, took turns passing their clear plastic pencil cases over this smoldering vessel to infuse their examination implements with magical power. Other worshippers waited their turn to draw lots (*chōuqiān*), a mantic practice common at temples. Subvocalizing their questions to the deity, these supplicants held large cups of numbered bamboo strips between their outstretched palms. In a gesture of prayerful entreaty, each lot drawer shook his or her cup until one of the numbered bamboo strips slowly extended outward and fell to the ground. Seated at a nearby table, a bored-looking "master of interpreting lots" (*jiěqiān shīfu*)—a middle-aged villager—cross-referenced the numbers on these strips against a series of cryptic poems, which were printed on small slips of thin pink paper that he handed out to each supplicant. Widely understood to be speaking with the voice of the deity, the master decoded these messages with reference to worshippers' questions about the future, which at this time of the year mainly revolved around the big test.

The teachers had already made a trip to Yongning in early April to submit a wish (*xǔyuàn*) for success on the examination. On that earlier trip, teachers had blessed the test-admission certificates of students at the incense urn. Kowtowing in front of the patriarch's effigy, they had offered sacrifices (*gòngpǐn*) of fruit, snacks, and wads of spirit money (*shòujīn*)—colorful pieces of paper that worshippers present as offerings to deities and ancestors. Afterward, the teachers had burned the spirit money along with a list of names of their students, thus transmitting a request for their success to the spirit world. Teachers had used official class funds to purchase the candies and crackers to be offered to the deity and, in some cases, taken up individual donations of two Chinese yuan (about twenty-five cents) per student so that the small minority of Christians could elect not to participate. After returning to the high school, the head teachers had distributed these sacrificial goods to the examinees, who ingested them to receive the protection (*bǎoyòu*) of the patriarch. For a small donation to the temple, teachers had also acquired protective wards—small pieces of red paper inscribed with magical glyphs—which they affixed above the inside of the main door to their classrooms. Unnoticed by the uninitiated, these wards form an inconspicuous but incongruous addition to classroom décor, which is otherwise exclusively dedicated to two messages—encouragement of students in their diligent study and praise for the Communist Party.

Now, a few days before the test, the teachers were conducting a pious renewal of their original request for examination success. As is typical of such occasions, this petition involved the promise to return to the temple after the deity had granted the request—a practice known as repaying the wish (*huányuàn*). The school planned to undertake this third trip to the temple in July after students received their Gaokao scores.

Ningzhou Number One is not the only high school to organize pilgrimages to religious sites. Much anecdotal evidence suggests that school-sponsored prayer trips—to Yongning and other temples—are common in southeastern China. Not every school, however, conducts them. As I outline below, their occurrence conforms to a clear geographical pattern. In my field sites, only rural schools and high-ranking urban schools generally sponsor pilgrimages.

At schools that undertake temple visits, they could be characterized as an open secret. Parents and students are aware of their existence. But at schools that do not organize them, people express incredulity that teachers would so blatantly contravene the principle of official atheism. As one Dragon Gate teacher told me, it would be impossible for schools to conduct prayer trips. Such activities would "violate the fundamental principles of education for quality," which, she said, include the obligation to inculcate students with a reverence for science and to inoculate them against feudalistic superstitions (*fēngjiàn míxìn*). "Obviously," she said, "praying for examination success would work against both purposes." As the Dragon Gate school counselor, Ms. Fu, told me, it was definitely illegal for teachers to encourage students in any religious belief, although she privately admitted that Yongning Temple was quite potent.

This testimony provides a demonstration of how backstage prayer clashes with frontstage secularism within high schools. High schools where prayer is not conducted seem to play a frontstage foil to high schools where it is. This sharp disparity is embarrassing to those in the know, constituting a form of cultural intimacy that cannot be easily shared with strangers (Herzfeld 2005). As people say, "Family scandals should not be revealed to outsiders" (*jiāchǒu bù kě wài chuán*).

I was in my field sites for nearly a year before I learned about school-sponsored prayer. When I asked insiders about it, they would often react with surprise that a foreigner could be aware of such things. A frequent response was "Yes, we do that. But who told you?" When I began my fieldwork, schools had appeared to be disenchanted places, devoid of religion and supernatural beliefs, but as I gradually learned, they are suffused with magic.

On the side of the Mountain County Number One courtyard, there is an awkwardly located banyan tree, which I initially saw merely as a sign of poor planning. As an administrator eventually divulged, however, no principal would dare remove the tree for fear of angering its resident spirit. An angry banyan god could be catastrophic for test scores. As time went on, I began to observe many other magical beliefs, including a ubiquitous obsession among students with luck and karmic merit or, as they called it, "earning character" (*zǎn rénpǐn*). But I did not see the magical protective glyph papers above every senior-three classroom door—evidence of school-sponsored pilgrimages—until a close friend pointed them out to me.

In retrospect, I should perhaps not have been so surprised to find such supernatural beliefs at high schools. The Gaokao is a magnet for magic. The activities that I describe above form only a small part of an extensive range of popular-religious practices that surround the examination both inside and beyond the school gates, including divination, prayer, possession, and exorcism, along with various test-day superstitions. But why are magic and religion so important in the Gaokao? And how does magical thinking square with the hyperrationalism of meritocracy? The objective and scientific operation of the exam seems out of joint with this pervasive obsession with luck and fate.

A comparative perspective offers an initial approach to this question. The use of magic during fateful rites of passage appears to be common among humans in general. Cross-culturally, many specialists in fateful action employ magic in their attempts to ward off bad luck and ensure a good outcome, including soldiers (Stouffer 1949), fishers (Malinowski 1935), baseball players (Gmelch 1978), gamblers (Lindner 1950), stock market investors (Lepori 2009), candidates for high office (Geshiere 2003), and even astronauts (O'Callaghan 2015). People do not employ magic lightly but reserve it for truly fateful situations. As Malinowski (1948, 32) observes, for example, the Trobriand Islanders require the performance of magic for open-sea fishing but not for lagoon fishing. The former represents a highly uncertain, high-stakes enterprise; the latter a more day-to-day occurrence.

In China, people resort to magic and prayer not only in exams but also in many of life's fateful moments. An inventory of such events can be tabulated by observing the range of reasons that people go to temples. When worshippers draw lots, temple minders normally dispense standardized prognostications, which are based on stock responses for each type of situation in which people typically seek divine assistance (figure 13). These categories usually include love, illness, family feuds, business decisions, and, of course, examinations. But in the range of fateful moments that an individual can face, few are of greater consequence than the Gaokao.

Here, however, lurks a paradox. These expressions of popular-religious belief not only contradict the public commitment of Chinese educational institutions to official state secularism, they also go against the emphasis in high schools on orthodox social reciprocity—the notion that diligence and good attitude alone account for success. In contrast to this orthodox interpretation of reciprocity, such religious activities incorporate the belief that transcendental cosmic forces such as fate and luck partly account for individual fortunes. "Heaven rewards

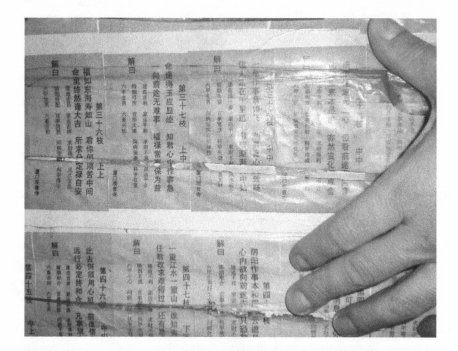

FIGURE 13. A catalog of lots at a temple to Guanyin, the Bodhisattva of Mercy. Each slip, which corresponds to the number of a lot, contains a few words of prophesy ("auspicious," "inauspicious," etc.) for the typical situations in which worshippers seek divine assistance. The slips are either handed to or read to worshippers. Photograph by the author.

hard work," as the saying goes, but apparently also more hidden virtues. Thus, although teachers frequently remind students that they must be masters of their own fate, the participation of teachers in school prayer represents a de facto concession that merit, as orthodoxly conceived, cannot by itself determine the outcome of the exam and thus of students' lives.

These cultural arrangements draw attention to an awkward fact. Despite widespread belief in meritocracy, people do not always experience one of its core tenets—orthodox social reciprocity—as fully persuasive. For one thing, they observe that random events like weather or guesswork can have fateful effects on test day and thus on life outcomes. For another, they note that relatively immutable aspects of personhood such as place of origin, class, gender, and ethnicity greatly influence educational outcomes. For these reasons, people understand that the result of the exam is not only determined by interpersonal competition on test day, ruled by what I term agonistic uncertainty (see chapter 1). It is also contingent on random occurrences and accidents of birth, or aleatory

uncertainty; that is, happenings outside individual control. To square this contradiction, people supplement orthodox social reciprocity with cosmic reciprocity. They attribute to luck and fate that which cannot be explained by diligence,
persistence, and composure alone. But in so doing, they tend to conflate two
types of phenomena that are analytically distinct. The accidents of social life that
precede the exam are not really aleatory in the same sense that happenstance
incidents that occur within the exam are. Although accidents of birth may not be
within individual control, they are part of social life. In a broader sense, therefore,
these accidents reflect the results of a competition that transcends the individual—
social competition. Thus, these accidents are also the result of agonistic uncertainty, although the timeframe for this competition far exceeds the scope of
any individual exam experience. But in attributing both random events and
the facts of personhood to luck and fate, people credit transcendental forces
with contingencies that are, in part, humanly (that is, socially) produced. In so
doing, they make social inequality appear as the natural and inevitable product
of fate.

Cosmic and orthodox reciprocity present different explanatory models
or cosmological frames for interpreting events (Goffman 1974). The former
is magico-religious and supernatural, the latter quotidian and scientific. But
despite this important difference, both conceptions of reciprocity follow similar
cultural logics of cause and effect. In both frames, people view success as a reward
for merit. In contrast to cosmic reciprocity, however, orthodox social reciprocity
restricts the definition of merit to individual diligence and character. This kind
of reciprocity follows the formula that "diligent efforts will be repaid with success" (fùchū de nǔlì yǒu huíbào). Cosmic reciprocity, on the other hand, expands
the spatial and temporal horizon of reciprocity to include the accumulation of
karmic merit (gōngdé) or secret virtue (yīndé). According to this view, good or
bad deeds in one domain of life can exert a fateful influence on other domains.
By "doing good to accumulate merit" (xíngshàn jīdé), one can acquire good luck,
thus tipping the scales of karmic justice: "Good repays good and evil repays evil"
(shàn yǒu shànbào, è yǒu èbào). Because people widely subscribe to a belief in
reincarnation, moreover, they understand cosmic reciprocity to incorporate
one's deeds in past lives. Finally, this conception of reciprocity extends beyond
the individual person to include the deeds of one's ancestors. In sum, as people
say, "no deed ever goes unreciprocated; it is merely that the time has not arrived"
(bù shì bù bào, shíhou wèi dào).

Chinese popular religion is multifarious, incorporating a wide variety of practices. But the belief in cosmic reciprocity is a fundamental if not the fundamental
commonality that unites them (Brokaw 1991). Few people can be found who,
in an unguarded moment, will not profess some theory of influencing luck and

changing fortune. This belief in cosmic reciprocity betrays the inherent lack or emptiness in the myth of meritocracy. Like other forms of rational, calculating apparatus, the exam cannot account for the singularity of each human existence (Derrida 1989). Although the exam presents itself as an objective, scientific form of selection, it actually represents a hegemonic negotiation of particular social interests. This contradiction results in a gap between ideal and reality—a gap that is simultaneously personal and social. The gnawing awareness of this incoherence produces tremendous anxiety, which magical beliefs help to salve.

Anxiety is not a side effect of meritocracy; it is integral to its functioning. Diligent exam preparation alone is not enough to sustain the myth of meritocracy. Restoring the appearance of coherence to the scales of reciprocity requires an additional form of labor: the magical labor of divination, pilgrimage, prayer, and the endless examination postmortems, in which fate and luck inevitably play an important role. These labors are not secondary or superficial to the exam experience. Indeed, the construction of fate through the examination forms a crux of its cultural meaning. The examination system is an engine for producing fate.

Cosmic reciprocity helps people come to terms with, or recognize, fate. Thus it might appear as if cosmic reciprocity merely works to shore up the ideology of individual merit and to stabilize the cultural gyroscope of the examination. At the same time, however, popular beliefs in fate and luck are a double-edged sword for those in power. They introduce a potential source of instability in social arrangements. By pointing toward the constitutive incoherence of the myth of meritocracy, these beliefs expand the scope for human agency. They provide people with openings for individual and social change.

Blending Cosmic and Orthodox Reciprocity
A Continuum of Magico-Religious Practices

Chinese popular religion draws from and overlaps with institutional religions like Buddhism and Daoism (and to a certain degree Christianity). But unlike these religions, it is diffused through a broad range of social contexts and institutions (family, workplace, schools, and so on) rather than being located in a single institutional locus, such as the church (C. K. Yang 1967). Whereas institutional religions are associated with high culture (the Great Tradition), popular religion incorporates popular culture (the Little Tradition), especially the legendary tales originally recorded in Ming-era (1368–1644 CE) vernacular novels such as *Investiture of the Gods*, *Three Kingdoms*, and *Journey to the West*. But the distinction between high and popular is contested. In everyday life, these two labels form the end points of a complex continuum of practices; moreover, the same person may oscillate between these different understandings of religion depending on the context (Sangren 2000).

Following this flexible approach, people in China tend to draw few sharp boundaries between magic and religion. They see all magico-religious practices as adhering to a common supernatural frame governed by the laws of cosmic reciprocity. Practices that people in other cultural contexts might label as magical, such as divination, are integrated seamlessly with the worship of deities.

Most believers see no conflict between mainstream or orthodox religious practices, such as prayer or the reading of scriptures, and what the state calls "heterodox" (*xié*) forms of communion with the spirit world like possession by ancestors or the appearance of omens in dreams. Indeed, spirit mediums are a regular fixture at many Chinese temples, and many ritualists, such as the masters of interpreting lots, mentioned above, understand themselves to be animating the voices of deities. By the same token, Buddhist and Daoist temples host solemn religious ceremonies even as they vend magical protective amulets and talismans. At the temple to the God of Examinations, for instance, visitors can, for a small donation, receive a lucky necklace or pen. Of course, some relatively pious adherents of institutional religion might consider such apotropaic talismans, along with mantic practices such as drawing lots, antithetical to the true teachings of scripture. But few ordinary people make such distinctions. Hence pious worship is regularly combined with what many might consider to be lowbrow forms of magic, if not superstition. This close association of religious and magical practices produces a demand for entrepreneurial ritualists who make a living on the fringes of orthodox religious life. After praying devoutly at a temple, worshippers frequently visit the fortunetellers who congregate outside many such places.

As a result of these arrangements, many who do not believe in any institutional religion nevertheless follow popular magico-religious practices. For example, many worshippers at the temple to the God of Examinations do not know whether the temple is Daoist or Buddhist, nor do they much care. Instead, as one middle-aged woman put it, they merely "jump on the bandwagon" (*gēnfēng*), glad to achieve any potential advantage for their children by any means possible. Such worshippers see prayer as a form of insurance policy. They say that one can never really know if the gods are real; thus, they reason, it is better to pray than not to pray.

To some degree, such agnosticism testifies to the decline of popular religion in mainland China. Under Communist Party rule, the popular religion underwent severe retrenchment—especially during the campaigns of the Cultural Revolution. In the Mao era, all religion was considered superstitious and thus subject to extirpation. In contemporary China, by contrast, people nominally enjoy freedom of religion, though in practice followers of institutional religion must submit to close supervision by the state. Although some ardent atheists continue to denigrate religion as superstition, in general people only use this term to describe popular-religious practices. But despite the slight air of disreputableness that surrounds the belief in cosmic reciprocity, it remains extremely common. Even many self-described skeptics, who purport to subscribe only to science, possess theories about how to influence luck.

Thus the degree of cultural loss is not as great as many think. The area of my field sites, southeastern China, has experienced a particularly strong resurgence of popular religion. Referring to the prevalence of superstitious beliefs in this region, migrants from other areas characterize this part of China as highly feudalistic. They marvel at how, for example, on the evening of the ninth day of the lunar new year the balconies of houses all over Ningzhou City light up as families burn carefully folded paper-money wheels in sacrifice to the Heavenly Emperor (*Tiāngōng*)—the patriarch of the Chinese pantheon of popular gods. Many families pray at temples and attend religious events, such as temple parades and rituals to banish evil influences, or exorcisms (*xiāozāi*). These public forms of worship are integrated into a regimen of household sacrifice to domestic deities and ancestors. Though they may be waning with increasing urbanization, these practices have been handed down and adapted to changing circumstances for hundreds of years and remain relatively vibrant in Fujian.

The Mixing of Orthodox and Popular Frames: Audits of Virtue and Karmic Bonus Points

The distinction between science (*kēxué*) and superstition (*míxìn*) became popularized in the aftermath of the self-strengthening (1861–95 CE) and May Fourth movements (1915–21 CE), when the country's elites fervently searched Western knowledge for solutions to society's problems (Duara 1995; Kwok 1965). These movements produced many new intellectual currents, including Chinese Marxism, which remains, in name at least, the official ideology of China. According to this ideology, which many scholars would consider a vulgar interpretation of Marxism, science is part of the rational material base of society whereas superstition is an irrational superstructure that must be vanquished through modernization.

Although science and superstition are relatively new, the contrast between rational and irrational beliefs is not. For one thing, China has its own scientific tradition, which for centuries surpassed that of Europe in many areas of technological achievement (Elman 2005). For another, the tension between the rational and irrational seems to have constituted an important aspect of Chinese cultural life long before the twentieth century. Since at least Song times (960–1279), the Chinese state has relied on a highly rationalized bureaucracy and market economy (see chapter 1). And as part of this culture of bureaucratic rationality, people have long drawn a distinction between orthodox and popular views of merit.

Orthodox currents of thought about merit can be traced through the Confucian writings of Mencius (372–289 BCE) and Neo-Confucian reinterpretations by Zhu Xi (1130–1200 CE) (Brokaw 1991). According to this thinking, human beings are endowed by Heaven with a fundamentally good nature or "pattern" (*lǐ*). To reach perfection, however, they must strive to overcome the conflicts inherent in their "material energy," or *qi*. This orthodox Confucian logic generally eschews notions of karma and reincarnation, focusing instead on the moral duty of all individuals to cultivate their fundamental goodness.

Whereas this orthodox Confucian view sees human nature as intrinsically good, the popular view of merit seems closer to alternative currents of Chinese thought, such as Mohist or Legalist philosophies, which stress the necessity of behavioral correctives and the vigilant avoidance of evil (Brokaw 1991). In the popular understanding, everyone's merit is judged by a pantheon of anthropomorphized god-bureaucrats, which is ruled by the supreme deity, the Heavenly Emperor. These god-bureaucrats tabulate and calculate every person's individual and family merit in this and past lives. To complete this task, they rely on communicating with spirits resident in the family (the kitchen god, for instance) and even in the body (the three worms, *sānchóng*). Just as human bureaucrats may be liable to graft and corruption, these spirits are sometimes petty and mean. On the whole, however, their panoptic view of human affairs enables them to make fair decisions on the allotment of individual success by assessing the secret virtue of every person.

Orthodox and popular conceptions of merit exhibit a clear contrast. The orthodox view restricts the agency of individuals to earnest and sincere self-cultivation. Within the ambit of this self-cultivation, however, they have perfect control over, and thus complete responsibility for, their lives. By contrast, the popular tradition gives people more scope for action. According to the popular logic, individuals have the power to affect fate by performing meritorious acts, thus tipping the scales of secret virtue in their favor. Paradoxically, however, the popular view of fate also attributes human success or failure to factors beyond individual control, such as the merit of ancestors, whereas the orthodox view of fate focuses exclusively on individuals' self-cultivation in the here and now.

The imperial-era tension between orthodox and popular views of merit closely resembles the contemporary tension between orthodox and cosmic reciprocity. In many respects, the former constitutes a close genealogical antecedent to the latter. As with the distinction between the Greater Tradition and the Lesser Tradition, however, these divisions should be understood as heuristic or ideal-typical. People tend to blend orthodox and cosmic accounts. For example, their approach to accounting for secret virtue may be highly rationalistic even when more orthodox thinkers brand it as irrational. Nevertheless, people themselves continue to make sharp distinctions between orthodox and popular accounts though these distinctions are in reality always contested and fuzzy.

Many examples can be provided to illustrate these cultural dynamics. The popularity of ledgers of merit in imperial times is a good starting point (Brokaw 1991). Resembling Benjamin Franklin's famous diary of virtue, these ledgers were moral account books that people used to tabulate and quantify good deeds, which were awarded scores according to a predetermined point system. The use of ledgers was neither isolated nor short lived. The phenomenon can be traced from medieval (that is, pre-Song) times, though it became popular during the Qing dynasty (1644–1911 CE). People saw ledgers as a way of achieving control over destiny. One particularly popular example of the genre was called "Determining Your Own Fate" (*Lì mìng piān*). Brokaw (1991) notes how these imperial-era audits of virtue blended popular obsessions with secret merit and orthodox concerns for individual self-cultivation. But orthodox Confucians generally looked down their nose at such practices. Ledgers combined popular and Confucian approaches in a way that orthodox thinkers tolerated but did not wholeheartedly embrace.

In the contemporary era, the Chinese Communist Party continued this tradition of tabulating merit by in its campaigns of political education. Registers of merit and demerit (*gōnggùbù*) encouraged people to self-create themselves by letting "merits . . . wash away demerits" (Brokaw 1991, n140). Similarly, the work-point system of collectivized agriculture awarded people for diligence and docked them for laziness and other sins, perceived or real. In the present, such concerns with quantifying merit are sustained in ubiquitous efforts to record and audit the quality of students, along with various other measurements of morality. A particularly chilling example of this phenomenon is the experimentation since the mid-2010s in many Chinese cities with a social credit system, in which each citizen is rated on their public morality with the assistance of facial recognition and artificial intelligence systems.[1] This system represents merely the most recent, if relatively Orwellian, manifestation of a long-standing cultural fascination in China with auditing human virtue. Although the merit that is recorded in such audits of virtue may not, on its face, be secret, the transitivity with which people understand merit in one domain of life to reflect on merit in another accords with popular, cosmic notions of reciprocity even as it brings to bear a calculating rationality on phenomena that are not easily quantified.

If the ledgers of merit represent a fusion of the orthodox and popular cosmological frames, other practices demonstrate the ability of people to shift from one frame to another depending on the context. After writing an examination essay on the niceties of orthodox Confucian philosophy, an imperial-era examinee could consult one of the many fortune tellers who tended to congregate outside examination halls (Elman 2000). As their demand for divination illustrates, many of these good Confucians were far from immune to popular beliefs. A wide range of imperial-era literature describes the supernatural obsessions of scholars, who frequently attributed success or failure in the exams to the influence of ghosts and karmic merit (Elman 2000; Miyazaki 1981). A favorite subject of such literature is the interpretation of dreams. The success of many a first-place examinee was said to be foretold in prescient visions.

In the present, too, the discursive clarity with which people draw the distinction between orthodox and cosmic reciprocity belies the syncretism of their practice, which frequently mixes the two frames. The policy of awarding extra points on the Gaokao to the sons and daughters of military veterans and martyrs is one example. Superficially, this practice might be understood as a form of affirmative action. However, it does not compensate awardees for a disadvantage but rather awards them for the merit of their parents. Such policies acknowledge the state's debt to the progeny of virtuous ancestors, which is tantamount to acknowledging the heritability of ancestral merit.

Frontstage and Backstage Cosmological Frames: Playing by the Chart

From the perspective of orthodox Marxist party-state rhetoric, the magico-religious frame of cosmic reciprocity continues to be regarded as a feudal superstition that must be surmounted as China develops toward the telos of modernity (see chapter 2). In schools, therefore, the eradication of superstition and promotion of science remains an important mission. As the frontline bureaucrats who are tasked with this mission, teachers must submit students to regular quality evaluations, though probably few are aware of the ironic genealogical linkage of such audits to imperial-era popular-religious ledgers of virtue. In these evaluations, teachers are supposed to rate students on their eschewal of superstitious belief. But because many teachers themselves are superstitious, they approach this task with ambivalence. Insofar as they judge students on their beliefs, this judgment mainly concerns the ability of students to suppress those beliefs appropriately by paying proper lip service in frontstage contexts to the orthodox rhetoric of secular modernity. In everyday high-school life, however, teachers in my field sites do not usually resort to the pejorative expression "superstition" to sanction inappropriate discussion of cosmic reciprocity in frontstage settings. Instead, they tend to prefer less muscular expressions of disapproval. For example, teachers may refer to such transgressions as "not playing by the chart" (bù kàopǔ), a relatively anodyne, jocular phrase that can refer broadly to any public expression of unorthodox sentiment.

In frontstage contexts, teachers reconcile prayer with atheism by offering scientific explanations for religious belief. They typically speak of worship as representing a "psychological comfort" to themselves and their students. This framing puts religious activity in psychological terms, providing everyone with a sanitized view that is acceptable in public situations. When further pressed to account for the efficacy of prayer, some teachers will employ one of a variety of closely related phrases that people commonly use to explain religious belief, such as "If your heart is sincere, then your prayer will be effective" (xīn chéng zé líng) or "If you believe, then your prayer will be effective" (xìn zé líng). Like the explanation of psychological comfort, such idioms encompass religion within the frame of natural-scientific explanation, suggesting that mind-over-body theories might help account for the effectiveness of religious belief. Unlike psychological comfort, however, the latter type of account ("if you believe, your prayer will be effective") incorporates a strong vein of agnosticism. This type of explanation is more often uttered by people who themselves genuinely believe in the effectiveness of deities, but prefer not to give voice to that belief. The agnostic view serves more as a sop to the skeptics than as a rebuttal to piety.

Both types of framing—the scientific and the agnostic—are compatible with presenting religious activities in pragmatic terms. According to the logic of these orthodox frames, religious activity serves as a mechanism for improving students' attitudes, helping them cope with examination pressure (see chapter 5). In adopting this view, people are close to the position of William James ([1902] 2002), the influential pragmatist philosopher, psychologist, and sociologist of religion who famously suggests that researchers bracket out the question of the existence of supernatural powers to focus on the psychological effects of religious belief. If asked about the efficacy of prayer, administrators and officials similarly choose not to debate the reality of the spirit world.

Privately, however, many teachers concede that they believe in the gods. One participant in the pilgrimage to Yongning, Ms. Ma, recounted praying to the local deities in her small town throughout her high-school and college years for academic success. She not only sacrificed to them but engaged them in continuous dialog, frequently saying prayers as she lay awake at night worrying about her studies.

As a result of this pious belief, Ms. Ma, like other pilgrimage participants, saw the mere act of praying to the Yongning ancestral patriarch to be a fateful event, one in which ritual missteps could have disastrous consequences for students' examination outcomes. For example, Ms. Ma fretted about having to visit the temple during her menses, which is considered ritually polluting (Seaman 1981). When the exam results of her class came out in July, she worried that the substandard performance of many of her students, including that of the police detective's daughter, Yuqing (see chapter 5), could be attributed to this ritual transgression. But she also expressed frustration about the double bind that such pollution taboos impose on women. If she had not prayed to the deity, it might have been angered; moreover, avoiding the pilgrimage would have been impossible, given that the event was mandatory for all senior-three head teachers.

Religious activities can have contradictory effects. On one hand, they provide people with comfort. On the other, they expand the sphere of fatefulness surrounding the examination to include activities that may seem only remotely related to the moment of the examination.

Balancing Ritual Efficacy with the Exigencies of Impression Management

The necessity to pay obeisance to school atheism in official contexts results in many contortions of impression management. People constantly strive to balance frontstage secularism with backstage belief. The incident of the missing door—famous at Ningzhou Number One—is a case in point.

A few weeks before the examination, some classmates at the school bought lottery tickets together, reasoning that their failure to win the lottery would help them succeed on the examination by tipping the scales of merit in their favor. They pasted these lottery tickets on the back of a classroom door, an addition to the class décor that their head teacher initially tolerated. But a vice principal noticed this unorthodox decoration and ordered the students to remove the tickets. Students complied by following the vice principal's instructions in fact but not in spirit—a form of strategic response that Chinese sometimes refer to as hitting an edge ball (see chapter 3). Instead of removing the tickets, the students removed the whole door, swapping it for another one that they found in a school attic. Their old classroom door then became a secret backstage shrine. In this way, the classroom was purified of this public display of not playing by the charts. Conspicuously, however, the vice principal did not ask this head teacher to remove the magical glyph from Yongning hanging over her door, which was de rigueur in all senior-three classrooms. The school's rejection of one magical display and endorsement of the other can be reconciled by recognizing that the glyph was both highly inconspicuous and deemed to be genuinely effective.

Another anecdote sheds further light on the politics of backstage belief. When a student committed suicide at one rural high school, the administration closed the school for a day so that a Daoist ritual specialist could be called in to conduct an exorcism. School administrators worried that the deceased student's spirit would contaminate other students, resulting in a negative influence on their examination performance. But any public announcement of these religious activities would seriously violate the principles of official secularism. In response to this dilemma, administrators settled on an ingenious approach. They conducted the exorcism under the guise of disinfecting the school following a flu outbreak—a fabrication that presumably suggested itself because of the close metaphorical association between spiritual and biological forms of contagion.

This last anecdote raises the question of how people perceive the relationship between magical and scientific frames of explanation. Usually, science is identified with the backstage efficacy of getting real work done. According to this cultural logic, science forms the opposite of the humanities, which are associated with the frontstage performance of orthodox rhetoric (see chapter 4). But in the case of the flu outbreak, science formed an acceptable frontstage packaging for the backstage reality of religious practice. In the backstage, the magic of exorcism overrode all scientific explanations.

This apparent contradiction between magic and science dissolves with recognition that people see the two domains as sharing a common concern with efficacious technique (Mauss [1902] 2006). The move from frontstage to backstage merely involves a shift in perspective on the primacy of science. In the frontstage, science is presented as transcending or encompassing the magico-religious domain, which is reduced to a psychological comfort. In the backstage, by contrast, religion is conceived as encompassing science and forming its transcendental container.

Geographical Variation in Pilgrimage Activities

The division between frontstage secularism and backstage belief is not merely internal to high schools. The rural-urban continuum—or, more accurately, the score-value hierarchy (see chapter 2)—is itself divided into a frontstage and backstage. In all points along the rural-urban hierarchy, schools conduct pilgrimages. But only in rural areas do non-elite high schools organize them. For example, all high schools in Mountain County "go to that place in Yongning," whereas few ordinary high schools in Ningzhou and, in particular, Xiamen embrace such religious practices. Surprisingly, however, high-ranking schools in Xiamen do conduct school-sponsored pilgrimages.

What accounts for this pattern of variation? Certainly, popular-religious belief is generally more common and widespread in rural places than it is in urban places, which contributes to rural places being perceived as feudalistic and traditional (see chapter 2). But if it were only a matter of rural-urban difference, all urban schools would avoid religious activities. The answer lies in just how important exam performance is to officialdom; in places where securing admission for students to top-ranking colleges influences official promotion, one tends to see backstage prayer.

In candid moments, many administrators and officials will admit to seeing education at ordinary low-ranking schools as mainly fulfilling a formulaic or ritualistic purpose. They say students at these schools should be made to feel that their examination performance matters, but in reality, it is relatively inconsequential in the grander scheme of things. Rather than producing high scores, a central purpose of such schools is to give the common people hope (see chapter 3).

At ordinary urban schools, recruiting students to believe in the myth of meritocracy supersedes the imperative that they excel on the examination. Granted, the principal and teachers at such low-ranking institutions can contribute to their own reputation and to that of their higher-ups through improving the examination performance of students. But the vast disparities in college admission rates along the score-value hierarchy ensure that no students at bad schools will do well enough on the examination to raise the reputation of the region as a whole. Not a single student from Dragon Gate has ever tested into Tsinghua or Peking University. Officials generally expect such schools to demonstrate only modest test score improvements on par with the general annual increase in college admission rates. As one Dragon Gate principal put it, his main goal lies in "displaying" (*zhǎnshì*) achievements in education for quality. Because the examination performance of such institutions is relatively inconsequential, the decision about whether or not to pray for examination success does not ordinarily rise to the level of an institutional imperative.

In a word, exam scores at low-ranking urban schools may be fateful to individual examinees and teachers, but not to officialdom or to the locality as a whole. Much as Trobriand Islanders do not require magic for lagoon fishing, the stakes of the Gaokao at low-ranking schools are generally too modest to compel them to seek divine intervention.

In rural and high-ranking urban schools, by contrast, educational authorities tacitly condone and in some cases encourage or even participate in official school pilgrimages. In the case of elite urban high schools, the exam performance of these schools is highly consequential not only to teachers and administrators but also to local officials. The reputation of educational officials is closely tied with the ability of these institutions to secure admission for their students to top colleges. In addition, the great prestige of administrators at high-ranking schools provides them with some immunization against the exigencies of paying obeisance to official secular ideology.

In rural areas, schools conduct pilgrimages for related but slightly differing reasons. As in centrally located places, examination success is highly consequential to the reputation of administrators and officials. But even low-ranking schools in rural areas are known to sponsor religious pilgrimages. The remoteness of these schools from central authorities partly protects them against the necessity to perform adherence to the tenets of education for quality. Not only is religious belief more common in rural places but "heaven is high and the emperor is far away" (see chapter 2).

Exams as Engines of Fatefulness: The Futility of Scientific Examination

This pragmatic attitude of teachers and administrators toward religion derives from a practical problem—the inability of orthodox reciprocity to offer a satisfactory account of exam performance. Students and teachers frequently complain about the chanciness of the examination, bemoaning the vicissitudes of weather, health, exam questions, guesswork, and seating arrangement (for example, being too close to a noisy or distracting neighbor). And much to the consternation of test researchers (many of whom seem to be in denial of this fact), head teachers report that it is ordinary for the scores of students to fluctuate by as much as twenty points or more even without such catastrophic occurrences as accidents, illness, sleeplessness, and so on (see chapter 1).

To combat these instabilities, the designers and organizers of the test are always in search of ways to create a more scientific assessment. For example, they attempt to balance the assessment of quality with the promotion of fairness and strive to homogenize the experience of examinees from school to school (see chapter 4). In practice, however, pursuing these goals poses many challenges. Consider the problem of the weather. During the Gaokao, the heat can be scorching, which has a significant effect on performance (Zivin et al. 2018). But not all schools have air conditioning. In many places, educational authorities pay lip service to fairness by saying that they require all schools in their jurisdiction to renounce climate control during the test if some lack this convenience. In practice, however, those schools that have air conditioners generally either just turn them on or hit an edge ball by cooling the examination hall before the exam.

Thus these attempts to create a scientific exam appear quixotic, if not misguided, on at least two fronts. For one thing, although it is surely noble to strive for impartiality, the exam—the result of a hegemonic negotiation—is inevitably biased toward certain social groups and thus can never be completely fair. For another, happenstance and random factors are an intrinsic part of fateful events. It is impossible to completely purge the aleatory from the Gaokao or, for

that matter, any fateful rite of passage. Not matter how frantically test designers try to remove all random factors from the test, they will always intrude on
the exam from the outside, if in no other fashion than through the accidents of
birth. In short, a perfectly scientific exam will never be found that can produce
an ideal measure of individual merit, as orthodoxically conceived. Unavoidably,
test takers will always have to appeal to the more encompassing frame of cosmic
reciprocity.

The efforts of examination researchers to create a more scientific examination
likewise appear naïve from another perspective. Far from being an extraneous or
inessential component of the examination's functioning, the aleatory component
of the examination enables people to suppose that it speaks for a higher power.
In using fate to account for failure or success, people infuse the whole experience
with transcendental authority. In this context, it is useful to recall that the exam's
main significance to people lies in how they see it as an opportunity to change
fate. As I note above, people identify fate with relatively immutable aspects of
personhood such as gender, place of origin, and family background—in short,
one's position in the social division of labor. Through competing in the exam,
people are striving to change their place in that division. But in so doing they also
produce fate as a causal explanation and force in their lives.

It is a short step from ascribing happenstance to the vicissitudes of fate to
accounting for one's place in the division of labor through fate. Analytically, these
two usages of fate are distinct. The former refers to random events, the latter
to arbitrary social relations, which reflect the results of cultural and historical
processes, including the social competition for scarce resources. But these two
aspects of the aleatory are rendered indistinguishable when people attribute
them both to a common transcendental cause.

The Lottery of College Selection, or
Tendering One's Aspiration

Test designers pay much obeisance to the ideal of designing a scientific assessment. However, not every aspect of the examination system has been arranged
to minimize its aleatory dimension. Much as a contradiction exists in the United
States between the ideal of political democracy and the byzantine reality of an
imperfect electoral system, a contradiction exists in China between the ideal of
selection by merit and the actual complexities of the college-selection process.

Bookstores in China usually dedicate a whole section to college-selection
guidebooks, and many high schools hold informational assemblies for parents
to help them navigate the process. But schools are generally more concerned
with their own reputations than with helping students fulfill their educational

and professional goals. Thus the advice that schools give to families frequently centers on ensuring that as many students as possible gain admission to first-tier colleges, because the rate of first-tier admissions forms the central metric by which schools are judged.

Following the Gaokao, students wait anxiously for three weeks before receiving their score. Afterward, they have two weeks to submit a ranked list of colleges and courses of study to which they seek admission—a process known as tendering one's aspiration (*tiánbào zhìyuàn*). Students' college and major are assigned to them through an opaque, backstage process that, from the perspective of the individual, appears extremely chancy.[2] These arrangements mean that students have relatively little control over this major decision, which has life-altering consequences. After starting college, it may be possible to change one's course of study, but this process is usually complicated and difficult.

For these reasons, tendering one's aspiration is widely compared to gambling. Like card players trying to make the most out of a hand, families employ various strategies to maximize their odds of achieving their desired result. And as in cards, the outcome is ultimately beyond their control. Until the 2000s, the college-selection process was even chancier for students, because they were required to tender their aspirations before receiving their Gaokao scores. This system has now been reformed, but people still see college selection as capricious and risky.

Parents routinely seek the advice of head teachers on college selection, but many head teachers, though they are presumed to be authorities, know little more about the process than well-informed parents. For these reasons, tendering one's aspiration creates an added layer of pitfalls for families with cultural-capital deficits. Just as US students who lack access to guidance counselors often pursue misguided college-selection strategies, Chinese families who have little understanding about the admissions process find themselves at a distinct disadvantage.

Not only is the process of tendering aspirations fraught with chanciness; it is also structured, almost as if by design, to increase the subordination of children to their elders. Parents dominate the college-selection process. The wishes of students—to the degree that they have any definite wishes—play only a secondary role. At this stage in their careers, the young scholars have been studying more or less nonstop for twelve years, but they have had little preparation for the moment of using their Gaokao score to determine their destinies. At the time of my field-work, they had been encouraged to develop their testing capacities as evenly as possible in all subjects, because a so-called bias toward one subject or another results in lowered test performance. As a result, they had little opportunity to cultivate their interests. But even after the recent round of reforms, teachers report that many students often select their subjects based on ease of study or strategic considerations rather than on any attraction. And as one student said, "Before the Gaokao, there is no time to think about the future; you have to put your whole heart into study." Moreover, having just completed the final battle, they are physically and emotionally exhausted, and many are plagued by anxiety as they await their final scores. Generally they are in no emotional state to think about the future. When they finally receive their scores, they must make a decision within two weeks. For all these reasons, parents usually decide for their children, often with fairly minimal consultation.

Despite the best preparations of parents, however, the result of the college-selection process lies largely outside their control. Depending on how the process pans out, a student may have to adapt to widely varying destinies. More and more universities are giving students some flexibility to change their majors, but this flexibility is far from absolute. For many, therefore, adjusting to their major incorporates a great measure of coming to terms with fate. Almost as if by design, the process of tendering one's aspiration heightens the uncertainty of the Gaokao selection process, making it an even more powerful engine for producing a belief in fate.

In this context, it is useful to note the resemblance between the secular process of tendering one's aspiration in the Gaokao and the sacred process of submitting a wish to a deity during prayer. This resemblance appears even more conspicuous when one considers possible alternative translations of "tendering one's aspiration." "Aspiration" (*zhìyuàn*) could also be translated as "wish" (*yuàn*). But it has a second meaning—"to volunteer." Thus the phrase possesses the additional connotation of volunteering for society—a terminological holdover from the era when college graduates were assigned jobs, and thus literally conceived to be volunteers for the country. Although I doubt if college applicants typically compare tendering one's aspiration to submitting a wish, the parallels are striking. Just as the worshipper promises to return the wish by paying back the deity, the college applicant (in principle, at least) promises to pay back the motherland for the education that she has provided.

In short, both worshippers and college applicants see themselves as supplicating an abstract, transcendental authority to grant them their wish. Similar to the attitude of worshippers toward the judgments of deities, moreover, most participants in the Gaokao believe more or less in the objectivity of the result, praising the examination as the only relatively fair social competition in China. As I suggest above, this conviction rests to an underappreciated degree on how people see the Gaokao as pronouncing the verdict of transcendental powers. The Gaokao is felt to represent the universalistic judgment of the national community, but also that of the ultimate transcendental power—fate. This transcendental category, which many associate with the authority of the supreme deity, Heaven, is understood to subsume all human effort and the workings of divine beings.

Changing Luck and Influencing Fate

As a general rule, people do not submit docilely to the prescriptions of fate. Rather, following in the tradition of the ledgers of merit, they take an active attitude toward their fortunes. They endeavor to influence the cosmic powers that they see as guiding their destinies by employing a variety of means and techniques for accumulating merit and changing luck.

Earning Character and Using Character: A Euphemized Form of Secret Virtue

The belief that good reciprocates good is ubiquitous. This conviction encourages people in various efforts to tip the karmic scales of virtue in their favor by performing good deeds. To a student's ear, however, the Buddhism-inflected language of doing good to accumulate merit sounds ridiculously old-fashioned—like something, as one student put it, that her grandmother would say. By the same token, this religious language is not regarded as appropriate within the cosmological frame of orthodox secular reciprocity that dominates everyday high-school life. Moreover, in contrast to their parents and teachers, most of whom are middle-aged, students have not reached a stage of life in which it is common to seek comfort and meaning in religious practices. Further, in accord with the macho ethos of self-mastery that prevails in high schools, they are encouraged on all sides to be diligent and take personal responsibility for their success or failure. Especially in public settings, most students adopt an agnostic if not skeptical attitude toward the religiosity of their elders, emphasizing that examination success does not depend on magic but on personal effort.

Privately, however, many students possess well-developed religious beliefs. Even those who do not identify with any institutional religion have a strong (if diffidently expressed) faith in the fundamental rules of cosmic reciprocity. They face a dilemma of impression management, even if they are not always clearly conscious of it. The examination invites, even demands, a consideration of cosmic reciprocity, but students avoid open displays of religiosity because such displays undermine their self-presentation as masters of their own fate. Many see traditional religion, which they associate with the older generations, as simply uncool.

These constraints have elicited a creative response—a sanitized or euphemized form of doing good to accumulate merit, which students term "earning character." In ordinary use, "character" (*rénpǐn*) is a close synonym with "quality" (*sùzhì*). In the mouths of students, however, the term has come to refer to a kind of invisible merit or secret virtue that can be "earned" (*zǎn*) and "used" (*yòng*). According to popular lore, character follows a law of conservation. Though it can be earned or used, it is never destroyed. One accumulates character not only through good deeds but also through inauspicious occurrences. Thus one can console an unfortunate classmate who gets caught cheating or who faces particularly difficult examination questions, because he or she has earned character for the next test. During my fieldwork, this karmic conception of character was very popular among students and younger teachers, particularly in urban areas. Character could be used to explain almost anything. As one teacher said, "If students cannot find a reason for something, they just say that their 'character' is bad."

The discussion of character is popular because the term packages secret virtue in a form inoffensive to official secularism. For example, one college student who had been honored with an invitation to join the Communist Party incorporated the rhetoric of earning character into a completely secular, scientific frame: "There is nothing superstitious or supernatural about earning character; you don't have to believe in ghosts and spirits to believe that good comes to good people and evil to evil people. That's just the law of the universe." Still, this statement conforms with the principles of cosmic reciprocity despite the secular veneer.

Unlike the idiom of accumulating merit, however, earning character has humorous connotations. For example, students who are bullied by their classmates can defend themselves by reminding their persecutors that unmeritorious conduct could cause them to lose character and become unlucky. Students who are labeled curve wreckers, or "academic overlords" (*xuébà*), can forestall this ridicule by claiming that their superior exam performance stemmed from good character rather than hard work. Gender frequently plays a role in such exchanges. Girls in particular may draw ridicule from boys for having high test scores, especially in subjects in which boys are presumed to possess a natural advantage, like math and science (see chapter 4). By assigning their superior test performance to character, girls may defuse the aggression that many boys exhibit when outperformed by someone of supposedly inferior ability.

Character also has other strategic uses, which similarly build on its humorous effect. Teachers sometimes soften a criticism of a student by jocularly attributing his or her poor test performance to poor character. They might say, "Why did you get such a simple question wrong? Your character must be awful!" And teachers and students may praise a classmate who gives an inexplicably good test performance by saying that his or her character surged (*rénpǐn bàofā chūlái*)— an explanation that invariably causes the whole class to burst into laughter. Of course, any unexpected good test result is described as a surge (see chapter 5), but when people say that someone's character surged, they are not merely commenting on a surprising performance but also offering an account of it. This account follows the laws of cosmic reciprocity, turning on notions of secret virtue similar to those promulgated in imperial ledger culture.

In obeisance to secular ideals, some will dismiss the discourse of character, saying that students merely employ this idiom as a humorous explanation. According to this view, students do not take this game so seriously. But many students really do strive to improve their secret virtue, even if they pretend a casual attitude toward these efforts. As one student said, "Of course you have to be kind. Of course you have to be good to other people. If you want character, you definitely have to be sincere in how you treat other people." Despite their pretense of irreverence, therefore, many students adopt a relatively sincere attitude to their character-earning activities.

The stereotypical method of earning character consists in performing acts of public virtue. As one student explained to me, "You can earn character, for example, by helping an old lady across the street." Students thus half-humorously associate earning character with various volunteer activities, such as those organized by schools as part of a government campaign during my fieldwork to resuscitate the spirit of Lei Feng, an archetypal paragon of moral virtue who was lionized in public campaigns during the Maoist era. But students also use many other methods to earn character. For example, college students report that various websites on which classmates provide one another with helpful advice experience a major uptick in activity before large examinations. In the days before a big exam, everyone is eager to earn character. Other efforts to acquire character seem at odds with public virtue. One student, describing her efforts to earn character during the Test of English as a Foreign Language (TOEFL), which students take to qualify for admission to college in the United States, said that she always went online promptly after taking the TOEFL exam to report all the questions and answers she could remember. Now largely computer based, such examinations as the TOEFL draw their questions from a limited pool, so publishing any remembered questions can be an effective method of helping others cheat. This student considered her mutual aid to be a particularly good way of earning character.

Other students couched more traditional forms of religiosity within the jocular idiom of earning character. One Xiamen student, for example, told me—to a chorus of laughter from her classmates—that she had a friend who prayed at a prominent Buddhist temple in Xiamen, Nanputuo Temple, to earn character. After seeing her examination scores improve, this friend began to pray at the temple regularly. Eventually, she was waitlisted at a Western university, to which, following further prayer, she eventually gained admission. Ordinarily, of course, people would describe such temple visits in the idiom of worship—submitting a wish and repaying a wish. But to be politically correct and cool, this student kept to the rhetoric of character.

The status of earning character as a euphemized form of secret virtue seems clear, but why does it evoke laughter? Use of the term "character" circumvents frontstage censorship rules by making karmic virtue acceptable in official contexts. In other words, it's an edge ball, enabling people to support official secularism while giving a nod to cosmic reciprocity. But it also reveals the resistance that students have toward acknowledging their superstitious beliefs, which they feel they ought to have surmounted. In deference to science and modernity, the rhetoric of earning character enables students to adopt a "half believing, half doubting" (bànxìn-bànyí) attitude toward cosmic retribution.

The humorous effect that this rhetoric achieves, however, tells a different story, belying any pretense of doubt. The reason that people laugh about character is that this idiom taps into a truth that is normally suppressed in frontstage contexts, namely, the limited explanatory power of orthodox social reciprocity. Orthodox conceptions of character—diligence, persistence, and composure—are insufficient to explain the outcome of the exam. The myth of meritocracy is incoherent. Teachers ordinarily attempt to suppress this truth in the interest of encouraging students to take personal responsibility for test scores, but the rhetoric of earning character switches the explanatory frame from orthodox reciprocity to cosmic reciprocity. Such reversals are normally inappropriate, but by reversing in a socially acceptable way, the idiom of character releases some of the tension that comes from suppressing the incoherence of meritocratic ideology. This tension is liberated as laughter (Freud [1905] 1960).

The idiom of character is an invention of the 2000s, and may fade quickly along with other fads that are spread through social media. But the need for this secularized idiom of cosmic reciprocity is structural to the institution of Chinese high schools. As long as tension exists between backstage and frontstage cosmologies, some form of secularized, sanitized rhetoric will be required to express deeply held beliefs in cosmic retribution. If the idiom of character disappears, it will eventually be replaced with a similar one.

Talking about character is mainly an informal and (on the surface) jocular affair. By contrast, other high-school religious practices are officially sponsored and treated with great earnestness, such as the official distribution and consumption of sacrificial goods following school-sponsored pilgrimages. During these moments, students become party to the institution's own officially organized backstage religious practices. As with character, students greet such occasions with laughter. Yet many admit to seeing such rituals as offering more than mere psychological comfort.

Backstage Magic: Gambling and Divination

Like specialists in fateful rites of passage cross-culturally, many students have private apotropaic rituals that they perform before the Gaokao. In addition to buying magical amulets or blessing their pencil cases, they may don a lucky shirt or pair of shoes. Similar to apotropaic customs like wearing red on test day, such practices are seen as consequential but not as chancy. By contrast, many other luck-bringing activities that people engage in at exam time mirror the structure of the fateful event itself, incorporating elements of both consequentiality and chanciness.

I refer here to a wide range of practices that includes, on the one hand, fortune-telling and divination, and on the other, mundane activities seen as predicting and influencing luck. People attribute divinatory power not only to temple practices such as drawing lots but also to games of chance, ranging from relatively orthodox ones, like the state-sponsored lottery or family mahjong games, to unorthodox ones, like sports gambling, the underground lotteries, and back-alley grifts (Bosco, Liu, and West 2009; Chu 2010; Festa 2007; Oxfeld 1993; Steinmüller 2013). In addition, people see their performance in chancy economic activities, such as stock market speculation, as a similar indicator of their luck in larger endeavors (Chumley and Jing 2013).[3]

All such activities possess the structure of fateful rites of passage. In this way, they mimic the fatefulness of the event that they are, in this context, meant to foresee and control—the Gaokao. This structural similarity is no accident. As in the Gaokao, the authority of these fateful activities is seen as coming from transcendental powers beyond any individual's control. What enables people to perceive these events as indicators of karmic merit is the aleatory quality or chanciness that they all share. As a result, people see gambling as a form of divination, and both gambling and divination as trials of merit. The ubiquitous interest in fateful activities may be attributed in part to the perception that merit in one branch of fatefulness relates to merit in all branches; one's accomplishment in any risky event provides an aggregate indication of divine favor and secret virtue more generally.

Coin-tossing games are relatively lighthearted divinatory games of chance. Similar to Western wishing wells, these games form a familiar sight in temples. People who pray at the Confucius Temple in Ningzhou may stop at the statue of Confucius on their way out to toss coins onto the platform created by the sage's folded arms. Attainment of this objective is said to bode well for one's examination performance. Planting one's projectile while dislodging those of previous aspirants is a particularly desirable result. In doing so, the candidate has "killed off" some of his or her competitors. To my knowledge, such games are not officially organized by temples; nevertheless, people rationalize them as a donation. Even if they fail to win the game, they can comfort themselves that they have increased their merit by contributing to the cult's coffers.

The attribution of divinatory significance to games of chance is not limited to those in the relatively sanctified space of temples. Not only students but many teachers, parents, and administrators see gambling as predictive of fortune. Many consider their performance in family games of mahjong or cards around the Chinese New Year to foretell their luck for the whole coming year. Many people in China are avid gamblers, and the games of chance in which they participate are legion. But in the region of my fieldwork, one chanceful recreation in particular has special significance in the context of examinations—that of "gambling for mooncakes" (*bóbǐng*), a Minnan custom with roots in the imperial era.

This activity takes place annually around Mid-Autumn Festival (the fifteenth day of the eighth lunar month). In gambling for mooncakes, people gather in groups, often organized by friends or employers, to play a game of dice for various prizes. Prizes include mooncakes—which are small, sweet pastries exchanged during this festival time—as well as other material and monetary awards. But the real import of gambling for mooncakes lies not in winning prizes but rather in what those prizes signify: good or bad luck in one's life more generally.

Intriguingly, gambling for mooncakes contains an explicit cultural reference to China's imperial civil examination system. The top three results in the game are named after the top three results in the civil exams. As in the old trial of mandarins, first place is termed "examination champion" (*zhuàngyuán*), second place the "eye of the announcement" (*bǎngyǎn*), and third the "scout of flowers" (*tànhuā*). The metaphorical equivalency that the game establishes between examinations and gambling is humorous, and, like the idiom of earning character, reveals a normally suppressed truth. This equivalency amounts to an oblique cultural acknowledgment of the aleatory dimension of exams. At the same time, it underscores how people can see games of chance as tests of merit.

Although the atmosphere around the game is jovial, many participants imbue it with significance. At Dragon Gate High School, teachers pool their money to buy prizes, then gather annually at a local restaurant to play. On one such occasion, senior-three head teacher Mr. Wei, whose daughter was about to take the Gaokao, became visibly distressed when he experienced bad luck during the game. As the dice continued to turn up abysmal results for him, this normally composed, soft-spoken educator started shaking his head and cursing under his breath. With both his daughter and his students facing the final battle, he considered his poor performance a bad omen. Other participants quarreled over whether or not certain configurations of the dice signified good or bad fortune. Toward the end of the night, I rolled six sixes, which my friends assured me was a particularly auspicious result—examination champion. But my good luck provoked the ire of others. In particular, a surly and intoxicated physical education teacher, appealing to certain disputed arcana of the rules, insisted that my throw actually demonstrated bad luck. He was mollified only after I donated one of my prizes to him—a carton of good cigarettes.

Given the structural similarities between examinations and gambling, it is unsurprising that historical linkages can be found between them. In imperial times, people used to bet on the outcome of the civil exams. In Guangdong (Canton) during the late Qing era, a popular lottery appeared that was based on guessing the surnames of successful candidates. Called Weixing, or *Vaeseng* in Cantonese, the game became immensely popular (E. Li 2015; Pina-Cabral 2002). But authorities cracked down on the practice because it threatened to undermine the legitimacy of the exam. Some examiners, who were in charge of ranking candidates and thus could be counted on to predict successful examinees with 100 percent accuracy, were caught buying tickets through a proxy. Although the Qing state banned the practice on the mainland, the game continued in Macau, which was under Portuguese control. The Macanese government, which was short on funds, provided lottery organizers with an official monopoly on the game, thereby helping to establish Macau's gambling industry (E. Li 2015; Pina-Cabral 2002).

Historical connections exist not only between gambling and examinations but also between examinations and divination. In early China, divination was an elite test of merit much like examinations became in later centuries. Many divinatory practices revolved around interpreting the Book of Changes, or Yijing—the oldest Chinese classic. Yijing divination, which remains widely practiced today, involves interpreting randomly selected passages of the classic text, each of which is associated with one of sixty-four Yijing hexagrams. In the Warring States period (475–221 BCE), perspicacious performance in this form of divination became an important test of moral acuteness among elites (Lewis 1999, 244). In light of this shared social function, contemporary examinations can be seen as genealogically related to such early fateful rites of passage. And the popular-religious descendants of elite divination—various forms of fortune-telling—continue to constitute an important domain of magical action, particularly around fateful events such as the Gaokao.

Fortune Tellers: Changing Luck by Accumulating Virtue

Fortune-telling—literally, "calculating fate" (*suànmìng*)—incorporates many different practices, including astrology (*suàn bāzì*), palmistry, face reading, drawing lots, and others. These techniques are pursued by an equally varied array of people, from informal practitioners to full-time professionals. The art is also practiced by private individuals, including many students. Full-time fortune tellers gather on the streets outside temples, but more professional grades of fortune teller also exist. Some entrepreneurial occultists even establish shops, renting inconspicuous storefronts on small streets in third- and fourth-tier cities.

Clients consult fortune tellers about a variety of fateful life events, including examinations. Students themselves rarely consult professional fortune tellers, but their parents do. Many of the uninitiated think fortune-telling mainly centers on prognostication, but clients are interested in influencing the future as well. Changing luck (*gǎi yùn*) is a primary goal of many consultations.

To help clients change their luck, fortune tellers suggest a variety of strategies. For example, they may counsel customers to improve the geomantic layout or fengshui of their homes, or they may suggest altering a child's name, both of which are assumed to affect fortune. But many seekers of advice are looking for a more personal touch. They hope to achieve insight into their character, family affairs, and interpersonal relationships. Sharing intimate details of their home life, some repeat customers develop a therapeutic relationship with their fortune tellers.

In addition to providing therapy, fortune tellers cater directly and explicitly to the needs of their clients for an explanatory frame that transcends orthodox social reciprocity. Parents and students seek out these soothsayers when orthodox explanations based on diligence break down. One practitioner—a blind astrologer who set up shop on the street outside the Guanyin Temple in Xiamen—explained the relationship between diligence and luck:

> Luck is like the weather. It changes. . . . If your luck is bad, it doesn't matter how good your horoscope is. . . . Diligence is also no good. Under normal circumstances, if you are lucky, you can get, let's say, one buck. If you work hard, you can get two. If you *really* work hard, you can get three. More work, more return. But if you are unlucky, you won't even get that first buck. . . . You can change luck by doing good, though. And merit also passes through generations.

As this explanation implies, changing luck involves various strategies for accumulating merit. Fortune tellers may advise clients on officially recognized channels for acquiring secret virtue, such as making temple donations or freeing captive animals, such as pet fish or turtles (*fàngshēng*). But in keeping with their therapeutic role, they also tell clients how to adjust their relationships in ways that will help accumulate virtue. For example, one fortune teller recalled how he was approached by a teenage girl who was having trouble with her parents and with school (such troubles frequently go together). The girl and her mother bickered constantly, and the girl's test performance was deteriorating.

Comforting the distraught examinee, the fortune teller advised her to perform acts of kindness toward her mother. Only then, he said, could she change her luck on examinations.

In many cases, people see hiring a fortune teller itself as a method for accumulating merit. Many professional occultists are afflicted with visible disabilities ranging from blindness to industrial injuries. Because of the widespread prejudice against people with disabilities in China, few other professions are available to them (Kohrman 2005). But the very quality that forms the pretense for discrimination against members of this group—their supposed unluckiness—constitutes an advantage to them in the fortune-telling profession. Clients can rationalize their payments as remuneration for services and as a donation to the unfortunate. Such charity is a way of earning secret virtue. But not just any misfortune qualifies the unlucky to serve as suitable recipients of charity and as instruments to accumulate merit. To fulfill this purpose, their misfortune must result from blows of fate that people perceive as lying outside the conscious control of the afflicted.

The same logic applies to beggars, whose social role resembles that of fortune tellers in several respects. Like occultists, beggars are often disabled and their misfortune is physically obvious. Those who are not visibly unfortunate must take great pains to exhibit, often through explanatory placards written in careful calligraphy, the various fateful setbacks that, despite their best efforts of diligence, have reduced them to their current fallen state. Such narratives display great variety, but typical themes include suffering a family illness, falling victim to violence or theft, or possessing unfilial children. Of course, donors worry that beggars may be fabricating such narratives, a suspicion that raises the philosophical conundrum of whether real merit can be earned through donating to a counterfeit beggar. The same question can be asked about many other common opportunities to accumulate merit. In many tourist destinations, for example, criminal gangs of counterfeit monks roam around asking travelers for alms.

Casting Divination Blocks and Drawing Lots

Pious pilgrims generally avoid the throngs of fortune tellers who gather outside temples, preferring instead to accumulate merit through the more orthodox means of worship and prayer. And prayer itself often involves a mantic component, obviating the need for further soothsaying. Drawing lots, also termed "asking lots" (wènqiān), is an example of such a component. When it is conducted at a temple, this practice is not considered fortune-telling. Rather, it constitutes a form of worship—one in which supplicants communicate directly with the temple's patron deity in the person of the interpreter of lots. As I note above, the aleatory component of divination enables worshippers to see it as revealing the verdicts of a higher power.

Because divination forms an important component of worship, people tend to employ "accuracy" (*zhǔn*) and "efficacy" (*líng*) interchangeably to describe the spiritual potency of deities. Saying that a temple is accurate is tantamount to saying that it is effective. Both qualities testify to the divine power of the deity, describing complementary aspects of that power. People understand deities to possess both great perspicacity and the ability to influence life's fateful events. In asking lots, worshippers appeal to both aspects of their authority.

The process of drawing lots usually involves two components, both of which incorporate an element of chance. Typically, worshippers first ask the deity whether or not they have its permission to draw a lot. They do so by casting divination blocks or "moon blocks" (in Minnan dialect, *poe*)—a pair of kidney-bean-shaped dice (figure 14). Casting the blocks may either be the first step toward drawing lots or constitute a self-contained divinatory activity. If both dice land right side up, the answer is no. If both land in an inverted position, then the answer is equivalent to a shoulder shrug, meaning maybe. Any other position indicates yes. Usually, worshippers keep casting the blocks until their question is answered with certainty.

FIGURE 14. A set of moon blocks. Photograph provided by Liak Koi Lau.

Note that an answer of yes is more than twice as likely as an answer of no. Supplicants are well aware of this fact, simultaneously taking account of and suspending disbelief in the statistical characteristics of moon blocks (Jordan 1982). Many worshippers frame their questions in a way that increases their chances of receiving the results that they desire. Nevertheless, they understand the activity to reveal the judgments of divine will.

After receiving verification that they may draw a lot (they rarely do not receive such verification), worshippers follow the procedure that I describe above, obtaining a cup of lots from the altar and shaking it in a prayer-like gesture until one falls out, which gives the uncanny effect of making the selected lot appear to have been plucked from its cup by invisible fingers. Following the selection of their lot, worshippers approach a temple caretaker, the interpreter of lots, who typically sits at a table near the altar.

The attitude of temple minders toward the interpretation of lots varies greatly. Although most Buddhist temples spurn the practice, many temples dedicated to the extremely popular Bodhisattva of Mercy, Guanyin, furnish worshippers with lot-drawing equipment. But temple caretakers privately dismiss lot drawing, scorning it as a vulgar corruption of Buddhist belief. In Guanyin temples, caretakers employ standardized sets of eighty or one hundred "Guanyin lots," each of which corresponds with a few vague words of canned guidance, which are either printed on small papers or directly on the temple walls. Given that the advice is standardized, its interpretation mainly involves offering words of encouragement. In the case of illiterate worshippers, the advice is read aloud.

In popular Daoist temples, like Yongning, the attitude toward lots is much different. In such temples, lots may form a unique cultural inheritance. In contrast to Guanyin lots, their interpretation is understood to require great skill, which may be handed down for generations within one village. Each lot corresponds not to a standardized explanation but to a highly ambiguous poem, the interpretation of which may change depending on the time of day, the season of the year, or the weather. Even the demeanor of the supplicant forms an important factor in interpretation. For instance, fierceness (*xiōng*) of expression may be inauspicious if the worshipper asks about luck, but the same expression may elicit the opposite judgment if he or she asks about examinations. For all these reasons, people say that such lots are dynamic or "alive" (*huó*). The interpretation of dynamic lots requires great experience and knowledge. This specialized expertise provides such lots with a greater aura of objectivity or accuracy than that of nondynamic lots. Lacking any control over their interpretation, worshippers have a heightened sense of communicating directly with a higher power.

In the broader region of Xiamen and Ningzhou, Yongning is considered particularly accurate. Stories about the perspicacity of the Yongning ancestral patriarch circulate widely, greatly increasing the temple's reputation. Although lot interpreters generally do not talk about their craft, ordinary temple workers gladly recount such stories. A common theme consists in how the deity predicts and accounts for small but consequential variations in test scores that orthodox social reciprocity cannot explain. People admiringly regard this uncanny accuracy as the mysterious (*xuán*) quality of successful interpretation. Once, for example, a lot interpreter predicted that a student would get into university, but, as the mystic said, "only by a little." Two months later, the student's parents returned to the lot interpreter to express their amazement and gratitude. Their child had indeed achieved admission to her desired university, but only by the slim margin of two points.

Prediction is almost invariably accompanied by prayer. On another occasion, a lot interpreter told a student that his examination score would fall just short of the mark. The master advised the examinee to pledge a wish to the deity. Following the interpreter's instructions, the boy asked the god for protection while making a small gift to the temple by lighting an oil lamp—a form of donation in which the worshipper, for a fee, places a lit candle in a special alcove. The student, who was plagued by examination anxiety, prayed for a steady disposition (*xīnqíng wěndìng*), promising to return to the temple to repay the wish after successful completion of the exam. On the fateful day, the student performed better than expected, exceeding the score cutoff for admission to his desired university.

Similar to fortune tellers in their therapeutic role, lot interpreters may have extended conversations with worshippers, whom they counsel on life choices. For example, when students draw inauspicious lots, the master may offer these disappointed diviners both spiritual and practical advice, instructing them on how to enlist the deity's support and exhorting them to be more diligent. Because believers see themselves communing directly with the deity, these occasions have great psychological force.

Pledging and Repaying Wishes:
The God of Examinations, Wenchang

Yongning is only one of many temples that people visit to enlist divine support for examinations, and drawing lots forms only one of many ways to do so. A wide variety of temples, ranging from small local shrines to major Buddhist monasteries, receive pilgrimages from examinees and their families. In the context of the Gaokao, one temple in particular deserves special comment, namely, the temple to the God of Examinations, Wenchang Dijun (literally, the "Emperor of Flourishing Culture"), commonly shortened to Wenchang.

The temple to Wenchang in downtown Ningzhou City draws worshippers from all over Ningzhou Prefecture and beyond. Worshippers not only hail from a wide geographical area but also represent socially diverse groups, ranging from street sweepers and factory workers to doctors and government officials. Since imperial times, a defining characteristic of the Wenchang cult has consisted in how it attracts supplicants from broad segments of society. Wenchang's natural constituency consists of anyone who is involved in the examination life—a group that includes both the rich and the poor but upwardly mobile (Kleeman 1994). The enormous popularity of the deity illustrates the socially cohering effect of national examinations.

During important examinations—the high-school entrance exam, the civil-service exam and, in particular, the Gaokao—the Wenchang temple overcrowds with pilgrims, who spill out onto the street. The cult has become so popular that the Ningzhou Bureau of Cultural Protection considers the great volume of incense that is burned there to be a danger to the building, which dates to the Qing dynasty.

But the temple has not always been so popular. Closed during the Mao era, it was not reopened until 2003, when local volunteers revived the cult following a surge of interest in Wenchang. These volunteers—now temple minders—attribute this surge to the expansion of higher education in the early 2000s, but remark that this period was also characterized by reviving interest in cultural protection and popular religion more generally.

Over the two days of the Gaokao, hundreds of worshippers pack the narrow alley outside the temple and crowd through the temple itself, kowtowing in front of the temple effigies and heaping long tables with symbolic sacrificial offerings, which include celery (*qíncài*, the first syllable of which is a homonym of the first syllable of "hard-working," or *qínfèn*), steamed dumplings (the name for which, *bāozi*, reminds people of the word for "preferential admission," *bǎosòng*), and green onions (*cōng*, which is a homonym of the word for "intelligent"). After being offered to the deity, these sacrifices are gathered up, taken home, and cooked by parents, whose children consume them to incorporate the protection of the god.

During the Gaokao, worshippers are required to burn incense outside. Most use large sticks, about two feet long, which must be placed in specially constructed metal frames in front of the temple. At the time of my fieldwork, all four sections of the Gaokao were held consecutively over two days, and the custom was to light one stick of incense for each section. Requiring a donation of fifty Chinese yuan (about seven US dollars) per stick, the purchase of incense constituted a significant expense for many families. But this outlay was the least of their inconveniences. To be able to light one stick of incense for each section of the exam, worshippers had to hurry back and forth between the temple and their child's examination hall, running themselves ragged in the scorching summer heat to balance the demands of prayer with those of feeding and caring for tired examinees. Parents from rural areas of Ningzhou sometimes appointed one parent to burn incense while the other accompanied their child.

Although the temple receives extra visitors on test days, it is busy throughout the year. In the months leading up to the examination, the temple holds several special ceremonies, which include celebrations of the deity's birthday and various rituals to exorcise families of evil influences. During these occasions, families can pledge a wish by becoming a "disciple" (*túdì*) of the deity in exchange for a donation. But visitors need not attend special ceremonies to pledge a wish. For a donation of fifty Chinese yuan, ordinary pilgrims can purchase a red cloth banner, which temple minders hang inside the temple to the left of the main altar. Embroidered in golden letters, these banners display messages like "Wishes will be reciprocated" (*yŏuqiú-bìyìng*) and "Rise to the heights step by step" (*bùbù-gāoshēng*). For an extra donation, parents can have these encouraging messages embroidered with their child's name and place of origin.

Following the exam, families repay the wish by donating money to hang a similar banner in thanks to the deity, this time to the right of the altar. Papering the wall, these banners display the names of successful examinees along with the institutions to which they gained admission. Spanning the educational hierarchy from peripherally located two-year colleges, like Ningzhou Vocational Technical Institute, to elite colleges and even overseas universities, like the University of California, Berkeley, the range of these institutions reflects the socioeconomically diverse constituency of Wenchang and attests to the broad social variation in what counts as examination success. Along with the name of the examinee and his or her college, the banners display congratulatory messages, such as "Wenchang is effective, studies have succeeded" (*Wénchāng língyàn, xuéyè yŏuchéng*) or "The name has appeared on the golden announcement" (*jīnbǎng-tímíng*), the latter of which alludes to the imperial-era practice of using gilded lettering to announce the names of advanced scholars—the highest level of achievement in the imperial civil exams.

Many regular visitors to the temple decide to accumulate further merit by becoming actively involved in temple life. But their degree and type of involvement vary according to their piety and financial ability. Participating in an exorcism costs 200 Chinese yuan, or about 30 US dollars—a fee that most devout parents can afford. More well-heeled worshippers may sponsor a theater performance around the deity's birthday during Chinese New Year—a meritorious deed that can cost several thousand Chinese yuan. But people of ordinary means may choose nonmonetary forms of service to express their devotion.

A middle-aged street peddler, Mr. Deng, whose daughter was finishing high school, regularly volunteered at the temple, emptying the troughs of hot incense ash that accumulated on test days.

The deity is known to reward loyal worshippers with various forms of divine assistance. Temple minders and worshippers can recount many examples of such supernatural intervention. Since the revival of the temple in the 2000s, Wenchang has become especially renowned for "entrusting dreams" (tuōmèng) to the faithful. In one case, Wenchang appeared to a local medical doctor in a recurring dream, complaining to her that she did not pray at the temple, whereas her husband and child visited regularly. In her dream, the doctor replied to the god that she had hesitated to expose the temple to the spiritual contamination of death and disease from her work. But following the dream, she became a frequent worshipper, and her daughter subsequently achieved unexpectedly high marks on the examination. In another case, the deity approached a father in a dream, telling him exactly how many points his daughter would score on the big test. As with the accuracy of Yongning, the power of the deity was demonstrated by its ability to make precise predictions.

Worshippers also use narratives of divine assistance to explain otherwise inexplicable test score increases. One student from Mountain County, whose mother frequently prayed at the temple, missed the score cutoff by thirty points on his final rehearsal exam but beat it by three points on the Gaokao. She was sure that the deity had helped her son. Another worshipper, whose son was studying in Hong Kong, said that his test score increased by an astounding sixty points after she began praying at the temple. It is difficult to estimate the number of people who believe that they have been assisted in this way. But the subjective impact of these narratives is evident. Their circulation inspires worshippers and increases the reputation of the deity.

Family Curses and Ancestral Sins: Materialist and Idealist Explanations

Of course, people may turn to divine powers not only to explain successful examination performances but also to account for bad outcomes. Deities and spirits are understood to not only help people but sometimes hinder them. Cosmic reciprocity, in other words, can explain terrible failures as well as spectacular successes.

Combining Confucian- and Daoist-inspired notions of ancestral virtue with Buddhist conceptions of karma, popular understandings of merit take an expansive view of the scales of cosmic reciprocity. The virtue of ancestors is often felt to affect one's life outcome as much as one's own merit. The above-mentioned blind fortune teller described accumulation of merit over many generations and lives in this way:

> You can do good to accumulate merit, but there is something else too that affects merit, namely, the things that you did in your past lives, and also the things that your ancestors did. . . . These explanations combine both Buddhist and Daoist views. There is no contradiction in them. The good and bad deeds that you do have two kinds of effects. They affect your future lives *and* your descendants.

This fortune teller further explained the workings of secret virtue with reference to the old saying that "riches and poverty do not pass beyond three generations" (*fù / qióng bùguò sāndài*). People in China invoke this idiom to explain the cycles of fortune and misfortune that families experience. As this fortuneteller explained, the cyclicity of family prosperity can be elucidated through karmic merit. Rich people tend to forget the poor, that is, they become greedy, neglecting to perform good deeds. In cosmic retribution for such greed, fate strips rich families of wealth. Similarly, the poor do not remain impoverished beyond three generations because poor people are generally kind.

The narrative of Mr. Li provides a vivid illustration of these principles of cosmic retribution. Mr. Li is a middle-aged migrant worker and army veteran from Jiangxi Province who was living in Xiamen during my fieldwork. Describing the decline of a prominent family in his village, Mr. Li attributed this decline to sins (*zuì*) committed by the family patriarch during the Cultural Revolution, retribution for which manifested itself in the disappointing fate of his offspring:

> During the Cultural Revolution, I was very little. I wasn't yet old enough to understand adult affairs (*dǒngshì*). But after finishing service in the army, I worked for a while in the village committee. This was around 1990 or so, long after collective land had been returned to families. I loved talking to the old men, so I heard lots of stories. During the Cultural Revolution, a village was called a production battalion. The battalion leader was in charge of the battalion, and he had a lieutenant whose job was to record points (*jìfēn*). People worked for points. For every day of work, men received ten work points, women eight. Grain was distributed on the basis of these points, plus the population of your household. But if you didn't have a good relationship with the battalion leader, he could decide to deduct points (*kòu fēn*). Then you would get less grain at the end of the month. The leaders took the excess grain for themselves. Everything looked fine from the outside—the village should have had plenty of grain—but in reality people were going hungry.

At this point in his narrative, Mr. Li paused to make a philosophical interjection. All phenomena in life have two types of explanation, he said—an orthodox or materialist explanation and an unorthodox, idealist one. To use an idealist explanation, Mr. Li said, the leaders had committed a sin:

> The leaders always had a justification for denying people grain, but having a justification didn't make it right. No matter what the justification, it is wrong to make people starve. But at the time, there was no retribution (*bàoyìng*) for their sins. The retribution came much later. The battalion leader had three sons. One of the sons was disabled (*cánjírén*). He was tormented by all kinds of illnesses. And in his whole family, none of the children were very good looking. They all looked really strange, and didn't do well in school. . . . Then, when the battalion leader got to be about sixty, he himself started suffering from strange illnesses. So when the old people tell stories like that, even though we haven't experienced this history ourselves, the stories will make us think. From an idealist perspective, all this misfortune was a form of retribution for his sins. We'll start analyzing them. How did the battalion leader's family get to be the way it is? So cosmic retribution is real. As they say, "It is not that there is no reciprocity, but that the time has not yet arrived." When the time arrives, there is always retribution. In the countryside, there are lots of realities (*xiànshí*) like this, lots of similar examples.

Mr. Li's narrative contained at least three points of relevance to the present discussion. First, as I mention above, there is a striking similarity between the work-point system of the collective era and other schemes for rationally calculating merit, including ledgers of merit, quality audits, and the Gaokao itself. Despite radical changes in political ideology, such schemes seem to be a relatively durable fixture of Chinese life.

Second, Mr. Li used orthodox Marxian terminology, which he studied in high school and in the military, to differentiate between the cosmological frames of orthodox materialism and cosmic idealism. By so doing, he avoided the term "superstition," which has a pejorative connotation, shifting the footing of the conversation instead to that of a philosophical discussion. In the conclusion to his story, moreover, Mr. Li emphasized that the cosmological logic of cosmic retribution constitutes reality. Without directly criticizing orthodox cosmology, therefore, he nevertheless implied that the materialist explanation, which ignores the reality of cosmic retribution, is empty and false. In this respect, Mr. Li's assessment resembled the pragmatic attitude toward popular religion that high schools adopt in the backstage, where teachers and administrators likewise acknowledge the reality of cosmic reciprocity. In the same way, Mr. Li reversed the polarity of the usual frontstage assessment. In his view, idealism described a higher-level reality than did materialism.

Third, the reality of cosmic retribution is such that it affects not just the perpetrator of karmic sins but also his or her offspring. As in orthodox social reciprocity, success reflects merit. But the temporal frame for that reciprocal relationship between success and merit expands to include multiple generations.

The Potency of Ancestors: Family Tragedy and Possession

Mr. Li's narrative described the general principles of cosmic retribution without offering a detailed account of the specific divine agents responsible for that retribution, whether ghosts, gods, ancestors, or some other supernatural power. When people feel personally afflicted by misfortune, however, they generally want to understand its precise mechanism, reasoning that this knowledge will empower them to take evasive or corrective action. And for many people in China, few greater calamities can occur than the educational failure of a child.

Particularly when children fail horribly, it can be difficult for families to account for this blow of fate within the orthodox cosmological frame. Parents may feel wronged, reasoning that they have exercised every effort of diligence to support their children through twelve years of schooling. Why should their fate now take such a sudden tragic turn? In some cases, the pressure to achieve educational success may be particularly acute for boys, who are shouldered with the burden of perpetuating the lineage. But for children of both genders, examination pressure can be too great to bear, resulting in mental and emotional breakdowns. The rebellion of Ms. Ma's brother, Junjie, forms one poignant example of such a family tragedy. His story illustrates the conundrums that such tragedies present, and the great lengths to which families will go to account for them.

Ms. Ma grew up in a village near the seat of a peripheral rural county. Her parents had three children—herself, her little sister, and a baby brother. As is typical of many rural families, Ms. Ma's parents kept having children until they had a boy. In this rural milieu, where extremely patriarchal views are common, Mr. Ma was unremarkable in describing his daughters as "scattered water" because they would marry out to other families (see chapter 4). In other respects, however, he was relatively progressive, encouraging his girls to pursue higher education. But he required the girls to become teachers, reasoning, as many parents do, that their pursuit of this profession would make them more marriageable. By contrast, he had much higher expectations for his son. He wanted Junjie to go to a good college, become an engineer, and support him and his wife in their old age.

During Junjie's senior-three year, however, an unfortunate incident precipitated a family crisis. In an act of rebellion, Junjie handed in a monthly exam paper without doing the Chinese essay. His Chinese teacher called Junjie's father, who came to the school in person, where he chastised the boy in front of his classmates. Humiliated, Junjie dropped out of school, refusing to take the Gaokao. He moved in with his maternal grandparents, eventually sitting for the exam the following year. He scored fairly well on the exam, qualifying for admission to a first-tier university, but decided to go to college in faraway Sichuan. Breaking off all contact with his natal family, he vowed never to speak to his father again. A couple years later, Ms. Ma received word that her brother had dropped out of university.

Fearing that Junjie's excommunication of his father would be too much for the man to bear, the rest of the family decided to keep the severity of the boy's estrangement secret from him. Ms. Ma frantically attempted to regain contact. Meanwhile, she contrived with her mother and sister to give her father the impression that his wayward son merely wished to take some time away from the family but was otherwise doing fine. The family patriarch was nevertheless highly distraught. He employed several local ritual specialists one after the other in attempts to ascertain the cause of his family's misfortune. Searching the whole house, the first specialist, a Daoist ritualist, found evidence of evil magic—a strange diagram that had been crammed into the wall in his son's room. The second ritualist, a fortune teller, produced a more compelling explanation. The spirit of a distantly related maternal grand-aunt was unhappy and had possessed the unwitting boy. To propitiate this angry ghost, the family would have to offer sacrifices on the family altar to the ancestor on the anniversary of her death. A third specialist, a famous and reclusive local fortune teller, recorded the whole family fortune on a cassette tape, including the specific dates on which each member of the family would die. At this point, Ms. Ma's mother became highly distressed. She complained to her husband that going to so many ritualists was negatively affecting their longevity. The family decided to cease further inquiries, and the tape, which had upset the whole family, was destroyed.

As of this writing, Junjie has never fully reconciled with his family. Despite some minimal contact with his sisters and mother, he still refuses to speak with his father, and has never returned home.

The ideal of the Gaokao as a fair, objective, and scientific measure of individual merit is contradicted by various kinds of aleatory uncertainty that intrude on the exam experience. These sources of chanciness range from happenstance factors that affect performance (for example, the weather, the position of one's seat, the accuracy of one's guesswork, and the state of one's health on exam day) to the process of college selection itself, which, almost as if by design, introduces an element of gambling into the Gaokao. Similarly, people are well aware that educational outcome is affected by accidents of birth, such as place of origin, social background, and gender. They rightfully perceive a fundamental contradiction between the ideal of individual merit and the reality of these social contingencies.

To cope with these contradictions, people supplement orthodox reciprocity with cosmic reciprocity. Magico-religious beliefs and practices are widespread. Despite official secularism, all stakeholders in the Gaokao—students, families, teachers, administrators, and officials—see magic and religion as effective means of improving examination performance. Even skeptics concede the psychological utility of religious faith. Such pragmatic considerations cause unorthodox practices to flourish in the institutional backstage.

But this backstage cosmic reciprocity is not a side effect of examination competition; rather, it is integral to its social effects. The examination is like an engine for generating belief in magic and fate. Given the constitutive incoherence of meritocracy, the work of diligent test preparation is not enough by itself to generate a belief in individual merit. Rather, students and families require the labors of divination, worship, prayer, and apotropaic ritual to construct a coherent narrative of examination outcome. These labors encourage them to conflate social differences, which are the contingent products of culture and history, with truly random events that lie outside human control. By prompting people to attribute both categories of phenomena to fate, the Gaokao has a socially stabilizing effect. The discourse of fate imbues social differences with the aura of necessity, thus making social inequality appear natural.

But magical signifiers like fate and luck do not merely paper over the contradictions of meritocratic ideology. They also draw attention to these contradictions. Just as no examination can scientifically purify itself of incoherence, no magical signifier—fate, luck, or fortune—can completely contain it (Siegel 2006). Pointing toward the paradoxes of meritocracy, these signifiers do not merely serve as ideological concepts that keep people down. Rather, they are double-edged swords. They enable people to reconcile the disconnects between myth and reality, but they also provide people with a language for engaging with the fundamental social contradictions that lie behind those disconnects. This engagement is not merely symbolic; it is material to people's everyday practices, in which they constantly strive to change luck and transform destiny.

In other words, people's conceptions of karmic virtue, luck, and fate provide important idioms in which they express and experience personal agency. In part, this agency manifests itself as psychological comfort. In an examination where "attitude determines knowledge" (see chapter 5), the importance of such comfort should not be underestimated. At the same time, however, magico-religious practices like divination, merit accumulation, and possession are important means by which people therapeutically negotiate among themselves about the fulfillment of cultural ideals, such as filiality. Finally, the idioms of fate and luck give people a way of directly addressing the paradoxes of meritocracy. When someone says that another test taker is just lucky, they are calling attention to the social and historical contingencies that inhere in individual merit even as they reach for an explanation to account for those contingencies. By the same token, the ideal of using the Gaokao to change fate indexes an awareness of the arbitrariness of the accidents of birth. In these cases, luck and fate do not merely speak the language of ideology but also that of social critique.

But the social significance of magico-religious thinking goes further than this. Under extraordinary circumstances, the volatility of the concept of fate can precipitate radical social change. Since early times, people in China have conceived of the authority of rulers as being granted by Heaven, the supreme Chinese deity (Shaughnessy 1999). According to this political culture, the right to govern derives from this Mandate of Heaven (*Tiānmìng*). Significantly, the Chinese word that scholars usually translate as "mandate" also means "fate" (*mìng*). In Chinese, these concepts are synonymous. Fate is Heaven's command. But just as Heaven does not bless the unmeritorious with a propitious fate, it does not bestow favor on rulers arbitrarily. Only those who possess great moral virtue can rightfully reign. This virtue largely consists in the ability to guarantee the social conditions of meritocracy—peace, prosperity, and opportunity. If the state fails to ensure the conditions of meritocracy, people interpret the Mandate of Heaven to imply the right of rebels to "prepare the way for Heaven" (*tì Tiān xíng dào*) (Muramatsu 1960; Perry 2002). When people cannot change fate through orthodox means, such as the Gaokao, they may seek unorthodox methods to do so—rebellion and revolution. Thus the mandate cuts both ways. What Heaven grants, Heaven can take away.

Throughout Chinese history, numerous rebellions have risen up against immoral leadership to seize Heaven's Mandate. The Great Helmsman Mao himself was popularly perceived as a rebel in this tradition, and many other examples of this historical pattern could be added. Perhaps most famously, in the waning years of the Qing dynasty an unsuccessful examination candidate, Hong Xiuquan (1814–64 CE), experienced a series of dreams and visions after his repeated failures to win a degree. Claiming that he was the little brother of Jesus, Hong led a millenarian sectarian uprising, the Taiping Rebellion (1850–64 CE) that harnessed widespread popular resentment against state corruption and rural poverty. This uprising of "God worshippers" became not only the most destructive war of the nineteenth century but perhaps the bloodiest civil war in world history, resulting in the deaths of at least twenty million people (Platt 2012; Weller 1994; Spence 1996).

Painfully aware of this history, the contemporary state continues to see sectarian movements as one of its greatest potential threats. In a striking historical parallel, one prominent contemporary sectarian group—Eastern Lightning (*Dōngfāng shǎndiàn*), also known as the Real Spirit (*Shíjìshén*), among other names—even appears to have deified a failed Gaokao candidate. Similar to Hong Xiuquan, this woman, a "female Christ," is rumored to have experienced visions after failing to realize her dream of examination success (Dunn 2009).

But an irony of rebel movements is how they replicate orthodox forms of state power. When rebels assume control, one of their first actions inevitably consists in establishing a new examination system. Even Hong Xiuquan, who fell just short of conquering China, declared special Christian examinations for his Heavenly Kingdom. In the twentieth century, the Communist Party continued this legacy of rebels-turned-rulers. By establishing the Gaokao so close on the heels of coming into power, the Communist Party joined a long lineage of Chinese examination states.

Although this cultural pattern is robust, the stability or longevity of any regime is not a given. The current conditions of economic slowdown in China raise questions about whether or not Chinese President Xi Jinping will be able to deliver on his meritocratic guarantee to guide the country past the middle-income trap into the rosy future of the Chinese Dream (see chapter 1). It is impossible to predict how this drama will unfold and whether or not it will have revolutionary consequences. But an immediate and more prosaic effect of these changing economic conditions is significant levels of educated unemployment and underemployment in China (Yanjie Huang 2013; Mok and Wu 2016). A growing tide of "lost and confused" (*mímáng*) young people are experiencing anomie and disillusionment as they fail to fulfill the promise of meritocracy.

LOST AND CONFUSED

The architects of the Gaokao face a momentous challenge. If the exam is to continue to serve as a fateful rite of passage, then people must perceive it as both consequential and chancy. But many in China's poor rural areas no longer see the exam as undetermined and thus fair. In response, they are dropping out of school; some even become possessed by spirits or join rebellious millenarian groups. Simultaneously, many in the middle classes no longer perceive the examination as consequential. Members of this relatively privileged group are voting with their feet, increasingly sending their children and capital abroad.

But the challenge of maintaining the fatefulness of the Gaokao is not intrinsic to the examination alone. It is also a problem of general social and economic policy. Even when young people put their faith in the exam, their faith is later eroded as they struggle to fulfill their life projects in the aftermath of the final battle. Facing this struggle, increasing numbers of people in their twenties and thirties describe themselves as lost and confused (*mímáng*).

This lostness and confusion is difficult to define, but refers to a general sense of purposelessness. For many high-school graduates, feeling this way starts right after the Gaokao, but it is not initially tied to economic pressures. Students use the term to describe the existential void that accompanies the sudden relaxation of discipline after the test. As one teacher said, "During high school, students are like a bow, strained to the breaking point under the pressure of the examination. After the examination, they are like an arrow. They shoot out of the bow, then fall to the earth, not knowing what to do with themselves." For twelve long years, students worry only about the final battle. After they finish the Gaokao, they resemble soldiers returning from combat. Confronting the absence of fatefulness in normal life, they feel a vacuum of existential meaning. In some respects, they are also like prisoners released from long-term incarceration. Overwhelmed by the lack of structure that their sudden freedom presents, they are beset by listlessness.

Many students respond to this loss of regimentation by sinking into depression. This depressive aimlessness that follows the Gaokao is such a common affliction that it has acquired its own name—"post-Gaokao disorder" (*Gāokǎo hòuyízhèng*). Every year after the test, psychologists and other mental health professionals hold forth in the media on how to treat this illness. Common cures include taking students on post-Gaokao vacations or encouraging them to take up a hobby.

For many, feeling purposeless does not abate much in college. College students widely complain that university education is empty. Whereas the Gaokao is a true trial of merit, examinations in college count for little. Once students matriculate, they are virtually guaranteed to graduate. Only those who plan to pursue postgraduate education overseas must worry about performing well. Employment is said to be determined not by one's grades but by the ranking of one's college and major, which is fixed at matriculation. Because the college that one attends forms a static aspect of personhood, people ironically refer to it as their birth status (*chūshēng*). In contrast to their hopeful expectation of the Gaokao, which they say can change fate, the college years seem devoid of fatefulness. They are hollow.

Because grades matter so little, many students spend their time in college preparing for further examinations, such as the national or provincial civil-service exams, the graduate-school entrance exam, or various tests required for study abroad. Other students pass their college years sojourning away from campus, working as migrant laborers in various temporary jobs only to return at the end of the semester to take their exams. Some start small businesses, selling products from their home towns. Still others earn money as "substitute examinees" or "sharpshooters," helping people cheat on the Gaokao. Those who are less entrepreneurial often describe large portions of their college experience as "frittering away the time" (*xūdù*), a description that includes playing video games, seeking amusement with friends, and chatting online.

After graduation, this feeling of emptiness may gradually transform into a more serious existential malaise. Most students have worked their whole lives with the expectation that a high score on the Gaokao will enable them to fulfill their parents' and grandparents' expectations of securing a good job and leading a stable, white-collar life. After college, however, many young people find themselves confronted with a disappointing reality. Graduates, especially of second- and third-tier universities, increasingly discover that the labor market will not reward them with jobs that can fulfill their parents' and other relatives' dreams for prosperity and stability (Yanjie Huang 2013; Mok and Wu 2016). Whereas those who receive a degree from a Project 985 university are enviously described as having a permit of passage (*tōngxíngzhèng*) to the good life, those without good "birth status" are less lucky. Young college grads from second-rate schools, who are predominantly of rural origin, may find themselves working as couriers, waiters, or security guards after studying finance, marketing, or economics. The majority of college graduates now earn less than an average migrant worker (Yanjie Huang 2013). The increase in graduate underemployment and unemployment means that the massification of higher education has exacerbated rural-urban income inequality despite expanding access to college (Mok and Wu 2016). For these reasons, many college graduates in their twenties and thirties report experiencing a fundamental "disconnect between ideal and reality" (*lǐxiǎng yǔ xiànshí tuōjié le*), which potentially presages growing discontent with China's established technocratic elite.

In some respects, this widespread existential crisis is structural to the Chinese examination system as it functions in the post-1980s period of labor-market liberalization. The system was designed for an era when every college graduate was assigned a job. Thus people frequently speak of a disconnect between the Gaokao and the labor market (which corresponds to the disconnect between ideal and reality). In many ways, the Gaokao, with its admission quotas and central planning, is a holdover of the planned economy, whereas the labor market has largely shifted to the invisible hand of supply and demand. It remains to be seen whether the current round of reforms to the Gaokao will help reconcile this contradiction. But there are grounds for skepticism. To some degree, the crisis is not just China's alone. Rather, it is merely the Chinese expression of a more general predicament of meritocracy under the changing economic and social conditions of the twenty-first century.

Hereditary Meritocracy: A Consolidating Trend in Authoritarian and Democratic Societies

At the end of the Cold War, social observers confidently declared the "end of history" (Fukuyama 1989). As the Soviet Union dissolved and the former Eastern Bloc states turned toward the West, liberal democracy appeared to have triumphed over authoritarianism. It would only be a matter of time, people thought, before

China, too, democratized. But at the beginning of the third decade of the twenty-first century, things look very different. Under Xi Jinping, China has shifted back to a more aggressive style of top-down rule and centralized control. Meanwhile, democracies around the world are in danger of deconsolidating; young people in many places, including traditional bastions of democracy, seem to prefer authoritarian styles of governance (Mounk 2018). And in what could be described as a Cold War hangover, the meritocratic authoritarianism of China is being touted as an alternative to liberal democracy.[1]

Proponents of this view admire how the ruling elite in China, including high government officials, are selected and promoted via a ladder of meritocratic assessments, of which the Gaokao forms an important foundation (chapter 1). They say that this system of political meritocracy, in which leaders are meritocratically selected rather than democratically elected, may not be suitable for every country, but that democracy is nevertheless not a panacea for every problem (Bell 2015). Authoritarian China has surpassed democratic India in pulling its people out of poverty and in providing access to basic social goods like health insurance and improved water sources and sanitation (Araral and Ratra 2016; Hsiao 2014; Ravallion 2011). Then there is Singapore, with its distinctive blend of capitalist meritocracy and single-party-dominant parliamentary rule. Considered by many Chinese officials to be a model of meritocratic authoritarianism, the island city-state possesses a widely envied public infrastructure and a subsidized housing system with one of the highest rates of home ownership on earth (Chua 2017; Ortmann and Thompson 2016).[2] Those who uphold liberal democratic values generally consider such goods to be human rights, but their provision is often woefully inadequate even in some wealthy democratic countries such as the United States (Alston 2017).

Even as meritocratic authoritarianism may guarantee social goods that liberals hold dear, democracy does not necessarily assure the protection of liberal values.[3] In the twenty-first century, xenophobic and racist populist movements have expanded in the United States, Europe, India, and other bastions of democracy. These movements seem to cast further doubt on the wisdom of democratic governance even as they point toward a growing preference for more autocratic forms of rule.

Populism, even when its politics are abhorrent, contains an important message—a critique of meritocracy. Populism is an assertion of the dignity of the people against the rule of a technocratic elite, who are assuming an increasingly prominent position not only in China but in societies around the world.[4] A meritocratically selected technocratic elite is a central feature of both political democracies and authoritarian regimes. In both systems, members of the technocratic elite fill bureaucracies of all types, whether in government or private business. As inequality within many countries rises and a new global class of plutocrats develops, popular discontent with the elite is also growing (Milanović 2016).

The emergence of discontent has complex causes. But slowing social mobility certainly plays a part. Meritocracies in both democratic and authoritarian countries are becoming hereditary. As I mention in chapter 1, places that embrace strong forms of the myth of meritocracy—which include both kinds of regimes—seem to tolerate higher levels of social inequality. The flip side of this equation may be that the "diploma disease" of meritocratic credentialism has become worse as inequality increases (Dore 1976). In hereditary meritocracies, the possession of an elite credential may assume special significance. On the one hand, it serves as a crucial marker of status because elite privilege, being largely inherited, appears increasingly arbitrary. On the other hand, it helps elites further consolidate their grip on power by making it increasingly difficult for outsiders to achieve the forms of quality that elite status requires.

With the reemergence of elite education and the growing wealth gap in the post-Mao era, China has become just such a hereditary meritocracy—a place where the university that one attends can be jocularly referred to as one's "birth status." This witticism points to not only the fateful significance of college prestige but also gnawing recognition of an unpleasant truth: despite the lip service paid to social mobility, one's place in the meritocracy is profoundly influenced by the opportunities and privileges that go with having the right parents, as, for example, the dominance of urban children in the Gaokao demonstrates. This reality, which is little acknowledged by proponents of the China model, tarnishes the sheen of political meritocracy as an ideal system.[5] It also puts China's rise in a different light. When people say that China's success in pulling people out of poverty proves the correctness of this model, a false dichotomy often results. According to this way of thinking, the world's leaders need to choose between the example of places like India, which are democratic but have failed to achieve China's success with poverty alleviation, or Chinese-style authoritarianism, which is repressive but gets the job done. This kind of debate constrains social and political imaginations to a narrow range of possibilities that appear disparate but share a common assumption: the correctness of developmentalism, the meritocratic ideology linking individual striving and national development (chapter 2). The resulting conversation often falls short in recognizing the negative consequences of developmentalism—such as economic exploitation, environmental degradation, and cultural loss—and fails to imagine the possibility of creating a society that is both less poor and more equal. Despite astronomical increases in conventional indexes of economic success like gross domestic product in post-Mao China, broader measures of personal well-being and quality of life have risen only marginally as the wealth gap widens (Kubiszewski et al. 2013). Achieving change requires thinking beyond the status quo.[6]

The status quo is increasingly unequal. In the twenty-first century, hereditary meritocracy is a consolidating global trend. In many places, meritocratic exams reinforce rather than counteract this trend. Such exams assume special cultural significance in countries with a Confucian legacy: China, Japan, Korea, Singapore, Taiwan, and Vietnam.[7] But examination-based meritocracy is much broader than that. In one form or another, this system is deployed in nearly every country on earth. It can provide an opening for mobility—for people to "change fate." But as economic disparities grow, it tends to bolster hereditary privilege. People often blame teachers and schools for the resulting gaps in achievement, but this argument puts the cart before the horse. Good teachers can accomplish much, but fundamental change requires addressing the underlying cause of achievement gaps: social inequality.

The Future of Meritocracy

Meritocracy—flawed, mythical, and yet integral to the social fabric of modern societies—today faces an onslaught of transformative forces that may bring about its ultimate demise: robotic labor and worker displacement, climate change, aging populations, and the evolving political structures of the near future. These changes may be nothing less than the kind of fundamental social transformation that occurred centuries ago in China and Europe with the transition from feudalism to meritocracy. Thus it would be a failure of political imagination to see hereditary meritocracy as the end of history. The very forms of economic and social change that are giving rise to this intensified form of meritocratic credentialism may also be bringing about a tectonic shift in the foundations of meritocracy.

In China alone, more than one hundred million jobs may be displaced (up to 12 percent of the workforce) by 2030 because of automation (Manyika et al. 2017). Although China is particularly vulnerable because of its reliance on agriculture and manufacturing, both of which are easily automated, many countries around the world are facing similar economic transformations. At the same time, in every region of the earth but Africa, the world's population is aging. By 2030, one in three people in China will be over sixty. Globally, from 2015 to 2030 the number of people aged sixty years or over is projected to rise 56 percent, from 901 million to 1.4 billion (United Nations 2015).

These changes signal a fundamental shift in the world's political economy. As workforces age and growing segments of the economy are automated, fewer and fewer jobs will likely be available for young people. Under such conditions, the hopeful promise of meritocracy pursued by rural Gaokao warriors increasingly seems like an impossible goal—a form of "cruel optimism" (Berlant 2011). As this hope slips from the grasp of rising numbers of people in China and elsewhere, lostness and confusion may become more common.

At the same time, the nature of work is changing. It appears likely that intelligent machines will take over many types of human labor, including not only blue-collar jobs like farming and driving but many white-collar jobs in accounting, medicine, and law (Susskind and Susskind 2015). These changing economic conditions raise questions about the future of work itself and, along with it, the future of meritocracy. Without the reward of better employment, the promise of meritocracy rings empty.

What might follow meritocracy? When Marx first conceived of communism, it was not as a system in which the state would merely take on the role of lead capitalist, as occurred in the "really-existing" communisms of China and the Soviet Union, among other places, in the twentieth century. Rather, what Marx had in mind was a science-fiction scenario in which the forces of production (technology and human labor) became so advanced that they would bring about a fundamental shift in the relations of production, that is, the division of labor. Marx ([1846] 1970, 52–53) imagined nothing less than the negation of that division, a world in which people could "do one thing today and another tomorrow," one kind of work "in the morning" and another "after dinner," without ever being defined by any single role.

Is the world getting closer to the society that Marx imagined? If the economy requires fewer and fewer people to work, and if the existing world of surplus and riches seems to be flowing to an ever-decreasing slice of the population, then how should societies respond? A common answer is that people should be prepared through constant retraining for frequent shifts of occupation. But this suggestion assumes that workers will still be needed—that there will, in other words, be enough traditional jobs for which people can retrain themselves. Others suggest that everyone should be paid a basic salary even when they are not working—a universal basic income (Ferguson 2015). Under this scenario, people should be encouraged to define for themselves what meaningful labor consists in. If we no longer need as many accountants, doctors, and lawyers, perhaps we will want more designers, poets, and scientists, or even new types of people who combine these roles. (I am biased, but I would certainly like to see more anthropologists!) And without doubt, we will require more caregivers for the very old (Greenhalgh 2010; Kleinman 2010). In any case, it seems likely that this redefinition of work will entail a massive redistribution of wealth. But a more equitable world would be a happier and more peaceful one—a rising tide that lifts all boats (Wilkinson and Pickett 2010).

In addition to automation, another human-caused difficulty bedevils the future of meritocracy: climate change (Frase 2016). A warming earth will affect different populations disproportionately and will result in increased conflicts over scare resources, like drinking water and arable land. Cultural conceptions of merit contribute to this problem. Just as the ideology of individual merit renders moot the contributions of parents, teachers, and society, the ideology of national merit overlooks the sacrifices of poor, marginalized, and subjugated peoples. Members of these groups disproportionately pay the costs and suffer the consequences of the industrial development that has warmed the planet and made some countries richer than others.

The way that humanity responds to the twin challenges of automation and climate change will determine what the future looks like: an apocalyptic future, in which the rich monopolize an increasing world of plenty while the poor struggle to survive; or a utopian one, in which the increasing productive capacities of humanity lift everyone up. Probably the reality will be somewhere in between. But the important thing is to see that the world has a choice (Frase 2016). All too often, the status quo presents itself as fate—a fait accompli, or the end of history. According to this view, the economic and political arrangements that people take for granted may be consequential, but they are predetermined by history or human nature and thus not subject to fateful transformation. Through imagination and collective action, however, the future can be changed. It is not a fait accompli but a fateful choice.

If hard work no longer guarantees success—and, indeed, if the very social system in which such a statement is intelligible ceases to exist—then meritocratic rites of passage such as the Gaokao may no longer be meaningful. But I believe that human beings will always need fateful rites of passage to create existential meaning and that societies will always require rituals to manage social transformations. It will be up to future generations, however, to define what that means in a world beyond the historical limits of meritocracy as conventionally conceived. One thing seems certain, though: change will not take place without political vision and will. The transformation of meritocracy into whatever follows it will come about only through a series of struggles, small and large, individual and social, which will themselves be fateful rites of passage.

Notes

PROLOGUE: THE FINAL BATTLE

1. The full name of the exam is "The People's Republic of China General Higher Education National Unified Student Recruitment Examination." The abbreviation, Gaokao, means "higher exam."

2. Predictions of China's future dominance are legion. Martin Jacques (2012) provides a popular account. For a more sober assessment, see Shambaugh (2016).

CHAPTER 1. A FATEFUL RITE OF PASSAGE

1. I take the term frontstage, which I discuss further in chapter 3, from Goffman (1959). On the "empty/full" or "false/real" distinction, see the useful edited volume by Susanne Bregnbæk and Mikkel Bunkenborg (2017). My essay in the volume contains further description of the rhetoric of emptiness/fullness and its relation to the Gaokao (Howlett 2017).

2. The initiation ritual of the Sambia people of Papua New Guinea supplies an example (Herdt 1981). As boys, Sambia initiates are taught to thrust stiff, sharp pieces of grass up their nose until the blood flows. They are first subjected to this practice by others, then learn to perform it on themselves. The ability to do so calmly becomes a test of Sambia masculinity. Such self-control is emblematic of the ability to face violence with equanimity—the hallmark of Sambia warriorhood (Herdt 1981, 204; 224; 246).

3. See my further discussion of promotion rates and the Gaokao system below.

4. See Lickona and Davidson (2005) for an influential formulation of this distinction, which has become popular in discussions of "character education" in the United States. "Ethical character" is usually termed "moral character," but I prefer the former because it highlights the social and cultural dimensions of personal character.

5. See also Lin Yi (2018).

6. The potlatch is an agonistic gift-giving ritual in which moieties and clans compete for control over powerful magical crests and aristocratic titles (Kan 2016). In Kula, participants "risk life and limb to travel across huge expanses of dangerous ocean" (Malinowski 1961) in a competition for the social recognition or "fame" that the exchange of ornamental objects confers (Munn 1986).

7. Nationwide, fewer than 2 percent of academic high school graduates attend Project 985 universities (see chapter 3), and, as I note below, less than half of China's children go to academic high school.

8. I am grateful to Emily Martin (personal correspondence) for pointing out this resemblance.

9. I take these numbers from *Sina Education* (2015).

10. See *Sohu* (2017). The category of first-tier includes Project 985, Project 211, and provincial keypoint universities.

11. University programs in China are divided into three tiers based on the "batches" (*pī*) in which they admit students, each tier having a different overall cutoff score. See Yu et al. (2012) for a comprehensive description.

12. New teachers may need to prove themselves before being granted the opportunity to teach the all-important senior-three year, and particularly effective teachers may be asked to specialize in teaching senior three.

13. The 3+1+2 system was preceded by brief experimentation in some provinces with a 3+3 system, in which students were tested in the three compulsory subjects (Chinese, math, and English) and could choose any three electives from the remaining six (biology, chemistry, geography, history, physics, and politics). But critics of the reform said that it led to students gaming the system by choosing combinations of electives in which it was relatively easy to score high. Few students chose physics because of its difficulty. In the 3+1+2 system, forcing students to choose between physics and history is a way of ensuring that there are adequate numbers of test takers in these relatively unpopular subjects. In a handful of provinces, students are already allowed to take the English section of the Gaokao twice per year starting in senior two, but this reform has been delayed in Fujian Province, my field site. A further reform allowing students similar flexibility with their elective-subject exams has been piloted in Zhejiang Province, but a national rollout is still uncertain. In Zhejiang, a common complaint is that this latter reform turns senior two and senior three into a protracted and exhausting Gaokao marathon, in which students retake what exams they can in the hope of improving their scores. Many of the new Gaokao reforms are still in flux and likely to undergo further changes.

14. During my fieldwork, my knowledge of the local Minnan dialect remained rudimentary. But Mandarin, which is the official language of school instruction, was adequate for my purposes. At schools, teachers and students stick almost exclusively to Mandarin. This is particularly true in cities, where many of them hail from other regions of Fujian and China (see chapter 2).

15. With permission, I made audio recordings of focus groups and some interviews. But generally my method consisted in jotting down records of conversations in a pocket notebook, which I transcribed into daily field notes. I sometimes reviewed my field notes with my interlocutors, adding a layer of commentary as we read them together.

16. I take the term from *The Economist* (2015), which uses it to refer to the United States. As I note below in the epilogue, people in China sometimes refer to one's college as one's "birth status," implying a similar critique.

17. To respond to this problem, the College Board—the company that administers the principle US college admissions test, the SAT—started including a so-called adversity index with its score reports in 2019 in an attempt to quantify the impact of neighborhoods and schools on student achievement. This initiative faced withering critique from many quarters and has since been rolled back. Now, admissions officers see school and neighborhood disadvantage scores rather than a single index of adversity, which critics felt to be an overly reductive measure of hardship and social background. Still, at least some commentators saw the adversity score as a step in the right direction of acknowledging the impact of social environment on test scores (Jack 2019).

CHAPTER 2. MOBILITY, TIME, AND VALUE

1. Precipitating causes included the 2008 Wenquan earthquake in Sichuan, which unleashed a wave of social protests after claiming the lives of many children after shoddily constructed schools collapsed, and ethnic riots in 2009 in Urumqi.

2. *Yuánfèn* is often translated as destiny, but I translate it as fortune to differentiate it from the closely related concepts of *mìng* and *mìngyùn*.

3. It is difficult to say how prevalent suicide is among rural students. Educational authorities closely guard this information. In general, however, suicide rates in rural areas,

particularly among women, are relatively high (Kleinman et al. 2011, 12–13). Moreover, suicide is not only a problem of rural areas but also one of the urban elite (Bregnbæk 2016).

4. For a discussion of extreme poverty in the United States, see the report of United Nations Special Rapporteur Philip Alston (2017).

5. I take the China figures from the Center for China and Globalization (2017). The US figures come the Institute of International Education (*Open Doors* 2017). After the 2016 presidential election, however, many US colleges started experiencing a marked drop off in enrollment of Chinese students.

6. In particular, Singapore's brand of meritocratic authoritarianism has long made the city-state a model for Chinese development (Ortmann and Thompson 2016).

7. Whereas in 2007 the ratio of returnees to new foreign students was only 35 percent, by 2017 it had risen to nearly 80 percent (Center for China and Globalization 2017). It is unclear, however, precisely how many of these returnees only decide to come back to China after they or a close family member have already acquired foreign residency or a foreign passport and thus a way out.

8. *The Economist* (2019) summarizes these trends.

9. Mobility produces similar effects in other cultural contexts. Young's (2004) study of marginalized black men in Chicago shows how those who have no exposure to the world outside of their own communities tend to blame themselves as individuals for the effects of social inequality and discrimination. Also writing about Chicago, Shedd (2015) reports similar findings. She documents how students from poor neighborhoods who bus to school in wealthy neighborhoods achieve a comparatively greater awareness of how access to resources and opportunities contributes to success.

CHAPTER 3. COUNTERFEIT FAIRNESS

1. In other regions, even some cities the size of Ningzhou pursue relatively aggressive tracking. But the general trend holds; the larger and more centrally located a city, the more likely it is to conform to centrally dictated norms.

2. Critics object that concepts like "misrecognition" (Bourdieu 1990) and "cynicism" (Žižek 2008; Sloterdijk 1988) falsely assume the reality of a unitary spoken ego—"a unified, bounded, sovereign individual" for whom meaning is fully formed before the act of speaking (Yurchak 2006, 18). Sharing a commitment to a broadly defined poststructural approach to social analysis, I agree that such essentialist notions of personhood should be avoided (see chapter 1). But a philosophically rigorous conception of personhood does not preclude retaining these concepts as useful tools of analysis. Further, sometimes such critiques can be overblown. For example, Goffman has himself been critiqued for subscribing to the essentialist view that a "real self" exists "behind the mask" (Butler 1988). But as Ian Hacking (2004) argues, Goffman's micropolitical approach to sociology is fully consistent with a social constructionist view of personhood that is complementary to Michel Foucault's genealogical approach to history.

3. I borrow the useful analytical distinction between "preferential" and "positive" policies from Zhou (2010). Most scholars refer to both types of policy as "preferential," directly translating the Chinese (*yōuhuì zhèngcè*). Hannum and Wang (2006) provide a useful analysis of regional disparities in education.

4. See Human Rights in China (2014).

5. In 2015, Shenzhen bucked this trend by publishing first-tier admission rates for all municipal high schools as part of a "sunshine policy." But the data appear to be no longer available.

6. Another big draw of private schools is the market for students who wish to repeat their senior-three year of high school to retake the examination (*fùdú*)—a service that only private schools can now legally provide.

7. Consider, for example, the nose-bleeding rite of the Sambia people of Papua New Guinea. When elders first subject initiates to this procedure, the terrified young boys believe that they are being viciously attacked by spirits (Herdt 1981, 224). From the perspective of individual initiates, the experience is genuinely fateful. They fear for their lives. But the elders know that the occasion is actually a well-choreographed ritual in which participants rarely suffer serious injury.

CHAPTER 4. DILIGENCE VERSUS QUALITY

1. See *Straits Times* (2017). Family firms have long contributed to the rise of distinctively Chinese forms of capitalism (Hamilton 1996).

2. Woronov (2008) notes that private urban schools for poor migrant children can emphasize quality because such schools do not need to prepare students to take examinations.

3. See World Economic Forum (2017).

4. The UN ranking can be found in United Nations Development Programme (2019: 334).

5. See, for example, *People's Daily Online* (2017).

6. Consider the controversy surrounding the admission of Asian Americans to Harvard (Mahdawi 2018).

CHAPTER 5. COURAGE UNDER FIRE

1. The linguistic theory of markedness (see, for example, Battistella 1990) provides a useful tool for describing such differences in predilection. I suggest that in ordinary Chinese pedagogical discourse, models based on the innate/learned distinction seem to be more marked whereas models based on the environment/personal distinction seemed to be unmarked. Conversely, in North American contexts, the opposite pertains.

2. Writing about life in a rural high school, M. H. Hansen (2015, 134–40) also describes how a similar modern-style pep rally was relatively well received in her field site.

3. See, for example, Cadwalladr (2015).

4. Many medical practitioners in China and worldwide employ this practice as a way for girls and women to reduce the timing and severity of endometriosis and premenstrual syndrome. Skeptics may regard such interventions as an unfortunate medicalization and even pathologization of menstruation (Martin 2001). In the global context, however, this use of birth control pills is common, and it is often regarded as medically necessary by patients and physicians.

5. The theories of Chinese teachers and students regarding somatization accord to some degree with anthropological approaches. In Arthur Kleinman's (1988) influential treatment of somatization, examination stress forms one prominent "social origin" of illness in China.

6. Entrance to the examination hall entails a mortification of self that is typical of asylums, the military, boarding schools, and other total institutions (Goffman 1962).

7. In the US context, both disadvantaged and affluent children experience high rates of depression and suicide (Luthar 1999; Luthar and Becker 2002). See also Rosin (2015) on suicide in wealthy Palo Alto, California, schools.

CHAPTER 6. MAGIC AND MERITOCRACY

1. On China's experiments with social credit systems, see, for example, Naughton (2018).

2. In a largely opaque process, universities set admission quotas for each province and major; then, based on these quotas, they admit top scorers (Yu et al. 2012). Of course, various direct admission programs also exist (see chapter 3).

3. The divinatory significance of gambling appears to be particularly great in Chinese cultural contexts, but it also constitutes an important yet understudied element of gambling more generally (Lindner 1950).

EPILOGUE: LOST AND CONFUSED

1. I take the term "meritocratic authoritarianism" from Ortmann and Thompson (2016).

2. It is unclear if the solutions of Singapore can be scaled up to a country as vast as China (Ortmann and Thompson 2016). Since the 2000s, moreover, the ways in which meritocracy reinforces social inequality have become a burning issue of public debate there (Teo 2018).

3. In the absence of strong constitutional protections, populists can use democracy to undermine basic liberal values, as in the case of Hungary's Fidesz Party (Schupmann 2019).

4. I thank Philip Gorski for sharing these thoughts on populism in a personal communication.

5. Mark Elliot (2012), debating from a historical perspective, makes a similar argument.

6. Such trends suggest the need to expand traditional definitions of development and poverty alleviation to encompass more comprehensive and diverse notions of human flourishing (Lau 2020).

7. Taiwan provides a fascinating case of parallel evolution to China. The country's national college entrance exam—termed the Liankao—developed separately from the Mainland Chinese system but resembles it in many respects (Zeng 1999). Korea and Vietnam, both of which were tributary states of China in imperial times and possessed their own civil exams modeled after that of their Chinese "big brother," have implemented similar meritocratic systems (Woodside 2006). In Vietnam, a high score on the examination is prerequisite for a good job. In South Korea, top colleges serve as a pipeline to coveted careers in Korea's top companies—the *chaebols*. In contrast to Vietnam and Korea, Japan did not introduce exams until the Meiji period (1868–1912), when that country transformed itself from a feudal system of samurai lords into a market society. Meiji reformers considered using China as a model for Japan's examination system but settled on Prussia as the prototype (Zeng 1999). Apparently unbeknownst to Japanese reformers, however, the Prussian system seems to have received inspiration from China (Jacobsen 2015). A similar irony underlies Singapore's experience with meritocracy. Scholars point out that the Singaporean education and public-service systems are influenced not only by Confucianism but also by British colonialism—a historical reality that national history sometimes ignores (Ortmann and Thompson 2016). But such arguments themselves overlook how the exam system in China seems to have provided stimulus for the uptake of meritocratic exams in colonial-era Britain (Teng 1943).

References

Alston, Philip. 2017. "Statement on Visit to the USA, United Nations Special Rapporteur on Extreme Poverty and Human Rights." Geneva: United Nations Office of the High Commissioner for Human Rights. https://www.ohchr.org/EN/NewsEvents/Pages/DisplayNews.aspx?NewsID=22533.

Anagnost, Ann. 1997. "Children and National Transcendence in China." In *Constructing China: The Interaction of Culture and Economics*, edited by Kenneth Lieberthal, Shuen-fu Lin, and Ernest P. Young, 195–222. Ann Arbor: Center for Chinese Studies, University of Michigan.

———. 2004. "The Corporeal Politics of Quality (Suzhi)." *Public Culture* 16 (2): 189–208. https://muse.jhu.edu/article/169125.

Andreas, Joel. 2004. "Leveling the Little Pagoda: The Impact of College Examinations, and Their Elimination, on Rural Education in China." *Comparative Education Review* 48 (1): 1–47. http://doi.org/10.1086/379840.

———. 2009. *Rise of the Red Engineers: The Cultural Revolution and the Origins of China's New Class*. Stanford, CA: Stanford University Press.

Araral, Eduardo, and Shivani Ratra. 2016. "Water Governance in India and China: Comparison of Water Law, Policy and Administration." *Water Policy* 18 (S1): 14–31. https://doi.org/10.2166/wp.2016.102.

Bakken, Børge. 2000. *The Exemplary Society: Human Improvement, Social Control, and the Dangers of Modernity in China*. Oxford: Oxford University Press.

Battistella, Edwin L. 1990. *Markedness: The Evaluative Superstructure of Language*. SUNY Series in Linguistics. Albany: SUNY Press.

Becker, Gary S. 1993. *Human Capital: A Theoretical and Empirical Analysis, with Special Reference to Education*. 3rd ed. Chicago: University of Chicago Press.

Bell, Daniel. 2015. *The China Model: Political Meritocracy and the Limits of Democracy*. Princeton, NJ: Princeton University Press.

Benney, Jonathan. 2016. "Weiwen at the Grassroots: China's Stability Maintenance Apparatus as a Means of Conflict Resolution." *Journal of Contemporary China* 25 (99): 389–405. https://doi.org/10.1080/10670564.2015.1104876.

Berg, Daria. 2002. "Marvelling at the Wonders of the Metropolis: Perceptions of Seventeenth-Century Chinese Cities in the Novel *Xingshi Yinyuan Zhuan*." In *Town and Country in China: Identity and Perception*, edited by David Faure and Tao Liu, 17–40. St. Antony's Series. Basingstoke, UK: Palgrave.

Berlant, Lauren Gail. 2011. *Cruel Optimism*. Durham, NC: Duke University Press.

Billioud, Sébastien, and Joël Thoraval. 2015. *The Sage and the People: The Confucian Revival in China*. Oxford: Oxford University Press.

Blum, Susan Debra. 2007. *Lies That Bind: Chinese Truth, Other Truths*. Lanham, MD: Rowman & Littlefield.

———. 2009. *My Word! Plagiarism and College Culture*. Ithaca, NY: Cornell University Press.

———. 2016. *"I Love Learning; I Hate School": An Anthropology of College*. Ithaca, NY: Cornell University Press.

Bol, Peter Kees. 1989. "Chu Hsi's Redefinition of Literati Learning." In *Neo-Confucian Education: The Formative Stage*, edited by Wm. Theodore De Bary, John W. Chaffee, and Bettine Birge, 151–85. Berkeley: University of California Press.

——. 2008. *Neo-Confucianism in History*. Cambridge, MA: Harvard University Asia Center.

Boretz, Avron Albert. 2011. *Gods, Ghosts, and Gangsters: Ritual Violence, Martial Arts, and Masculinity on the Margins of Chinese Society*. Honolulu: University of Hawai'i Press.

Bosco, Joseph, Lucia Huwy-Min Liu, and Matthew West. 2009. "Underground Lotteries in China: The Occult Economy and Capitalist Culture." In *Economic Development, Integration, and Morality in Asia and the Americas*, edited by Donald Wood, 31–62. Research in Economic Anthropology 29. Bingley, UK: Emerald Group.

Bourdieu, Pierre. 1977. *Outline of a Theory of Practice*. Translated by Richard Nice. London: Cambridge University Press.

——. 1984. *Distinction: A Social Critique of the Judgement of Tastes*. Translated by Richard Nice. Cambridge, MA: Harvard University Press.

——. 1986. "The Forms of Capital." In *Handbook of Theory and Research for the Sociology of Education*, edited by John G. Richardson, translated by Richard Nice, 241–58. Westport, CT: Greenwood.

——. 1990. *The Logic of Practice*. Translated by Richard Nice. Stanford, CA: Stanford University Press.

——. 1991. *Language and Symbolic Power*. Cambridge, MA: Harvard University Press.

——. 2001. *Masculine Domination*. Stanford, CA: Stanford University Press.

Bourdieu, Pierre, and Jean-Claude Passeron. 1977. *Reproduction in Education, Society, and Culture*. London: SAGE.

Boyer, Dominic. 2010. "On the Ethics and Practice of Contemporary Social Theory: From Crisis Talk to Multiattentional Method." *Dialectical Anthropology* 34 (3): 305–24. https://doi.org/10.1007/s10624-009-9141-6.

Brandt, Loren, Debin Ma, and Thomas G. Rawski. 2014. "From Divergence to Convergence: Reevaluating the History behind China's Economic Boom." *Journal of Economic Literature* 52 (1): 45–123. https://doi.org/10.1257/jel.52.1.45.

Bregnbæk, Susanne. 2016. *Fragile Elite: The Dilemmas of China's Top University Students*. Stanford, CA: Stanford University Press.

Bregnbæk, Susanne, and Mikkel Bunkenborg, eds. 2017. *Emptiness and Fullness: Ethnographies of Lack and Desire in Contemporary China*. Integration and Conflict Studies 2. New York: Berghahn.

Brokaw, Cynthia Joanne. 1991. *The Ledgers of Merit and Demerit: Social Change and Moral Order in Late Imperial China*. Princeton, NJ: Princeton University Press.

——. 2007. *Commerce in Culture: The Sibao Book Trade in the Qing and Republican Periods*. Cambridge, MA: Harvard University Asia Center.

Brook, Timothy. 1998. *The Confusions of Pleasure: Commerce and Culture in Ming China*. Berkeley: University of California Press.

Buchmann, Claudia, and Thomas A. DiPrete. 2006. "The Growing Female Advantage in College Completion: The Role of Family Background and Academic Achievement." *American Sociological Review* 71 (4): 515–41. https://doi.org/10.1177/000312240607100401.

Butler, Judith. 1988. "Performative Acts and Gender Constitution: An Essay in Phenomenology and Feminist Theory." *Theatre Journal* 40 (4): 519–31. http://www.jstor.org/stable/3207893.

——. 1997. *The Psychic Life of Power: Theories in Subjection*. Stanford, CA: Stanford University Press.

Cadwalladr, Carole. 2015. "Students Used to Take Drugs to Get High. Now They Take Them to Get Higher Grades." *Observer*, February 14, 2010. https://www.theguardian.com/society/2015/feb/15/students-smart-drugs-higher-grades-adderall-modafinil.

Carrico, Kevin. 2017. *The Great Han: Race, Nationalism, and Tradition in China Today.* Oakland: University of California Press.

Center for China and Globalization. 2017. *Report on Employment and Entrepreneurship of Chinese Returnees.* Beijing: Center for China and Globalization. http://en.ccg.org.cn/uploads/2019/09/041611142933.pdf.

Chaffee, John W. 1995. *The Thorny Gates of Learning in Sung China: A Social History of Examinations.* New ed. Albany: SUNY Press.

Chan, Christina Y., and Stevan Harrell. 2010. "School Consolidation in Rural Sichuan." In *Affirmative Action in China and the U.S.: A Dialogue on Inequality and Minority Education*, edited by Minglang Zhou and Ann Maxwell Hill, 144–64. New York: Macmillan.

Charles, Maria. 2011. "A World of Difference: International Trends in Women's Economic Status." *Annual Review of Sociology* 37 (1): 355–71. https://doi.org/10.1146/annurev.soc.012809.102548.

Chau, Adam Yuet. 2006. *Miraculous Response: Doing Popular Religion in Contemporary China.* Stanford, CA: Stanford University Press.

Cherng, Hua-Yu Sebastian, and Emily Hannum. 2013. "Community Poverty, Industrialization, and Educational Gender Gaps in Rural China." *Social Forces* 92 (2): 659–90. https://doi.org/10.1093/sf/sot084.

Chow, Kai-wing. 2004. *Publishing, Culture, and Power in Early Modern China.* Stanford, CA: Stanford University Press.

Chu, Julie Y. 2010. *Cosmologies of Credit: Transnational Mobility and the Politics of Destination in China.* Durham, NC: Duke University Press.

Chua, Beng Huat. 2017. *Liberalism Disavowed: Communitarianism and State Capitalism in Singapore.* Ithaca, NY: Cornell University Press.

Chumley, Lily. 2016. *Creativity Class: Art School and Culture Work in Postsocialist China.* Princeton, NJ: Princeton University Press.

Chumley, Lily, and Wang Jing. 2013. "'If You Don't Care for Your Money, It Won't Care for You': Chronotypes of Risk and Return in Chinese Wealth Management." In *Qualitative Research in Gambling: Exploring the Production and Consumption of Risk*, edited by Rebecca Cassidy, Andrea Pisac, and Claire Loussouarn, 202–17. New York: Routledge.

Chung, Carol, and Mark Mason. 2012. "Why Do Primary School Students Drop Out in Poor, Rural China? A Portrait Sketched in a Remote Mountain Village." *International Journal of Educational Development* 32 (4): 537–45. https://doi.org/10.1016/j.ijedudev.2012.02.012.

Cohen, David, and Nathan Beauchamp-Mustafaga. 2014. "Anti-Privilege Campaign Hits the Chinese Middle Class." *China Brief* 14 (17): 1–3. https://jamestown.org/program/anti-privilege-campaign-hits-the-chinese-middle-class/.

Cohen, Myron L. 1970. "Developmental Process in the Chinese Domestic Group." In *Family and Kinship in Chinese Society*, edited by Ai-li S. Chin and Maurice Freedman, 21–36. Stanford, CA: Stanford University Press.

Cohen, Paul A. 1984. *Discovering History in China: American Historical Writing on the Recent Chinese Past.* New York: Columbia University Press.

Csikszentmihalyi, Mihaly. 1991. *Flow: The Psychology of Optimal Experience.* New York: Harper Collins.

Davis, Deborah. 2014. "Privatization of Marriage in Post-Socialist China." *Modern China* 40 (6): 551–77. https://doi.org/10.1177/0097700414536528.

De Weerdt, Hilde Godelieve Dominique. 2007. *Competition over Content: Negotiating Standards for the Civil Service Examinations in Imperial China (1127–1279)*. Cambridge, MA: Harvard University Asia Center.

Demerath, Peter. 2009. *Producing Success: The Culture of Personal Advancement in an American High School*. Chicago: University of Chicago Press.

Derrida, Jacques. 1989. "Force of Law: The Mystical Foundation of Authority." *Cardozo Law Review* 11:919–51.

Dickens, William T., and James R. Flynn. 2001. "Heritability Estimates versus Large Environmental Effects: The IQ Paradox Resolved." *Psychological Review* 108 (2): 346–69. https://doi.org/10.1037/0033-295X.108.2.346.

Dore, Ronald. 1976. *The Diploma Disease: Education, Qualification, and Development*. Berkeley: University of California Press.

Duara, Prasenjit. 1995. *Rescuing History from the Nation: Questioning Narratives of Modern China*. Chicago: University of Chicago Press.

Duckworth, Angela L., Christopher Peterson, Michael D. Matthews, and Dennis R. Kelly. 2007. "Grit: Perseverance and Passion for Long-Term Goals." *Journal of Personality and Social Psychology* 92 (6): 1087–1101. https://doi.org/10.1037/0022-3514.92.6.1087.

Dunn, Emily C. 2009. "'Cult,' Church, and the CCP: Introducing Eastern Lightning." *Modern China* 35 (1): 96–119. https://doi.org/10.1177/0097700408320546.

Economist. 2015. "An Hereditary Meritocracy," January 22, 2015. https://www.economist.com/briefing/2015/01/22/an-hereditary-meritocracy.

———. 2019. "The Growing Ranks of Unemployed Graduates Worry China's Government," August 1, 2019. https://www.economist.com/china/2019/08/01/the-growing-ranks-of-unemployed-graduates-worry-chinas-government.

Elliott, Mark. 2012. "Opinion: The Real China Model." *New York Times*, November 13, 2012. https://www.nytimes.com/2012/11/14/opinion/the-real-china-model.html.

Elman, Benjamin A. 2000. *A Cultural History of Civil Examinations in Late Imperial China*. Berkeley: University of California Press.

———. 2005. *On Their Own Terms: Science in China, 1550–1900*. Cambridge, MA: Harvard University Press.

———. 2013. *Civil Examinations and Meritocracy in Late Imperial China*. Cambridge, MA: Harvard University Press.

Fanon, Frantz. 2008. *Black Skin, White Masks*. New ed. New York: Grove.

Farquhar, Judith. 2002. *Appetites: Food and Sex in Postsocialist China*. Durham, NC: Duke University Press.

Fei, Xiaotong. [1947] 1992. *From the Soil, the Foundations of Chinese Society: A Translation of Fei Xiaotong's Xiangtu Zhongguo, with an Introduction and Epilogue*. Translated by Gary G. Hamilton and Zheng Wang. Berkeley: University of California Press.

Feng, Wang. 2010. "China's Population Destiny: The Looming Crisis." *Current History* 109 (728): 244–51. http://search.proquest.com/docview/749603801/abstract/C1CB19B5EC7C42A9PQ/1.

Ferguson, James. 1990. *The Anti-Politics Machine: "Development," Depoliticization, and Bureaucratic Power in Lesotho*. Cambridge: Cambridge University Press.

———. 2015. *Give a Man a Fish: Reflections on the New Politics of Distribution*. Durham, NC: Duke University Press.

Festa, Paul E. 2007. "Mahjong Agonistics and the Political Public in Taiwan: Fate, Mimesis, and the Martial Imaginary." *Anthropological Quarterly* 80 (1): 93–125. https://doi.org/10.1353/anq.2007.0004.

Feuchtwang, Stephan. 1992. *The Imperial Metaphor: Popular Religion in China*. New York: Routledge.

Fincher, Leta Hong. 2016. *Leftover Women: The Resurgence of Gender Inequality in China.* London: Zed.

Finn, Chester E., Jr. 2010. "A Sputnik Moment for U.S. Education." *Wall Street Journal,* December 8, 2010. https://www.wsj.com/articles/SB10001424052748704156304 576003871654183998.

Fiskesjö, Magnus. 1999. "On the 'Raw' and the 'Cooked' Barbarians of Imperial China." *Inner Asia* 1 (2): 139–68. https://doi.org/10.1163/146481799793648004.

———. 2006. "Rescuing the Empire: Chinese Nation-Building in the Twentieth Century." *European Journal of East Asian Studies* 5 (1): 15–44. https://doi.org/10.1163/ 157006106777998106.

Flynn, James R. 1987. "Massive IQ Gains in 14 Nations: What IQ Tests Really Measure." *Psychological Bulletin* 101 (2): 171–91. https://doi.org/10.1037/0033-2909.101. 2.171.

Foley, Douglas E. 1990. *Learning Capitalist Culture: Deep in the Heart of Tejas.* Philadelphia: University of Pennsylvania Press.

Fong, Vanessa L. 2002. "China's One-Child Policy and the Empowerment of Urban Daughters." *American Anthropologist* 104 (4): 1098–1109. https://doi.org/10.1525/ aa.2002.104.4.1098.

———. 2006. *Only Hope: Coming of Age under China's One-Child Policy.* Stanford, CA: Stanford University Press.

———. 2011. *Paradise Redefined: Transnational Chinese Students and the Quest for Flexible Citizenship in the Developed World.* Stanford, CA: Stanford University Press.

Foucault, Michel. 1995. *Discipline and Punish: The Birth of the Prison.* New York: Vintage.

Frank, Robert H. 2016. *Success and Luck: Good Fortune and the Myth of Meritocracy.* Princeton, NJ: Princeton University Press.

Frase, Peter. 2016. *Four Futures: Life after Capitalism.* London: Verso.

Freud, Sigmund. [1905] 1960. *Jokes and Their Relation to the Unconscious.* New York: W. W. Norton.

———. [1919] 2005. *Civilization and Its Discontents.* New York: W. W. Norton.

Friedman, Sara. 2006. *Intimate Politics: Marriage, the Market, and State Power in Southeastern China.* Cambridge, MA: Harvard University Asia Center.

Fu, Yiqin. 2013. "China's Unfair College Admissions System." *Atlantic,* June 19, 2013. https://www.theatlantic.com/china/archive/2013/06/chinas-unfair-college-admissions-system/276995/.

Fukuyama, Francis. 1989. "The End of History?" *National Interest,* no. 16, 3–18. https:// www.jstor.org/stable/24027184.

Gaetano, Arianne M. 2014. "'Leftover Women': Postponing Marriage and Renegotiating Womanhood in Urban China." *Journal of Research in Gender Studies* 4 (2): 124–49. https://www.ceeol.com/search/article-detail?id=2960.

Geshiere, Peter. 2003. "On Witch Doctors and Spin Doctors: The Role of 'Experts' in African and American Politics." In *Magic and Modernity: Interfaces of Revelation and Concealment,* edited by Birgit Meyer and Peter Pels, 159–82. Stanford, CA: Stanford University Press.

Gladney, Dru C. 2004. *Dislocating China: Reflections on Muslims, Minorities, and Other Subaltern Subjects.* Chicago: University of Chicago Press.

Gmelch, George. 1971. "Baseball Magic." *Trans-action,* 8 (8): 39–41. https://link.springer. com/article/10.1007/BF02908325.

Goffman, Erving. 1959. *The Presentation of Self in Everyday Life.* Garden City, NY: Doubleday.

———. 1962. "On the Characteristics of Total Institutions." In *Asylums: Essays on the Social Situation of Mental Patients and Other Inmates,* 1–124. Chicago: Aldine.

——. 1967. "Where the Action Is." In *Interaction Ritual: Essays in Face-to-Face Behavior*, 149–270. Chicago: Aldine.

——. 1974. *Frame Analysis: An Essay on the Organization of Experience*. Cambridge, MA: Harvard University Press.

Goodman, David S.G. 2014. *Class in Contemporary China*. China Today Series. Cambridge: Polity.

Gorski, Philip S. 2003. *The Disciplinary Revolution: Calvinism and the Rise of the State in Early Modern Europe*. Chicago: University of Chicago Press.

Gramsci, Antonio. 1971. *Selections from the Prison Notebooks of Antonio Gramsci*. Edited and translated by Quintin Hoare and Geoffrey N. Smith. New York: International Publishers.

Greenhalgh, Susan. 2010. *Cultivating Global Citizens: Population in the Rise of China*. Cambridge, MA: Harvard University Press.

Guillory, John. 1993. *Cultural Capital*. Chicago: University of Chicago Press.

Guinier, Lani. 2015. *The Tyranny of the Meritocracy: Democratizing Higher Education in America*. Boston: Beacon.

Guo, Congbin, Mun C. Tsang, and Xiaohao Ding. 2010. "Gender Disparities in Science and Engineering in Chinese Universities." Special issue in Honor of Henry M. Levin, *Economics of Education Review*, 29 (2): 225–35. https://doi.org/10.1016/j.econedurev.2009.06.005.

Hacking, Ian. 2004. "Between Michel Foucault and Erving Goffman: Between Discourse in the Abstract and Face-to-Face Interaction." *Economy and Society* 33 (3): 277–302. http://www.tandfonline.com/doi/abs/10.1080/0308514042000225671.

Hamilton, Gary G. 1996. "Overseas Chinese Capitalism." In *Confucian Traditions in East Asian Modernity: Moral Education and Economic Culture in Japan and the Four Mini-Dragons*, edited by Weiming Tu, 328–42. Cambridge, MA: Harvard University Press.

Hannum, Emily C. 1999. "Political Change and the Urban-Rural Gap in Basic Education in China, 1949–1990." *Comparative Education Review* 43 (2): 193–211. http://www.jstor.org/stable/1189018.

Hannum, Emily C., and Jennifer Adams. 2007. "Girls in Gansu, China: Expectations and Aspirations for Secondary Schooling." In *Exclusion, Gender and Schooling: Case Studies from the Developing World*, edited by Maureen Lewis and Marlaine Lockheed, 71–98. Washington, DC: Center for Global Development.

Hannum, Emily C., and Meiyan Wang. 2006. "Geography and Educational Inequality in China." *China Economic Review* 17 (3): 253–65. https://doi.org/10.1016/j.chieco.2006.04.003.

Hansen, Anders Sybrandt. 2017. "Guanhua! Bejing Students, Authoritative Discourse and the Ritual Production of Political Compliance." In Bregnbæk and Bunkenborg 2017, 35–51.

Hansen, Mette Halskov. 2015. *Educating the Chinese Individual: Life in a Rural Boarding School*. Seattle: University of Washington Press.

Hansen, Mette Halskov, and Terry E. Woronov. 2013. "Demanding and Resisting Vocational Education: A Comparative Study of Schools in Rural and Urban China." *Comparative Education* 49 (2): 242–59. https://doi.org/10.1080/03050068.2012.733848.

Hanson, F. Allan. 1993. *Testing: Social Consequences of the Examined Life*. Berkeley: University of California Press.

Harding, Sandra. 1998. "Women, Science, and Society." *Science* 281 (5383): 1599–1600. http://www.jstor.org/stable/2896353.

Harrell, Stevan. 1985. "Why Do the Chinese Work So Hard?" *Modern China* 11 (2): 203–26. https://doi.org/10.1177/009770048501100203.

——. 1987. "The Concept of Fate in Chinese Folk Ideology." *Modern China* 13 (1): 90–109. http://www.jstor.org/stable/189148.

——. 1995. "Introduction." In *Cultural Encounters on China's Ethnic Frontiers*, edited by Stevan Harrell, 17–27. Seattle: University of Washington Press.

Hartwell, Robert M. 1982. "Demographic, Political, and Social Transformations of China, 750–1550." *Harvard Journal of Asiatic Studies* 42 (2): 365–442. http://www.jstor.org/stable/2718941.

Harvey, David. 2005. *A Brief History of Neoliberalism*. Oxford: Oxford University Press.

Herdt, Gilbert H. 1981. *Guardians of the Flutes: Idioms of Masculinity*. New York: McGraw-Hill.

Herzfeld, Michael. 2005. *Cultural Intimacy: Social Poetics in the Nation-State*. 2nd ed. New York: Routledge.

Hesketh, Therese, Li Lu, and Zhu Wei Xing. 2005. "The Effect of China's One-Child Family Policy after 25 Years." *New England Journal of Medicine* 353 (11): 1171–76. https://doi.org/10.1056/NEJMhpr051833.

Ho, Ping-Ti. 1962. *The Ladder of Success in Imperial China: Aspects of Social Mobility, 1368–1911*. New York: Columbia University Press.

Hobart, Mark, ed. 2002. *An Anthropological Critique of Development: The Growth of Ignorance*. New York: Routledge.

Howlett, Zachary M. 2017. "China's Examination Fever and the Fabrication of Fairness: 'My Generation Was Raised on Poisoned Milk.'" In Bregnbæk and Bunkenborg 2017, 15–34.

——. 2020. "Tactics of Marriage Delay in China: Education, Rural-to-Urban Migration, and 'Leftover Women.'" In Inhorn and Smith-Hefner 2020, 177–99.

Hsiao, William C. 2014. "Correcting Past Health Policy Mistakes." *Daedalus* 143 (2): 53–68. https://doi.org/10.1162/DAED_a_00272.

Huang, Yanjie. 2013. "China's Educated Underemployment." *East Asian Policy* 5 (2): 72–82. https://doi.org/10.1142/S1793930513000172.

Huang, Yasheng. 2008. *Capitalism with Chinese Characteristics: Entrepreneurship and the State*. Cambridge: Cambridge University Press.

——. 2015. "Policy Model and Inequality: Some Potential Connections." In *China's Challenges*, edited by Jacques DeLisle and Avery Goldstein, 83–104. Philadelphia: University of Pennsylvania Press.

Human Rights in China. 2014. *New Citizens Movement Briefing Note*. New York: Human Rights in China, https://www.hrichina.org/sites/default/files/new_citizens_movement_briefing_note_2014.pdf.

United Nations Development Programme. 2019. *Human Development Report 2019*. New York: United Nations Development Programme. http://hdr.undp.org/sites/default/files/hdr2019.pdf, accessed July 8, 2020.

Inhorn, Marcia C. 2020. "The Egg Freezing Revolution? Gender, Education, and Reproductive Waithood in America." In Inhorn and Smith-Hefner 2020.

Inhorn, Marcia C., and Nancy Smith-Hefner, eds. 2020. *Waithood: Gender, Education, and Global Delays in Marriage*. New York: Berghahn.

Jack, Anthony Abraham. 2016. "(No) Harm in Asking: Class, Acquired Cultural Capital, and Academic Engagement at an Elite University." *Sociology of Education* 89 (1): 1–19. https://doi.org/10.1177/0038040715614913.

——. 2019. "I Was a Low-Income College Student. Classes Weren't the Hard Part." *New York Times*, September 10, 2019, https://www.nytimes.com/interactive/2019/09/10/magazine/college-inequality.html.

Jacka, Tamara. 2009. "Cultivating Citizens: Suzhi (Quality) Discourse in the PRC." *Positions* 17 (3): 523–35. https://doi.org/10.1215/10679847-2009-013.

Jackson, Michael. 2005. *Existential Anthropology: Events, Exigencies, and Effects*. New York: Berghahn.

Jacobsen, Stefan Gaarsmand. 2015. "Prussian Emulations of a Chinese Meritocratic Ideal? Early Modern Europe Debating How China Selected Civil Servants." *Journal for Eighteenth-Century Studies* 38 (3): 425–41. https://doi.org/10.1111/1754-0208.12222.

Jacques, Martin. 2012. *When China Rules the World: The End of the Western World and the Birth of a New Global Order*. 2nd ed. London: Penguin.

James, William. [1902] 2002. *Varieties of Religious Experience: A Study in Human Nature*. Centenary ed. London: Routledge.

Ji, Yingchun. 2015. "Between Tradition and Modernity: 'Leftover' Women in Shanghai." *Journal of Marriage and Family* 77 (5): 1057–73. https://doi.org/10.1111/jomf.12220.

Jing, Jun. 1998. *The Temple of Memories: History, Power, and Morality in a Chinese Village*. Stanford, CA: Stanford University Press.

Jordan, David K. 1982. "Taiwanese *Poe* Divination: Statistical Awareness and Religious Belief." *Journal for the Scientific Study of Religion* 21 (2): 114–18. https://doi.org/10.2307/1385496.

Judd, Ellen R. 1996. *Gender and Power in Rural North China*. Stanford, CA: Stanford University Press.

Kajanus, Anni. 2015. *Chinese Student Migration, Gender and Family*. Basingstoke, UK: Palgrave Macmillan.

Kan, Sergei. 2016. *Symbolic Immortality: The Tlingit Potlatch of the Nineteenth Century*. Second edition. Seattle: University of Washington Press, 2016.

Karabel, Jerome. 2006. *The Chosen: The Hidden History of Admission and Exclusion at Harvard, Yale, and Princeton*. Boston: Houghton Mifflin Harcourt.

Keimig, Rose Kay. 2017. "Growing Old in China's New Nursing Homes." PhD diss., Yale University.

Khor, Niny, Lihua Pang, Chengfang Liu, Fang Chang, Di Mo, Prashant Loyalka, and Scott Rozelle. 2016. "China's Looming Human Capital Crisis: Upper Secondary Educational Attainment Rates and the Middle-Income Trap." *China Quarterly*, no. 228, 905–26. https://doi.org/10.1017/S0305741016001119.

Kipnis, Andrew B. 2001. "The Disturbing Educational Discipline of 'Peasants.'" *China Journal*, no. 46, 1–24. http://www.jstor.org/stable/3182305.

———. 2006. "Suzhi: A Keyword Approach." *China Quarterly*, no. 186, 295–313. https://doi.org/10.1017/S030574100600026.

———. 2008. "Audit Cultures: Neoliberal Governmentality, Socialist Legacy, or Technologies of Governing?" *American Ethnologist* 35 (2): 275–89. https://doi.org/10.1111/j.2008.1548-1425.00034.x.

———. 2011. *Governing Educational Desire: Culture, Politics, and Schooling in China*. Chicago: University of Chicago Press.

———. 2016. *From Village to City: Social Transformation in a Chinese County Seat*. Oakland: University of California Press.

———. 2017. "Urbanization and the Transformation of Kinship Practice in Shandong." In *Transforming Patriarchy: Chinese Families in the Twenty-First Century*, edited by Gonçalo D. Santos and Stevan Harrell, 113–28. Seattle: University of Washington Press.

Kleeman, Terry F. 1994. *A God's Own Tale: The Book of Transformations of Wenchang, the Divine Lord of Zitong*. Albany: SUNY Press.

Kleinman, Arthur. 1988. *Social Origins of Distress and Disease: Depression, Neurasthenia, and Pain in Modern China*. New Haven, CT: Yale University Press.

———. 2010. "Caregiving: Its Role in Medicine and Society in America and China." *Ageing International* 35 (2): 96–108. https://doi.org/10.1007/s12126-010-9054-3.

Kleinman, Arthur, Yunxiang Yan, Jing Jun, Sing Lee, Everett Zhang, Tianshu Pan, Fei Wu, and Jinhua Guo. 2011. "Introduction: Remaking the Moral Person in New China." In *Deep China: The Moral Life of the Person—What Anthropology and Psychiatry Tell Us about China Today*, 1–35. Berkeley: University of California Press.

Ko, Dorothy. 1994. *Teachers of the Inner Chambers: Women and Culture in Seventeenth-Century China*. Stanford, CA: Stanford University Press.

———. 2005. *Cinderella's Sisters: A Revisionist History of Footbinding*. Berkeley: University of California Press.

Kohn, Alfie. 2000. *The Case against Standardized Testing: Raising the Scores, Ruining the Schools*. Portsmouth, NH: Heinemann.

Kohrman, Matthew. 2005. *Bodies of Difference: Experiences of Disability and Institutional Advocacy in the Making of Modern China*. Berkeley: University of California Press.

Kraus, Michael W., and Jacinth J. X. Tan. 2015. "Americans Overestimate Social Class Mobility." *Journal of Experimental Social Psychology* 58 (May): 101–11. https://doi.org/10.1016/j.jesp.2015.01.005.

Kuan, Teresa. 2015. *Love's Uncertainty: The Politics and Ethics of Child Rearing in Contemporary China*. Oakland: University of California Press.

Kubiszewski, Ida, Robert Costanza, Carol Franco, Philip Lawn, John Talberth, Tim Jackson, and Camille Aylmer. 2013. "Beyond GDP: Measuring and Achieving Global Genuine Progress." *Ecological Economics* 93 (September): 57–68. https://doi.org/10.1016/j.ecolecon.2013.04.019.

Kuhn, Philip A. 2002. *Origins of the Modern Chinese State*. Stanford, CA: Stanford University Press.

———. 2008. *Chinese among Others: Emigration in Modern Times*. State and Society in East Asia. Lanham, MD: Rowman & Littlefield.

Kwok, D. W. Y. 1965. *Scientism in Chinese Thought, 1900–1950*. New Haven, CT: Yale University Press.

Lacan, Jacques. 2006. "The Function and Field of Speech and Language in Psychoanalysis." In *Ecrits: The First Complete Edition in English*, translated by Bruce Fink, 197–268. New York: W. W. Norton.

Lakoff, George, and Mark Johnson. 1981. *Metaphors We Live By*. Chicago: University of Chicago Press.

Lam, Willy Wo-Lap. 2019. "'Stability Maintenance' Gets a Major Boost at the National People's Congress." *China Brief* 19 (6). https://jamestown.org/program/stability-maintenance-gets-a-major-boost-at-the-national-peoples-congress/.

Lau, Ting Hui. 2020. "Colonial Development and the Politics of Affliction on the China-Myanmar Border." PhD diss., Cornell University.

Lemann, Nicholas. 1999. *The Big Test: The Secret History of the American Meritocracy*. New York: Farrar, Straus and Giroux.

Lepori, Gabriele M. 2009. "Dark Omens in the Sky: Do Superstitious Beliefs Affect Investment Decisions?" SSRN Scholarly Paper ID 1428792. Rochester, NY: Social Science Research Network. http://papers.ssrn.com/abstract=1428792, accessed February 15, 2016.

Lévi-Strauss, Claude. 1963. "The Effectiveness of Symbols." In *Structural Anthropology*, 181–201. Translated by Claire Jacobson and Brooke Grundfest Schoepf. New York: Basic.

Lewis, Mark Edward. 1999. *Writing and Authority in Early China*. Albany: SUNY Press.

———. 2007. *The Early Chinese Empires: Qin and Han*. Cambridge, MA: Belknap Press of Harvard University Press.

Li, Bingqin. 2015. "China's Hukou Reform a Small Step in the Right Direction." *East Asia Forum* (blog), January 13, 2015. https://www.eastasiaforum.org/2015/01/13/chinas-hukou-reform-a-small-step-in-the-right-direction/.

Li, En. 2015. "Betting on Empire: A Socio-Cultural History of Gambling in Late-Qing China." PhD diss., University of Washington in St. Louis.

Li, Jinbo, and Jun Yang. 2015. "Gaokao chengji chengxiang chayi ji qi fazhan qushi fenxi" [An analysis of rural-urban differences in Gaokao scores and developing trends]. *Zhongguo kaoshi* [Examinations in China], no. 12, 19–23.

Liang, Chen, James Z. Lee, Danqing Ruan, Hao Zhang, Cameron D. Campbell, Shanhua Yang, and Lan Li. 2012. "Wusheng de geming: Beijing daxue yu Suzhou daxue shehui laiyuan yanjiu, 1952–2002" [Silent revolution: The origins of Peking University and Soochow University undergraduates, 1952–2002]. *Zhongguo shehui kexue* [Social science in China] 1:101–21.

Lickona, Thomas, and Matthew Davidson. 2005. *Smart and Good High Schools: Integrating Excellence and Ethics for Success in School, Work, and Beyond*. Cortland, NY: Center for the 4th and 5th Rs/Character Education Partnership.

Lindner, Robert M. 1950. "The Psychodynamics of Gambling." *Annals of the American Academy of Political and Social Science* 269 (May): 93–107. http://www.jstor.org/stable/1027822.

Ling, Minhua. 2015. "'Bad Students Go to Vocational Schools!': Education, Social Reproduction and Migrant Youth in Urban China." *China Journal*, no. 73, 108–31. https://doi.org/10.1086/679271.

———. 2017. "Returning to No Home: Educational Remigration and Displacement in Rural China." *Anthropological Quarterly* 90 (3): 715–42. https://doi.org/10.1353/anq.2017.0041.

Linton, Ralph. 1936. *The Study of Man: An Introduction*. The Century Social Science. New York: D. Appleton-Century.

Liu, Haifeng. 2007. *Gaokao gaige de lilun sikao* [Theoretical reflections on reform of the Chinese College Entrance Examination]. Wuhan: Central China Normal University Press.

Liu, Limin, Wolfgang Wagner, Bettina Sonnenberg, Xiwei Wu, and Ulrich Trautwein. 2014. "Independent Freshman Admission and Educational Inequality in the Access to Elite Higher Education: Evidence from Peking University." *Chinese Sociological Review* 46 (4): 41–67. http://www.tandfonline.com/doi/abs/10.2753/CSA2162-0555460403.

Liu, Xiaoyuan. 2004. *Frontier Passages: Ethnopolitics and the Rise of Chinese Communism, 1921–1945*. Stanford, CA: Stanford University Press.

Liu, Xin. 1997. "Space, Mobility, and Flexibility: Chinese Villagers and Scholars Negotiate Power at Home and Abroad." In *Ungrounded Empires: The Cultural Politics of Modern Chinese Transnationalism*, edited by Aihwa Ong and Donald Macon Nonini, 91–114. New York: Routledge.

Liu, Ye. 2013. "Meritocracy and the Gaokao: A Survey Study of Higher Education Selection and Socio-Economic Participation in East China." *British Journal of Sociology of Education* 34 (5–6): 868–87. https://doi.org/10.1080/01425692.2013.816237.

Lora-Wainwright, Anna. 2013. *Fighting for Breath: Living Morally and Dying of Cancer in a Chinese Village*. Honolulu: University of Hawai'i Press.

Loveless, Tom. 2014. "Lessons from the PISA-Shanghai Controversy." Washington, DC: Brookings Institution. http://www.brookings.edu/research/reports/2014/03/18-pisa-shanghai-loveless, accessed April 29, 2014.

Luthar, Suniya S. 1999. *Poverty and Children's Adjustment*. London: SAGE.

Luthar, Suniya S., and Bronwyn E. Becker. 2002. "Privileged but Pressured? A Study of Affluent Youth." *Child Development* 73 (5): 1593–1610. http://www.ncbi.nlm.nih.gov/pmc/articles/PMC3524830/.

Luthar, Suniya S., Dante Cicchetti, and Bronwyn Becker. 2000. "The Construct of Resilience: A Critical Evaluation and Guidelines for Future Work." *Child Development* 71 (3): 543–62. http://www.ncbi.nlm.nih.gov/pmc/articles/PMC1885202/.

Ma, Liping, You You, Yu Xiong, Lu Dong, Mengshan Zhu, and Kunzhao Guan. 2016. "Daxue zhuanye xuanze de xingbie chayi—jiyu quanguo 85 suo gaoxiao de diaocha yanjjiu" [The gender difference in college students' choice of majors—based on a survey of 85 universities]. *Gaodeng jiaoyu yanjiu* [Higher education research] 37 (5): 36–42.

Mahdawi, Arwa. 2018. "Harvard Sued for Alleged Discrimination against Asian American Applicants." *Guardian*, June 15, 2018. https://www.theguardian.com/education/2018/jun/15/harvard-sued-discrimination-against-asian-americans.

Mahmood, Saba. 2012. *Politics of Piety: The Islamic Revival and the Feminist Subject.* 2nd ed. Princeton, NJ: Princeton University Press.

Makley, Charlene. 2018. *The Battle for Fortune: State-Led Development, Personhood, and Power among Tibetans in China.* Ithaca, NY: Cornell University Press.

Malinowski, Bronislaw. 1935. *Coral Gardens and Their Magic: A Study of the Methods of Tilling the Soil and of Agricultural Rites in the Trobriand Islands.* London: Allen & Unwin.

———. 1948. *Magic, Science and Religion.* Garden City, NY: Doubleday.

———. 1961. *Argonauts of the Western Pacific: An Account of Native Enterprise and Adventure in the Archipelagoes of Melanesian New Guinea.* New York: E. P. Dutton.

Mann, Susan. 1997. *Precious Records: Women in China's Long Eighteenth Century.* Stanford, CA: Stanford University Press.

Manyika, James, Susan Lund, Michael Chui, Jacques Bughin, Jonathan Woetzel, Parul Batra, Ryan Ko, and Saurabh Sanghvi. 2017. *Jobs Lost, Jobs Gained.* New York: McKinsey Global Institute. https://www.mckinsey.com/featured-insights/future-of-organizations-and-work/jobs-lost-jobs-gained-what-the-future-of-work-will-mean-for-jobs-skills-and-wages.

Martin, Emily. 2001. *The Woman in the Body: A Cultural Analysis of Reproduction.* Boston: Beacon.

Marx, Karl. [1846] 1970. *The German Ideology.* Edited by Christopher John Arthur. New York: International Publishers.

Mauss, Marcel. [1925] 2000. *The Gift: The Form and Reason for Exchange in Archaic Societies.* New York: W. W. Norton.

———. [1902] 2006. *A General Theory of Magic.* London: Routledge.

Mazzarella, William. 2015. "Totalitarian Tears: Does the Crowd Really Mean It?" *Cultural Anthropology* 30 (1): 91–112. https://doi.org/10.14506/ca30.1.06.

McNamee, Stephen J. 2009. *The Meritocracy Myth.* Rev. ed. Lanham, MD: Rowman & Littlefield.

Medina, Jennifer, Katie Benner, and Kate Taylor. 2019. "Actresses, Business Leaders and Other Wealthy Parents Charged in U.S. College Entry Fraud." *New York Times*, March 12, 2019, sec. U.S. https://www.nytimes.com/2019/03/12/us/college-admissions-cheating-scandal.html.

Mijs, Jonathan B. 2016. "Stratified Failure: Educational Stratification and Students' Attributions of Their Mathematics Performance in 24 Countries." *Sociology of Education* 89 (2): 137–53. https://doi.org/10.1177/0038040716636434.

Milanović, Branko. 2016. *Global Inequality: A New Approach for the Age of Globalization.* Cambridge, MA: Belknap Press of Harvard University Press.

Miyakawa, Hisayuki. 1955. "An Outline of the Naito Hypothesis and Its Effects on Japanese Studies of China." *Far Eastern Quarterly* 14 (4): 533–52. http://www.jstor.org/stable/2941835.

———. 1960. "The Confucianization of South China." In Wright 1960, 241–67.

Miyazaki, Ichisada. 1981. *China's Examination Hell*. Translated by Conrad Schirokauer. New Haven, CT: Yale University Press.

Mok, Ka Ho, and Alfred M. Wu. 2016. "Higher Education, Changing Labour Market and Social Mobility in the Era of Massification in China." *Journal of Education and Work* 29 (1): 77–97. https://doi.org/10.1080/13639080.2015.1049028.

Mounk, Yascha. 2018. *The People vs. Democracy: Why Our Freedom Is in Danger and How to Save It*. Cambridge, MA: Harvard University Press.

Munn, Nancy D. 1986. *The Fame of Gawa: A Symbolic Study of Value Transformation in a Massim (Papua New Guinea) Society*. Cambridge: Cambridge University Press.

Munro, Donald J. 2001. *The Concept of Man in Early China*. Michigan Classics in Chinese Studies 6. Ann Arbor: Center for Chinese Studies, University of Michigan.

Muramatsu, Yuji. 1960. "Some Themes in Chinese Rebel Ideologies." In Wright 1960, 241–67.

Murphy, Rachel. 2004. "Turning Peasants into Modern Chinese Citizens: 'Population Quality' Discourse, Demographic Transition and Primary Education." *China Quarterly*, no. 177, 1–20. http://www.jstor.org/stable/20192302.

———. 2014. "Study and School in the Lives of Children in Migrant Families: A View from Rural Jiangxi, China." *Development and Change* 45 (1): 29–51. http://onlinelibrary.wiley.com/doi/10.1111/dech.12073/abstract.

Naughton, John. 2018. "China Is Taking Digital Control of Its People to Unprecedented and Chilling Lengths." *Guardian*, May 27, 2018. https://www.theguardian.com/commentisfree/2018/may/27/china-taking-digital-control-of-its-people-to-unprecedented-and-chilling-lengths.

Nyíri, Pál. 2010. *Mobility and Cultural Authority in Contemporary China*. Seattle: University of Washington Press.

Obendiek, Helena. 2016. *"Changing Fate": Education, Poverty and Family Support in Contemporary Chinese Society*. Halle Studies in the Anthropology of Eurasia 33. Münster, Germany: Lit Verlag.

O'Callaghan, Jonathan. 2015. "The Superstitions of Space Travel Revealed." *Mail Online*, January 7, 2015. https://www.dailymail.co.uk/sciencetech/article-2822436/The-superstitions-space-travel-revealed-Fear-number-13-peeing-tyres-tapping-Snoopy-s-nose-bizarre-rituals.html.

Ong, Aihwa. 1999. *Flexible Citizenship: The Cultural Logics of Transnationality*. Durham, NC: Duke University Press.

Open Doors. 2017. New York: Institute of International Education. https://www.iie.org/en/Research-and-Insights/Open-Doors/Data/International-Students.

Ortmann, Stephen, and Mark R. Thompson. 2016. "China and the 'Singapore Model.'" *Journal of Democracy* 27 (1): 39–48. http://www.journalofdemocracy.org/sites/default/files/Thompson-27-1.pdf.

Ortner, Sherry B. 1972. "Is Female to Male as Nature Is to Culture?" *Feminist Studies* 1 (2): 5–31. http://www.jstor.org/stable/3177638.

Osburg, John. 2013. *Anxious Wealth: Money and Morality among China's New Rich*. Stanford, CA: Stanford University Press.

———. 2015. "Morality and Cynicism in a 'Grey' World." In Steinmüller and Brandtstädter 2015, 47–62.

Oxfeld, Ellen. 1993. *Blood, Sweat, and Mahjong: Family and Enterprise in an Overseas Chinese Community*. Anthropology of Contemporary Issues. Ithaca, NY: Cornell University Press.

———. 2010. *Drink Water, but Remember the Source: Moral Discourse in a Chinese Village*. Berkeley: University of California Press.

———. 2017. *Bitter and Sweet: Food, Meaning, and Modernity in Rural China*. Oakland: University of California Press.

People's Daily Online. 2017. "Women Dominate Higher Education in China," October 28, 2017. http://en.people.cn/n3/2017/1028/c90000-9285962.html.

Perry, Elizabeth J. 2002. *Challenging the Mandate of Heaven: Social Protest and State Power in China*. Armonk, NY: M. E. Sharpe.

———. 2014. "Growing Pains: Challenges for a Rising China." *Daedalus* 143 (2): 5–13.

———. 2020. "Educated Acquiescence: How Academia Sustains Authoritarianism in China." *Theory and Society* 49 (1): 1–22. https://doi.org/10.1007/s11186-019-09373-1.

Piketty, Thomas. 2013. *Capital in the Twenty-First Century*. Cambridge, MA: Harvard University Press.

Pina-Cabral, João de. 2002. *Between China and Europe: Person, Culture and Emotion in Macao*. London School of Economics Monographs on Social Anthropology 74. London: Continuum.

Platt, Stephen R. 2012. *Autumn in the Heavenly Kingdom: China, the West, and the Epic Story of the Taiping Civil War*. New York: Alfred A. Knopf.

Pomeranz, Kenneth. 2000. *The Great Divergence*. Princeton, NJ: Princeton University Press.

Postiglione, Gerard A. 2014. "China: Reforming the Gaokao." *International Higher Education*, no. 76, 17–18. https://doi.org/10.6017/ihe.2014.76.5527.

Puett, Michael J. 2006. "Innovation as Ritualization: The Fractured Cosmology of Early China." *Cardozo Law Review* 28: 23–36.

———. 2014. "Ritual Disjunctions: Ghosts, Anthropology, and Philosophy." In *The Ground Between: Anthropologists Engage Philosophy*, 218–33. Durham, NC: Duke University Press.

———. 2015. "Ritual and Ritual Obligations: Perspectives on Normativity from Classical China." *Journal of Value Inquiry* 49 (4): 543–50. https://doi.org/10.1007/s10790-015-9524-7.

Qiuye, Yuqian. 2015. *Fangyang de nühai shang Hafo* [How a free-range daughter got into Harvard]. Xiamen, China: Xiamen University Press.

Ravallion, Martin. 2011. "A Comparative Perspective on Poverty Reduction in Brazil, China, and India." *World Bank Research Observer* 26 (1): 71–104. https://doi.org/10.1093/wbro/lkp031.

Ravitch, Diane. 2010. *The Death and Life of the Great American School System: How Testing and Choice Are Undermining Education*. New York: Basic Books.

Readings, Bill. 1996. *The University in Ruins*. Cambridge, MA: Harvard University Press.

Robinson, William I. 2012. "Global Capitalism Theory and the Emergence of Transnational Elites." *Critical Sociology* 38 (3): 349–63. https://doi.org/10.1177/0896920511411592.

Rosin, Hanna. 2015. "The Silicon Valley Suicides." *Atlantic*, December 2015. https://www.theatlantic.com/magazine/archive/2015/12/the-silicon-valley-suicides/413140/.

Rowe, William T. 1994. "Education and Empire in Southwest China." In *Education and Society in Late Imperial China, 1600–1900*, edited by Benjamin A. Elman and Alexander Woodside, 417–57. Berkeley: University of California Press.

Sangren, P. Steven. 2000. *Chinese Sociologics*. London: Athlone.

———. 2013. "The Chinese Family as Instituted Fantasy: Or, Rescuing Kinship Imagi-naries from the 'Symbolic.'" *Journal of the Royal Anthropological Institute* 19 (2): 279–99. https://doi.org/10.1111/1467-9655.12033.

Santos, Gonçalo D., and Stevan Harrell. 2017. "Introduction." In *Transforming Patriar-chy: Chinese Families in the Twenty-First Century*, edited by Gonçalo D. Santos and Stevan Harrell, 3–36. Seattle: University of Washington Press.

Schupmann, Benjamin A. 2019. "Constraining Political Extremism and Legal Revolution." *Philosophy & Social Criticism*, June 2019. https://doi.org/10.1177/0191453719856652.

Seaman, Gary. 1981. "The Sexual Politics of Karmic Retribution." In *The Anthropology of Taiwanese Society*, edited by Emily M. Ahern and Hill Gates, 381–96. Stanford, CA: Stanford University Press.

Seligman, Adam B., Robert P. Weller, Michael J. Puett, and Benett Simon. 2008. *Ritual and Its Consequences: An Essay on the Limits of Sincerity*. Oxford: Oxford University Press.

Seth, Michael J. 2002. *Education Fever: Society, Politics, and the Pursuit of Schooling in South Korea*. Honolulu: University of Hawai'i Press.

Shambaugh, David L. 2016. *China's Future*. Cambridge: Polity.

Shaughnessy, Edward L. 1999. "Western Zhou History." In *The Cambridge History of Ancient China: From the Origins of Civilization to 221 B.C.*, edited by Michael Loewe and Edward L. Shaughnessy, 292–351. Cambridge: Cambridge University Press.

Shedd, Carla. 2015. *Unequal City: Race, Schools, and Perceptions of Injustice*. New York: Russell Sage Foundation.

Shi, Lihong. 2017. *Choosing Daughters: Family Change in Rural China*. Stanford, CA: Stanford University Press.

Siegel, James T. 2006. *Naming the Witch*. Stanford, CA: Stanford University Press.

Sina Education. 2015. "1977–2014 linian quanguo Gaokao renshu he luqulü tongji" [1977–2014 historical national statistics of College Entrance Examination num-bers and admission rates]. June 18, 2015. http://edu.sina.com.cn/gaokao/2015-06-18/1435473862.shtml.

Skinner, G. William. 1964–65. "Marketing and Social Structure in Rural China," parts 1–3. *Journal of Asian Studies* 24 (1): 3–43, 195–228, 363–99. https://doi.org/10.2307/2050412.

———. 1976. "Mobility Strategies in Late Imperial China." In *Regional Analysis*, vol. 1: *Economic Systems*, edited by C. A. Smith, 327–64. New York: Academic.

———. 1980. "Marketing Systems and Regional Economies: Their Structure and Devel-opment." Paper presented at the Symposium on Social and Economic History in China from the Song Dynasty to 1900, Chinese Academy of Social Sciences, Beijing.

Sleeboom-Faulkner, Margaret. 2010. "Eugenic Birth and Fetal Education: The Friction between Lineage Enhancement and Premarital Testing among Rural House-holds in Mainland China." *China Journal*, no. 64, 121–41. http://www.jstor.org/stable/20749249.

Sloterdijk, Peter. 1988. *Critique of Cynical Reason*. Translated by Andreas Huyssen. Min-neapolis: University of Minnesota Press.

Snyder, Timothy. 2018. *The Road to Unfreedom: Russia, Europe, America*. New York: Tim Duggan.

Soares, Joseph A. 2007. *The Power of Privilege: Yale and America's Elite Colleges*. Stanford, CA: Stanford University Press.

Sohu. 2017. "2017 nian 985, 211 Daxue zai quanguo gesheng luqulü paihang" [The 2017 national ranking of every province according to admission rates for Project 985 and 211 universities]. October 17, 2017. www.sohu.com/a/198431528_507475.

Spence, Jonathan D. 1996. *God's Chinese Son: The Taiping Heavenly Kingdom of Hong Xiuquan*. New York: W. W. Norton.

Stafford, Charles. 1995. *The Roads of Chinese Childhood*. Cambridge: Cambridge University Press.

Steinmüller, Hans. 2011. "The State of Irony in China." *Critique of Anthropology* 31 (1): 21–42. https://doi.org/10.1177/0308275X10393434.

———. 2013. *Communities of Complicity: Everyday Ethics in Rural China*. New York: Berghahn.

Steinmüller, Hans, and Susanne Brandtstädter, eds. 2015. *Irony, Cynicism and the Chinese State*. New York: Routledge.

Stevens, Mitchell L. 2009. *Creating a Class: College Admissions and the Education of Elites*. Boston: Harvard University Press.

Stouffer, Samuel Andrew. 1949. *The American Soldier*. Princeton, NJ: Princeton University Press.

Straits Times. 2017. "China's Family Firm Successions Power Massive Wealth Transfer." September 28, 2017. https://www.straitstimes.com/asia/east-asia/chinas-family-firm-successions-power-massive-wealth-transfer.

Strathern, Marilyn. 1988. *The Gender of the Gift: Problems with Women and Problems with Society in Melanesia*. Berkeley: University of California Press.

Susskind, Richard, and Daniel Susskind. 2015. *The Future of the Professions: How Technology Will Transform the Work of Human Experts*. Oxford: Oxford University Press.

Teixeira, Lauren. 2017. "China's Middle Class Anger at Its Education System Is Growing." *Foreign Policy* (*China U* blog), February 6, 2017. https://foreignpolicy.com/2017/02/06/chinas-middle-class-anger-at-its-education-system-is-growing-gaokao-quota-protest-resentment-study-abroad/.

Temin, Peter. 2017. *The Vanishing Middle Class: Prejudice and Power in a Dual Economy*. Cambridge, MA: MIT Press.

Teng, Ssu-yü. 1943. "Chinese Influence on the Western Examination System: I. Introduction." *Harvard Journal of Asiatic Studies* 7 (4): 267–312. http://www.jstor.org/stable/2717830.

Teo, Youyenn. 2018. *This Is What Inequality Looks Like*. Singapore: Ethos.

Thøgersen, Stig. 1990. *Secondary Education in China after Mao: Reform and Social Conflict*. Aarhus, Denmark: Aarhus University Press.

Tomba, Luigi. 2014. *The Government Next Door: Neighborhood Politics in Urban China*. Ithaca, NY: Cornell University Press.

Turner, Terence. 1977. "Transformation, Hierarchy and Transcendence: A Reformulation of Van Gennep's Model of the Structure of Rites de Passage." In *Secular Ritual*, edited by Sally Falk Moore and Barbara G. Myerhoff, 53–70. Assen, Netherlands: Van Gorcum.

Ulfstjerne, Michael Alexander. 2017. "The Tower and the Tower: Excess and Vacancy in China's Ghost Cities." In Bregnbæk and Bunkenborg 2017, 67–84.

United Nations. 2015. *World Population Ageing 2015*. New York: United Nations, Department of Economic and Social Affairs, Population Division. http://www.un.org/en/development/desa/population/publications/pdf/ageing/WPA2015_Report.pdf.

Van Gennep, Arnold. [1909] 1960. *The Rites of Passage*. London: Routledge & Paul.

Wallace, Jeremy L. 2014. *Cities and Stability: Urbanization, Redistribution, and Regime Survival in China*. New York: Oxford University Press.

Wan, Minggang, and Ling Jiang. 2016. "Lun wo guo shaoshu minzu jiaoyu zhong de 'ligongke wenti'" [Discussion of the 'STEM problem' among China's ethnic minorities]. *Jiaoyu yanjiu* [Education research], no. 2, 96–101.

Wang, Qinghua. 2014. "Crisis Management, Regime Survival and 'Guerrilla-Style' Policy-Making: The June 1999 Decision to Radically Expand Higher Education in China." *China Journal*, no. 71, 132–52. https://doi.org/10.1086/674557.

Wang, Xiaobing, Chengfang Liu, Linxiu Zhang, Yaojiang Shi, and Scott Rozelle. 2013. "College Is a Rich, Han, Urban, Male Club: Research Notes from a Census Survey of Four Tier One Colleges in China." *China Quarterly*, no. 214, 456–70. https://doi.org/10.1017/S0305741013000647.

Wang, Yuhua, and Carl Minzner. 2015. "The Rise of the Chinese Security State." *China Quarterly*, no. 222, 339–59. https://doi.org/10.1017/S0305741015000430.

Wang, Zheng. 2012. *Never Forget National Humiliation: Historical Memory in Chinese Politics and Foreign Relations*. Contemporary Asia in the World. New York: Columbia University Press.

Warikoo, Natasha K. 2016. *The Diversity Bargain: And Other Dilemmas of Race, Admissions, and Meritocracy at Elite Universities*. Chicago: University of Chicago Press.

Weber, Max. [1905] 1992. *The Protestant Ethic and the Spirit of Capitalism*. Translated by Talcott Parsons. London: Routledge.

——. 1946. "The Sociology of Charismatic Authority." In *From Max Weber: Essays in Sociology*, 245–53. Edited and translated by Hans H. Gerth and C. Wright Mills. New York: Oxford University Press.

Wedeen, Lisa. 1999. *Ambiguities of Domination: Politics, Rhetoric, and Symbols in Contemporary Syria*. Chicago: University of Chicago Press.

Weller, Robert P. 1994. *Resistance, Chaos and Control in China: Taiping Rebels, Taiwanese Ghosts, and Tiananmen*. Seattle: University of Washington Press.

Whyte, Martin King. 2010. *Myth of the Social Volcano: Perceptions of Inequality and Distributive Injustice in Contemporary China*. Stanford, CA: Stanford University Press.

Wiens, Herold J. 1954. *China's March toward the Tropics*. Hamden, CT: Shoe String.

Wilkinson, Richard G., and Kate Pickett. 2010. *The Spirit Level: Why Greater Equality Makes Societies Stronger*. New York: Bloomsbury.

Willis, Paul E. 1981. *Learning to Labor: How Working Class Kids Get Working Class Jobs*. New York: Columbia University Press.

Winnicott, Donald W. 1991. *Playing and Reality*. London: Routledge.

Wong, Roy Bin. 1997. *China Transformed: Historical Change and the Limits of European Experience*. Ithaca, NY: Cornell University Press.

Woodside, Alexander. 2006. *Lost Modernities: China, Vietnam, Korea, and the Hazards of World History*. Cambridge, MA: Harvard University Press.

World Economic Forum. 2017. *The Global Gender Gap Report*. Geneva: World Economic Forum. https://www.weforum.org/reports/the-global-gender-gap-report-2017/.

Woronov, Terry E. 2008. "Raising Quality, Fostering 'Creativity': Ideologies and Practices of Education Reform in Beijing." *Anthropology & Education Quarterly* 39 (4): 401–22. http://onlinelibrary.wiley.com/doi/10.1111/j.1548-1492.2008.00030.x/abstract.

——. 2015. *Class Work: Vocational Schools and China's Urban Youth*. Stanford, CA: Stanford University Press.

Wright, Arthur F., ed. 1960. *The Confucian Persuasion*. Stanford, CA: Stanford University Press.

Wu, Jinting. 2016. *Fabricating an Educational Miracle: Compulsory Schooling Meets Ethnic Rural Development in Southwest China*. Albany: State University of New York Press.

Xinhua Net. 2018. "Xiamen kinyibu fangkuan gaoxiao biyesheng luohu tiaojian" [Xiamen further relaxes household registration conditions for college graduates]. October 1, 2018. http://www.xinhuanet.com/fortune/2018-10/01/c_129964567.htm.

Xu, Duoduo. 2018. "Is Gender Equality at Chinese Colleges a Sham?" *Sixth Tone*, April 5, 2018. https://www.sixthtone.com/news/1002051/is-gender-equality-at-chinese-colleges-a-sham%3F.

Yamada, Naomi C. F. 2012. "Education as Tautology: Disparities, Preferential Policy Measures and Preparatory Programs in Northwest China." PhD diss., University of Hawai'i at Manoa.

Yan, Hairong. 2008. *New Masters, New Servants: Migration, Development, and Women Workers in China*. Durham, NC: Duke University Press.

Yan, Yunxiang. 2003. *Private Life under Socialism: Love, Intimacy, and Family Change in a Chinese Village, 1949–1999*. Stanford, CA: Stanford University Press.

———. 2012. "Food Safety and Social Risk in Contemporary China." *Journal of Asian Studies* 71 (3): 705–29. https://doi.org/10.1017/S0021911812000678.

Yang, C. K. 1967. *Religion in Chinese Society: A Study of Contemporary Social Functions of Religion and Some of Their Historical Factors*. Berkeley: University of California Press.

Yang, Dongping. 2006. *Zhongguo jiaoyu gongping de lixiang he xianshi* [The ideal and reality of Chinese educational fairness]. Beijing: Peking University Press.

Yang, Jie. 2015. *Unknotting the Heart: Unemployment and Therapeutic Governance in China*. Ithaca, NY: Cornell University Press.

Yang, Mayfair Mei-hui. 1994. *Gifts, Favors, and Banquets*. Ithaca, NY: Cornell University Press.

Yeh, Wen-Hsin. 1990. *The Alienated Academy: Culture and Politics in Republican China, 1919–1937*. Cambridge, MA: Council on East Asian Studies, Harvard University.

Yeung, Wei-Jun Jean. 2013. "Higher Education Expansion and Social Stratification in China." *Chinese Sociological Review* 45 (4): 54–80. http://www.tandfonline.com/doi/abs/10.2753/CSA2162-0555450403.

Yi, Hongmei, Linxiu Zhang, Renfu Luo, Yaojiang Shi, Di Mo, Xinxin Chen, Carl Brinton, and Scott Rozelle. 2012. "Dropping Out: Why Are Students Leaving Junior High in China's Poor Rural Areas?" *International Journal of Educational Development* 32 (4): 555–63. https://doi.org/10.1016/j.ijedudev.2011.09.002.

Yi, Lin. 2008. *Cultural Exclusion in China: State Education, Social Mobility, and Cultural Difference*. New York: Routledge.

———. 2011. "Turning Rurality into Modernity: Suzhi Education in a Suburban Public School of Migrant Children in Xiamen." *China Quarterly*, no. 206, 313–30. https://doi.org/10.1017/S0305741011000282.

———. 2018. "Individuality, Subjectivation, and Their Civic Significance in Contemporary China: The Cultivation of an Ethical Self in a Cultural Community." *China Information*, September 2018, 1–21. https://doi.org/10.1177/0920203X18800877.

Young, Alford A. 2004. *The Minds of Marginalized Black Men: Making Sense of Mobility, Opportunity, and Future Life Chances*. Princeton Studies in Cultural Sociology. Princeton, NJ: Princeton University Press.

Yu, Kai, Andreas Lynn Stith, Li Liu, and Huizhong Chen. 2012. *Tertiary Education at a Glance: China*. Rotterdam, The Netherlands: Sense. https://link.springer.com/openurl?genre=book&isbn=978-94-6091-746-2.

Yurchak, Alexei. 2006. *Everything Was Forever, Until It Was No More: The Last Soviet Generation*. Princeton, NJ: Princeton University Press.

Zeng, Kangmin. 1999. *Dragon Gate: Competitive Examinations and Their Consequences*. Frontiers of International Education. London: Cassell.

Zhang, Li. 2010. *In Search of Paradise: Middle-Class Living in a Chinese Metropolis*. Ithaca, NY: Cornell University Press.

———. 2012. "Economic Migration and Urban Citizenship in China: The Role of Points Systems." *Population and Development Review* 38 (3): 503–33. https://doi.org/10.1111/j.1728-4457.2012.00514.x.

Zhang, Zoey Ye. 2019. "China Is Relaxing Hukou Restrictions in Small and Medium-Sized Cities." *China Briefing*, April 17, 2019. https://www.china-briefing.com/news/china-relaxing-hukou-restrictions-small-medium-sized-cities/.

Zhao, Ruohui, and Hongwei Zhang. 2017. "Family Violence and the Legal and Social Responses in China." In *Global Responses to Domestic Violence*, edited by Eve S. Buzawa and Carl G. Buzawa, 189–206. Cham, Switzerland: Springer. https://doi.org/10.1007/978-3-319-56721-1_10.

Zhao, Xu. 2015. *Competition and Compassion in Chinese Secondary Education*. New York: Palgrave Macmillan.

Zhao, Yihai. 2012. "Zao 'shen' chaojizhongxue de yuanqi yu yinyou" [The origins and private worries of 'god'-creating super high schools]. *Nanfang Zhoumo*, November 15, 2012. http://www.infzm.com/contents/82926.

Zhao, Yong. 2014. *Who's Afraid of the Big Bad Dragon: Why China Has the Best (and Worst) Education System in the World*. San Francisco: Jossey-Bass.

Zheng, Ruoling. 2011. *Gaokao gaige de kunjing yu yupo* [Difficulties and breakthroughs in the reform of the Gaokao]. Yangzhou, China: Jiangsu Educational.

Zheng, Tiantian. 2009. *Red Lights: The Lives of Sex Workers in Postsocialist China*. Minneapolis: University of Minnesota Press.

Zhou, Minglang. 2010. "China's Positive and Preferential Policies." In *Affirmative Action in China and the U.S.: A Dialogue on Inequality and Minority Education*, edited by Minglang Zhou and Ann Maxwell Hill, 47–70. New York: Macmillan.

Zivin, Joshua S. Graff, Yingquan Song, Qu Tang, and Peng Zhang. 2018. "Temperature and High-Stakes Cognitive Performance: Evidence from the National College Entrance Examination in China." Cambridge, MA: National Bureau of Economic Research. https://doi.org/10.3386/w24821.

Žižek, Slavoj. 2008. *The Sublime Object of Ideology*. London: Verso.

Index

admission rates, 23, 86–87, 98–100, 106, 199

Advanced Scholar (*jìnshì*) degree, 22–23, 101, 217. *See also* civil exams (imperial era)

agency, 8–9, 14–18, 20, 133, 190, 193, 222–25. *See also* existential meaning; self-efficacy

Alibaba Group, 144

ant tribe, the, (*yǐzú*), 66

anxiety, 20, 60, 114, 174–77, 190, 203, 215

assemblies to pledge resolution. *See* mobilization rallies

atheism. *See* secularism

Australia, 60

automation, 231–33

autonomous admission examinations (*zìzhǔzhāoshēng*), 79, 111–12

backstage, 5, 30, 84–85; collusion between parents and teachers, 176; competition for resources, 106–113; inequality, 91–92, 95, 98–99; male domination in, 130, 134; manipulation of exam scores, 35, 98; popular-religious beliefs, 186, 195–99, 207, 208–210, 223. *See also* edge balls (*cābiānqiú*); fairness; frontstage; Goffman, Erving

beggars, 212

Beijing, 4–5, 48, 51, 59, 63, 66–67, 71, 73, 84, 86, 91–92, 99, 103, 114

Beijing University. *See* Peking University

birth-planning policy. *See* one-child policy; two-child policy

boarding schools, 107–110, 116–18, 153–56, 162

Bodhisattva of Mercy (Guanyin), 188, 211, 214

bonus points (*jiāfēn*), 79, 86, 88, 93, 100, 139, 179, 195

Book of Changes (Yijing), 210

Bourdieu, Pierre, 6, 8–9, 31, 83, 147, 158

brain drain, 52, 107–12

Brokaw, Cynthia Joanne, 194

Buddhism, 178–79, 190–91, 204, 206, 214–15, 218–19

Canada, 60

Canton, 65, 210

capitalism, 26, 50, 56–57, 60, 81, 229, 232

Celestial Stems, 49

Central Kingdom, 43, 56–59

central-place hierarchy, 36–37, 41–42; celestial bureaucracy of gods as reflecting the, 41–42, 101–2; developmentalism objectified in, 45–50, 52–53, 56; as emic and etic, 73–76; funneling of value up the, 94–95, 111, 113; as a hierarchy of talent, 22, 45–50, 75, 101, 154–56; migration up the, 22, 65, 68–70; increasing objectivity of examinations along, 102–3; overlap of administrative hierarchy with, 41–42, 94–95; variations in educational policy implementation along, 111–12, 127–28, 162, 198–200. *See also* developmentalism; migration; score-value hierarchy; spatial variation; value

Certified Public Accounting Exam, 29

character: composure as ideal of, 147–49; diligence and quality as ideals of, 19, 39, 121–22, 125–26, 136, 141–45, 181; intelligence considered as an aspect of, 157–59; performance versus ethical, 12–14; paradox of, 14–16. *See also* composure as performance characteristic; diligence as performance characteristic; existential meaning; filial piety (*xiào*); IQ (*zhìshāng*); luck as performance characteristic; persistence as performance characteristic; quality (*sùzhì*)

cheating efforts, 23–24, 83, 179, 205–6, 227

Chinese Civil War, 35

Chinese Communist Party, 26, 28, 31–33, 35, 44, 50, 55, 58–61, 79, 90, 93, 185, 191, 194, 205, 225

Chinese Dream, 123, 225

Chinese New Year, 64, 69, 209, 217

Chongqing, 66

Christianity, 49, 185, 190, 225

Chu, Julie, 45